Europe, 1945 to the Present

Other Volumes Available from Oxford University Press

Europe
1945 to the Present

Robin W. Winks
Late of Yale University

John E. Talbott
University of California, Santa Barbara

New York   Oxford
OXFORD UNIVERSITY PRESS
2005

Oxford University Press

Oxford   New York
Auckland   Bangkok   Buenos Aires   Cape Town   Chennai
Dar es Salaam   Delhi   Hong Kong   Istanbul   Karachi   Kolkata
Kuala Lumpur   Madrid   Melbourne   Mexico City   Mumbai
Nairobi   São Paulo   Shanghai   Taipei   Tokyo   Toronto

Published by Oxford University Press, Inc.
198 Madison Avenue, New York, New York, 10016
http://www.oup.com

Oxford is a registered trademark of Oxford University Press

Library of Congress Cataloging-in-Publication Data
Winks, Robin W.
   Europe 1945 to the present / by Robin W. Winks and John E. Talbott.
   p. cm.
   Includes bibliographical references and index.
   ISBN-13: 978-0-19-515691-1 — ISBN-13: 978-0-19-515692-8 (pbk.)
   ISBN-10: 0-19-515691-9 — ISBN-10: 0-19-515692-7 (pbk.)
   1. Europe—History—1945–   I. Talbott, John E. II. Title.

D1051.W56 2005
940.55—dc22   2004058321

Printing number: 9 8 7 6 5 4 3 2 1

Printed in the United States of America
on acid-free paper

Contents

Maps and Boxes

Maps

Boxes

Preface

The Value of History

History is a series of arguments to be debated, not a body of data to be recorded or a set of facts to be memorized. Thus controversy in historical interpretation—over what an event actually means, over what really happened at an occurrence called "an event," over how best to generalize about the event—is at the heart of its value. Of course history teaches us about ourselves. Of course it teaches us to understand and to entertain a proper respect for our collective past. Of course it transmits to us specific skills—how to ask questions, how to seek out answers, how to think logically, cogently, lucidly, purposefully. Of course it is, or ought to be, a pleasure. But we also discover something fundamental about a people in what they choose to argue over in their past. When a society suppresses portions of its past record, that society (or its leadership) tells us something about itself. When a society seeks to alter how the record is presented, well-proven facts notwithstanding, we learn how history can be distorted to political ends.

Who controls history, and how it is written, controls the past, and who controls the past controls the present. Those who would close off historical controversy with the argument either that we know all that we need to know about a subject, or that what we know is so irrefutably correct that anyone who attacks the conventional wisdom about the subject must have destructive purposes in mind, are in the end intent upon destroying the very value of history itself—that value being that history teaches us to argue productively with each other.

Obviously, then, history is a social necessity. It gives us our identity. It helps us to find our bearings in an ever more complex present, providing us with a navigator's chart by which we may to some degree orient ourselves. When we ask who we are, and how it is that we are so, we learn skepticism and acquire the beginnings of critical judgment. Along with a sense of narrative, history also provides us with tools for explanation and analysis. It helps us to find the particular example, to see the uniqueness in a past age or past event, while also helping us to see how the particular and the unique contribute to the general. History thus shows us humanity at work and play, in society, changing through time. By letting us experience other lifestyles, history shows us the values of both subjectivity and objectivity—those twin conditions of our individual view of the world in which we live, conditions between which we constantly, and usually almost without knowing it, move. Thus, history is both a form of truth and a matter of opinion, and the close study of history should help us to distinguish between the two. It is important to make such distinctions, for as Sir Walter Raleigh wrote, "It is not truth but opinion that can travel the world without a passport." Far too often what we read, see, and hear and believe to be the truth—in our newspapers, on our television sets, from our friends—is opinion, not fact.

History is an activity. That activity asks specific questions as a means of arriving at general questions. A textbook such as this is concerned overwhelmingly with general questions, even though at times it must ask specific questions or present specific facts as a means of stalking the general. The great philosopher Karl Jaspers once remarked, "Who I am and where I belong, I first learned to know from the mirror of history." It is this mirror that any honest book must reflect.

To speak of "civilization" (of which this book is a history) is at once to plunge into controversy, so that our very first words illustrate why some people are so fearful of the study of history. To speak of "Western civilization" is even more restrictive, too limited in the eyes of some historians. Yet if we are to understand history as a process, we must approach it through a sense of place: our continuity, our standards, our process. Still, we must recognize an inherent bias in such a term as "Western civilization," indeed two inherent biases: first, that we know what it means to be "civilized"and have attained that stature; and second, that the West as a whole is a single unitary civilization. This second bias is made plain when we recognize that most scholars and virtually all college courses refer not to "Eastern civilization" but to "the civilizations of the East"—a terminology that suggests that while the West is a unity, the East is not. These are conventional phrases, buried in Western perception of reality, just as our common geographical references show a Western bias. The Near East or the Far East are, after all, "near" or "far" only in reference to a geographical location focused on western Europe. The Japanese do not refer to London as being in the far West, or Los Angeles as being in the far East, although both references would be correct if they saw the world as though they stood at its center. Although this text will accept these conventional phrases, precisely because they are traditionally embedded in our Western languages, one of the uses of history—and of the writing of a book such as this one—is to alert us to the biases buried in our language, even when necessity requires that we continue to use its conventional forms of shorthand.

But if we are to speak of civilization, we must have, at the outset, some definition of what we mean by "being civilized." Hundreds of books have been written on this subject. The average person often means only that others, the "noncivilized," speak a different language and practice alien customs. The Chinese customarily referred to all foreigners as barbarians, and the ancient Greeks spoke of those who could not communicate in Greek as *bar-bar*—those who do not speak our tongue. Yet today the ability to communicate in more than one language is one hallmark of a "civilized" person. Thus definitions of civilization, at least as used by those who think little about the meaning of their words, obviously change.

For our purposes, however, we must have a somewhat more exacting definition of the term, since it guides and shapes any book that attempts to cover the entire sweep of Western history. Anthropologists, sociologists, historians, and others may reasonably differ as to whether, for example, there is a separate American civilization that stands apart from, say, a British or Italian civilization, or whether these civilizations are simply particular variants on one larger entity, with only that larger entity—the West—entitled to be called "a civilization." Such an argument is of no major importance here, although it is instructive that it should occur. Rather, what is needed is a definition sufficiently clear to be used throughout the narrative and analysis to follow. This working definition, therefore, will hold that "civilization" involves the presence of several (although not necessarily all) of the following conditions within a society or group of interdependent societies:

1. There will be some form of government by which people administer to their political needs and responsibilities.
2. There will be some development of urban society, that is, of city life, so that the culture is not nomadic, dispersed, and thus unable to leave significant and surviving physical remnants of its presence.
3. Human beings will have become toolmakers, able through the use of metals to transform, however modestly, their physical environment, and thus their social and economic environment as well.
4. Some degree of specialization of function will have begun, usually at the workplace, so that pride, place, and purpose work together as cohesive elements in the society.
5. Social classes will have emerged, whether antagonistic to or sustaining of one another.
6. A form of literacy will have developed, so that group may communicate with group and, more important, generation with generation in writing.
7. There will be a concept of leisure time—that life is not solely for the workplace, or for the assigned class function or specialization—so that, for example, art may develop beyond (although not excluding) mere decoration and sports beyond mere competition.
8. There will be a concept of a higher being, although not necessarily through organized religion, by which a people may take themselves outside themselves to explain events and find purpose.
9. There will be a concept of time, by which the society links itself to a past and to the presumption of a future.
10. There will have developed a faculty for criticism. This faculty need not be the rationalism of the West, or intuition, or any specific religious or political mechanism, but it must exist, so that the society may contemplate change from within, rather than awaiting attack (and possible destruction) from without.

A common Western bias is to measure "progress" through technological change and to suggest that societies that show (at least until quite recently in historical time) little dramatic technological change are not civilized. In truth, neither a written record nor dramatic technological changes are essential to being civilized, although both are no doubt present in societies we would call civilized. Perhaps, as we study history, we ought to remember all three of the elements inherent in historical action as recorded by the English critic John Ruskin: "Great nations write their autobiographies in three manuscripts, the book of their deeds, the book of their words, and the book of their art."

The issue here is not whether we "learn from the past." Most often we do not, at least at the simple-minded level; we do not, as a nation, decide upon a course of action in diplomacy, for example, simply because a somewhat similar course in the past worked. We are wise enough to know that circumstances alter cases and that new knowledge brings new duties. Of course individuals "learn from the past"; the victim of a mugging takes precautions in the future. To dignify such an experience as "a lesson of history," however, is to turn mere individual growth from child into adult into history when, at most, such growth is a personal experience in biography.

We also sometimes learn the "wrong lessons" from history. Virtually anyone who wishes to argue passionately for a specific course of future action can find a lesson from the past that will convince the gullible that history repeats itself and therefore that the past is a map to the future. No serious historian argues this, however. General patterns may, and sometimes do, repeat themselves, but specific chains of events do not. Unlike those subjects that operate at the very highest level of generalization (political science, theology, science), history simply does not believe in ironclad laws. But history is not solely a series of unrelated events. There are general patterns, clusters of causes, intermediate levels of generalization that prove true. Thus, history works at a level uncomfortable to many: above the specific, below the absolute.

If complex problems never present themselves twice in the same or even in recognizably similar form—if, to borrow a frequent image from the military world, generals always prepare for the last war instead of the next one—then does the study of history offer society any help in solving its problems? The answer surely is yes—but only in a limited way. History offers a rich collection of clinical reports on human behavior in various situations—individual and collective, political, economic, military, social, cultural—that tell us in detail how the human race has conducted its affairs and that suggest ways of handling similar problems in the present. President Harry S. Truman's secretary of state, a former chief of staff, General George Marshall, once remarked that nobody could think about the problems of the 1950s who had not reflected upon the fall of Athens in the fifth century B.C. He was referring to the extraordinary history of the war between Athens and Sparta written just after it was over by Thucydides, an Athenian who fought in the war. There were no nuclear weapons, no telecommunications, no guns or gunpowder in the fifth century B.C., and the logistics of war were altogether primitive, yet twenty-three hundred years later one of the most distinguished leaders of

American military and political affairs found Thucydides indispensable to his thinking.

History, then, can only approximate the range of human behavior, with some indication of its extremes and averages. It can, although not perfectly, show how and within what limits human behavior changes. This last point is especially important for the social scientist, the economist, the sociologist, the executive, the journalist, or the diplomat. History provides materials that even an inspiring leader—a prophet, a reformer, a politician—would do well to master before seeking to lead us into new ways. For it can tell us something about what human material can and cannot stand, just as science and technology can tell engineers what stresses metals can tolerate. History can provide an awareness of the depth of time and space that should check the optimism and the overconfidence of the reformer. For example, we may wish to protect the environment in which we live—to eliminate acid rain, to cleanse our rivers, to protect our wildlife, to preserve our majestic natural scenery. History may show us that most peoples have failed to do so and may provide us with some guidance on how to avoid the mistakes of the past. But history will also show that there are substantial differences of public and private opinion over how best to protect our environment, that there are many people who do not believe such protection is necessary, or that there are people who accept the need for protection but are equally convinced that lower levels of protection must be traded off for higher levels of productivity from our natural resources. History can provide the setting by which we may understand differing opinions, but recourse to history will not get the legislation passed, make the angry happy, or make the future clean and safe. History will not define river pollution, although it can provide us with statistics from the past for comparative measurement. The definition will arise from the politics of today and our judgments about tomorrow. History is for the long and at times for the intermediate run, but seldom for the short run.

So if we are willing to accept a "relevance" that is more difficult to see at first than the immediate applicability of science and more remote than direct action, we will have to admit that history is "relevant." It may not actually build the highway or clear the slum, but it can give enormous help to those who wish to do so. And failure to take it into account may lead to failure in the sphere of action.

But history is also fun, at least for those who enjoy giving their curiosity free reign. Whether it is historical gossip we prefer (how many lovers did Catherine the Great of Russia actually take in a given year, and how much political influence did their activity in the imperial bedroom give them?), the details of historical investigation (how does it happen that the actual treasures found in a buried Viking ship correspond to those described in an Anglo-Saxon poetic account of a ship-burial?), more complex questions of cause-and-effect (how influential have the writings of revolutionary intellectuals been upon the course of actual revolutions?), the relationships between politics and economics (how far does the rise and decline of Spanish power in modern times depend upon the supply of gold and silver from New World colonies?), or cultural problems (why did western Europe choose to revive classical Greek and Roman art and literature instead of turning to some altogether new experiment?), those who enjoy history will read almost greedily to discover what they want to know. Having discovered it, they may want to know how we know what we have learned and may want to turn to those sources closest in time to the persons and questions concerned—to the original words of the participants. To read about Socrates, Columbus, or Churchill is fun; to read their own words, to visit with them as it were, is even more so. To see them in context is important; to see how we have taken their thoughts and woven them to purposes of our own is at least equally important. Readers will find the path across the mine-studded fields of history helped just a little by extracts from these voices—voices of the past but also of the present. They can also be helped by chronologies, bibliographies, pictures, maps—devices through which historians share their sense of fun and immediacy with a reader.

In the end, to know the past is to know ourselves—not entirely, not enough, but a little better. History can help us to achieve some grace and elegance of action, some cogency and completion of thought, some harmony and tolerance in human relationships. Most of all, history can give us a sense of excitement, a personal zest for watching and perhaps participating in the events around us that will, one day, be history too.

History is a narrative, a story; history is concerned foremost with major themes, even as it recognizes the significance of many fascinating digressions. Because history is largely about how and why people behave as they do, it is also about patterns of thought and belief. Ultimately, history is about what people believe to be true. To this extent, virtually all history is intellectual history, for the perceived meaning of a specific treaty, battle, or scientific discovery lies in what those involved in it and those who came after thought was most significant about it. History makes it clear that we may die, as we may live, as a result of what someone believed to be quite true in the relatively remote past.

We cannot each be our own historian. In everyday life we may reconstruct our personal past, acting as detectives for our motivations and attitudes. But formal history is a much more rigorous study. History may give us some very small capacity to predict the future. More certainly, it should help us arrange the causes for given events into meaningful patterns. History also should help us to be tolerant of the historical views of others, even as it helps to shape our own convictions. History must help us sort out the important from the less important, the relevant from the irrelevant, so that we do not fall prey to those who propose simple-minded solutions to vastly complex human problems. We must not yield to the temptation to blame one group or individual for our problems, and yet we must not fail to defend our convictions with vigor.

To recognize, indeed to celebrate, the value of all civilizations is essential to the civilized life itself. To understand that we see all civilizations through the prism of our specific historical past—for which we feel affection, in which we may feel comfortable and secure, and by which we interpret all else that we encounter—is simply to recognize that we too are the products of history. That is why we must study history and ask our own questions in our own way. For if we ask no questions of our past, there may be no questions to ask of our future.

Robin W. Winks

Acknowledgments

Thanks to Linda Harris and Peter Coveney for their help, the readers for their comments, my daughter Ann for her suggestions on the artwork, Sam Hynes for his example, and my family for its patience.

John E. Talbott

ONE

Europe in a Bipolar World

A Continent in Ruins

In the autumn of 1945, a few months after the German surrender ended World War II in Europe, an American intelligence officer named Felix Gilbert drove his jeep to a once-leafy neighborhood of Berlin. The German-born Gilbert was looking for the apartment building he had lived in as a boy. The German Army's headquarters, only one building removed from his apartment, had made the neighborhood a particular target of Allied bombing. Now he saw how thorough the air campaign had been: "the area . . . was as far as the eye could see a flat, stony desert." Yet amid the rubble he could still discern the blue and white cobblestones that had marked the driveway of his apartment house. Their survival evoked childhood memories of turn-of-the century Berlin, the imperial capital of Wilhelm II.

Berlin in 1945 was the former capital of a defeated Nazi Germany. At their zenith the German Army's conquests had stretched from the Atlantic coast of France to Stalingrad, deep inside the Soviet Union, and from the Arctic Circle to North Africa. In autumn 1942 Allied offensives in the south and east began to turn the tide. The landing of Anglo-American armies in northern France in June 1944 marked the beginning of the end for the regime of Adolf Hitler. If the beginning took longer than expected, by April 1945 these forces reached the Elbe River, deep in the heart of Germany, scarcely sixty miles west of Berlin. On the order of General Dwight D. Eisenhower they halted at the Elbe, a decision the supreme allied commander's critics never allowed to be forgotten. In their view Eisenhower's decision left Berlin the Red Army's for the taking. Rarely had an army believed it had as many scores to settle against an enemy. The Soviet Union had borne the brunt of the land war. As they thrust into Germany from the east in the early months of 1945, Soviet forces wreaked havoc for the devastation the German Army had inflicted on the Soviet Union and its people. The Battle of Berlin, the climactic event of the European war, was waged with the utmost savagery. In April the Red Army closed in on a city defended by remnants of the shattered German forces and hastily thrown-together units comprised mostly of old men and young boys.

On April 30 Hitler committed suicide in his bunker. On May 8 Germany's unconditional surrender took effect, ending World War II in Europe.

Not only Berlin but also nearly every major German city of industrial, administrative, military, or economic significance—as well as some of little or no strategic importance—lay in ruins. The targets of intense British and American bombing campaigns, they suffered civilian casualties in the hundreds of thousands. Of the millions of survivors of these air raids and firestorms, a great many no doubt suffered lasting psychological injuries. Despite, or perhaps because of, these appalling losses and their lingering effects among those who survived the devastation that fell on them from the air, the Allied bombing campaigns left little or no trace in Germany's cultural memory. Silence hung over this issue for decades, deepened perhaps by Germans' awareness that their country's actions in Britain, France, the Netherlands, the Balkans, the Soviet Union and elsewhere set off the annihilation of their own cities.

The landscape of urban ruins that characterized Germany in 1945, if not as extensive elsewhere in Europe, was nevertheless widespread. German bombing ravaged London, Plymouth, and other major English cities, as well as Rotterdam and Amsterdam in the Netherlands. Paris, occupied by the Germans between 1940 and 1944, escaped large-scale damage, but other French cities and towns were pounded by Allied air and ground forces during and after the landings in Normandy. Stretches of the Italian countryside were laid waste as the Allies ground their way up the peninsula against tenacious German defenders. Nowhere, however, was the loss of life higher and the destruction greater than in the Soviet Union. An estimated 8.5 million Soviet soldiers and nearly 17 million Soviet civilians died, a total greater than the number of military and civilian deaths among all the other European belligerents and their allies combined (the U.S. share of military deaths was 265,000, a sum greater than those sustained in any American conflict except the Civil War, but 3 percent of Soviet military losses in World War II).

If the Soviet Union was the epicenter of World War II in Europe, the war's economic consequences were felt throughout the continent. France, for instance, although spared the horrendous loss of life and property meted out to the Soviet Union, had nevertheless been plundered by the Germans. The occupation had been a form of organized looting. In 1945 French industrial production stood at only 40 percent of the level reached in 1938, which in turn, owing to the Great Depression, had declined 15 percent since 1928. Railways were at a standstill, highways in disrepair, and fuel in short supply. As in Germany, in France most of the bridges over the major rivers had been destroyed. There were shortages of everything, stimulating black markets in necessities (such as food) and luxuries (such as nylon stockings).

Unlike states throughout the European continent, Britain had not suffered the hard hand of an occupier. Still, the island nation had sustained substantial material damage. By 1943 fully 55 percent of gross domestic product (GDP) was being sucked into the war effort. Wartime losses of capital, human and material, ran to around 20 percent of prewar wealth. Britain was no

> ## Doing History

ANTHONY BEEVOR, *THE FALL OF BERLIN 1945*

The French medievalist Marc Bloch was one of the greatest historians of the twentieth century. "A good historian," he once wrote, "resembles the ogre of the legend. Wherever he smells human flesh, he knows that there he will find his prey." Stressing the experience of ordinary people as well as the actions of holders of power, Anthony Beevor's *The Fall of Berlin 1945* (New York: Viking, 2002) illustrates the force of Bloch's remark.

In the centre of Berlin, the intensely claustrophobic life of those trapped in bomb shelters and cellars continued. With the total collapse of a structured existence, people tried to calm themselves by creating some sort of routine. In one cellar quite close to the government district, a tailor's wife spread a napkin on her lap at precisely set times, then cut small pieces of bread and covered them with a little jam. She then distributed these to her husband, daughter and disabled son.

Many were on the edge of nervous breakdown. A young woman with a thin little son could not stop talking about her husband, a fireman who had been sent to the front. She had not seen him for two years. Her way of coping with the anxiety had been to make a list of jobs for him to do in the apartment—to replace a door handle, a window catch. But now their house had burned down in the shelling. 'The boy was making painful grimaces,' the interpreter Rzhevskaya noted while waiting for the Reich Chancellery to be captured. 'It was apparently difficult for him to put up with his mother's story for the hundredth time.'

The fear of unjustified reprisal in the chaos of the fighting made everyone afraid. Women, when they had a chance to slip back upstairs to their apartment, tore up and burned photographs of Hitler or anything else which might indicate support for the regime. They even felt obliged to destroy their most recent photographs of husbands, brothers or fiancés because they were taken in Wehrmacht uniform.

longer the financial capital of the world; it had long since ceased being the world's preeminent political and naval power. Its global empire remained intact, but time was running out on the exercise of European control of lands overseas. Britain emerged from the war victorious but impoverished.

Millions of refugees roamed to and fro over the ruins of central Europe. Ethnic Germans, especially, fled the westward advance of the Red Army. East Prussia, homeland of Germans for centuries, ceased to exist. Allied agreements compelled other Germans to leave Poland and Czechoslovakia and resettle in western regions of a greatly truncated Germany. Upward of 10 million "displaced persons" hit the road between 1945 and 1947, the largest and most reluctant human migration in European history, war-tossed, destitute, and miserable.

Aside from the defeat of Nazi Germany, the cardinal event in Europe in 1945 was the Red Army's advance to the center of the continent. A huge Soviet force, bearer and protector of the ideology of communism, now stood at the door of western Europe. On May 1 a Soviet soldier planted a flag atop the Reichstag, the German parliament building in Berlin. The Western democracies that had pursued the war against the Nazis had little choice but to acknowledge the Soviet conquest. Less than three weeks later, three American agents slipped into the city to see what the Russians were up to. In June 1945 defeated Germany was divided into four occupied sectors—American, British, French, and Soviet. The Soviet sector extended from eastern Germany to west of Berlin, which, as the former capital, was also divided into four occupation zones, one for each of the Allies. The chief surviving Nazi leaders were tried at Nuremberg in 1946; twelve were sentenced to death for war crimes, establishing legal precedents that have continued in force to our own day.

Soviet forces did not withdraw from some of the territories they occupied at the end of World War II until the early 1990s, or nearly half a century later. Throughout, Berlin remained the pivot of what the English historian A. J. P. Taylor, writing of an earlier time, called "the struggle for mastery in Europe." The struggle between the United States and the Soviet Union was soon pursued throughout the world, and with far greater intensity elsewhere than in Europe. Nevertheless, Europe remained the chief prize in the struggle and Berlin the chief arena.

The Cold War Breaks Out

By the time Felix Gilbert drove his jeep into Berlin in the autumn of 1945, whatever goodwill remained from the wartime alliance was rapidly petering out. Winston Churchill, Britain's wartime prime minister, recognized the chill in relations in a speech in Fulton, Missouri, in March 1946, when he spoke of an "Iron Curtain" descending in a north-south line across central Europe. Before long, a "cold war" was said to exist between the Americans and the Soviets and their respective associates, clients, and followers in Europe and around the world. The disparity between the military and economic strength of the United States and the Soviet Union and that of all the rest was so great that the two principal rivals came to be called superpowers.

The term "cold war" expressed a condition short of a shooting war but far from peace: Each side became an armed camp defending itself, by its lights, from the encroachments of the other side. In Europe tensions between the two sides were greatest between 1946 and the mid-1950s. At length, the Americans and the Russians both tacitly acknowledged that the Iron Curtain was a border too dangerous to cross without risking a general war. After the mid-1950s the struggle shifted from Europe to the developing world, where wars could be fought by proxy armies without so directly threatening the vital interests of either side.

Western historians' interpretations of the origins and course of the cold war went through three successive phases. In the first or orthodox phase, the

Winston Churchill, the indomitable wartime prime minister of Britain, flashes the "V for Victory" sign. The bowler hat, bow tie, and ever-present cigar were trademarks of the jaunty but deadly serious Churchill, leader of Britons in what he called "their finest hour." Called to office in the crisis provoked by the German attack on France in May 1940, he served as prime minister for the remainder of World War II. (Getty Images.)

United States was seen as reacting defensively to the aggressive moves of the Soviet Union, especially in Europe. The second phase of interpretation, which ran throughout the 1960s, the middle period of the cold war, was marked by intense controversy. Revisionists, disquieted by the American conduct of the Vietnam War, shifted attention to American initiatives. They regarded the dropping of atomic bombs on Hiroshima and Nagasaki, for instance, as intended to intimidate the Soviet Union as much as to force the surrender of Japan. The primary aim of American foreign policy, revisionists insisted, was to keep the world open to American trade, not to make it safe for democracy. The end of the cold war, and the opening of the Soviet archives, heralded a third phase of interpretation, in which the aggressive

A Closer Look

GEORGE F. KENNAN'S DISPATCH FROM MOSCOW: THE SOVIET UNION AND THE ATLANTIC PACT

In the so-called Long Telegram of 1946 (later published in the journal *Foreign Affairs* as "The Sources of Soviet Conduct") the American diplomat George F. Kennan laid down a policy for "containing" the Soviet Union within the frontiers it had attained at the end of World War II. By military, economic, and political means, the United States and its European allies pursued a policy of containment throughout the cold war. One manifestation of the policy was the North Atlantic Treaty Organization (NATO), established in 1949 as a response to the military threat the Soviet Union was thought to pose to western Europe. In a 1952 dispatch to the U.S. State Department Kennan, then ambassador to the Soviet Union, commented on the Soviet Union and the Atlantic Pact.

It was the spring of 1948, and particularly the period on the heels of the Czech developments, that saw the rise of a strong wave of military anxiety throughout the Western countries, and even a species of "war scare," supported particularly by reports from Western observers in Berlin. To date there has never been any evidence that would tend to confirm that Moscow had any thought at that time of launching its armed forces against the West or that its views on this subject were in any way different from those described above. Nevertheless, a firm opinion crystallized in Western circles there was danger of a Soviet attack; and with this opinion came a feeling that rather than, or at least together with, consolidating the political gains that had been achieved in the past year and proceeding to the crushing of the Western European Communist parties in conjunction with the restoration of decent economic conditions in the countries concerned, the thing to do was to proceed to the formation of a Western military alliance against the Soviet Union. As will be recalled, the negotiations in this direction, namely the negotiations for the Atlantic Pact, were begun in June 1948 and concluded in December of that year.

I do not mean to say that there was no justification for the conclusion of the Atlantic Pact. Large numbers of people, both in Western Europe and in the United States, were incapable of understanding the Russian technique of penetration and "partial war" or of thinking in terms of this technique. They were capable of thinking about international developments only in the old-fashioned terms of full-fledged war or full-fledged peace. It was inconceivable to them that there could be real and serious threats to the independence of their countries that did not come to them in the form of foreign armies marching across frontiers; and it was natural that in undertaking to combat what they conceived to be a foreign threat they should have turned to the old-fashioned and familiar expedient of military alliance. They had understood that there was a threat; but they had not understood the nature of that threat, and were hardly capable of doing so.

Nor was it possible for anyone to argue that this outlook was wholly wrong. In the first place, the use of violence had never been ruled out of the Soviet bag of tricks; violence occupied, in fact, a prominent place in that collection. One could not even say that international violence—that is, war—had been fully ruled out. The Soviet outlook still allowed for the use of violence on the international scale in certain circumstances. Its lack of plans for instigating major warfare at that particular time rested primarily on the peculiarities of a given situation which rendered such an idea unpromising and inexpedient. Were the Western world to fall into a state of military weakness that constituted a direct invitation to cheap and easy aggression, it was quite possible that Soviet thinking might change. Or again, were the political war to progress favorably enough from the Soviet standpoint, it was always possible that a decision might be taken to use the Red Army in the wake of successful political operations, for purposes of giving the decisive push or conducting the mopping-up operations at minor cost. Any drastic alteration in the terms and course of the cold war, either to Soviet advantage or disadvantage, might in fact have operated to alter the Soviet attitude on war.

Furthermore, it was clear that any marked disparity between the armed strength of the Communist and non-Communist world, to the disadvantage of the latter, would be mercilessly if subtly exploited by the Kremlin for purposes of intimidating Western European peoples and inflicting them with uncertainty and lack of confidence in resisting Communist political pressures. In fact, the mere existence of such a disparity would have this effect even in the absence of any deliberate, overt Soviet effort to exploit it. There was thus a clear, legitimate and undeniable need for strong military strength in the West. And this, in terms of modern armament, meant arrangements for pooling in many ways the military resources and territorial facilities necessary for the conduct of modern war on the grand scale by the Western powers as a group.

. . . The present situation has in it several of those tremendous dilemmas which in the past have been the makings of great wars, and there is as yet no visible prospect of a solution of these dilemmas by nonmilitary means. It is easy, in these circumstances, to argue for the inevitability of war and to sell one's soul to it. Unquestionably, the events of the past four or five years have brought war much further into the realm of possibility and have heightened the danger of its imminent outbreak, not so much as a result of any deliberate desire of either side that it should break out, but rather as a result of the inability of people in given possible contingencies to find any acceptable alternative solution. Yet an intensive scrutiny of the Moscow scene yields no reason to believe that war is yet inevitable, and provides no justification for those who would sell their souls to this assumption. We have, as an anchor of reassurance, the overwhelmingly important fact that there is no evidence that the Soviet leaders, obsessed as they are with hatred of the West and deaf as they are to the voice of reason, regard the turmoil and suffering of another world war as the preferred milieu in which to seek the satisfaction of their aspirations; and the contemporary development of weapons is hardly such as to impel them in that direction. For the moment, they seem content to continue to maintain the contest on their curious level of "partial war"; and I, for one, am reluctant to believe that they cannot be successfully coped with by us on this terrain. Whether, in the event the "partial war" should go badly for them, they would retain their preference for contest on the political level, or how long they would retain it, I cannot say. But I think we can say of them, as they now say of us, that if they were to be forced by political reverses to a point of great desperation, their military power would by that time have been appreciably deflated in its real capabilities, and their effort, in turn, would then be the sharp but unpromising struggle of the cornered animal.

actions of the Soviet Union in the mid- to late-1940s regained the spotlight. On balance, according to the neo-orthodox position, American moves in the early years of the cold war were reactions to Soviet provocation.

In the immediate aftermath of World War II, the Soviet Union moved rapidly to consolidate its territorial hold on central and eastern Europe. Under Soviet military domination, Poland, Romania, Hungary, and Bulgaria were made into "people's republics," or Soviet satellites. In the lands between the Elbe and Oder rivers, roughly one third of the old Germany, Soviet rule continued for a time. The Soviets annexed to the USSR a strip of territory east of the line established by the Oder and Neisse rivers and handed the rest over to a Polish satellite. Finland remained independent but eager not to offend its gigantic and truculent Soviet neighbor. Austria reverted to a qualified independence, detached from Germany, to which it had been joined in 1938, but divided, like Germany, into four occupation zones.

All these moves in the remaking of states and boundaries happened between 1945 and 1947. In 1948 the communists seized power in Czechoslovakia, ousting the freely elected democratic government of Eduard Benes. The leaders of each satellite—all, with the notable exception of Josip Tito of Yugoslavia, more or less willingly under the thumb of the Soviet leadership—mimicked Soviet policies. Under the guise of a command economy, where the allocation of resources fell to a centralized government bureaucracy, not the workings of the market, the communists moved quickly to collectivize agriculture, impose forced industrialization, and dominate cultural life, all under the fearsome eye of an omnipresent secret police.

The United States Pursues a Policy of Containment

The Western democracies had no means of directly challenging the Soviet Union's efforts at satellite building in those areas of central and eastern Europe directly under its military control. The United States, however, was determined to keep western Europe from falling into the Soviet sphere (whether the Soviets had either the intention or the capability of making this happen was long debated among policy makers and historians). The one Western democracy to emerge from World War II far stronger, in both military and economic terms, than it had been before the war broke out, the United States deployed a combination of economic and military policies to counter what it perceived as the aggressive and possibly expansionist aims of the Soviet Union, not only in Europe but also around the world.

Soviet intentions aside, the United States required strong western European trading partners in order to sustain its own economic health. In 1947 Secretary of State George C. Marshall announced a program of economic aid to help Europe recover from the ruin of the war. Marshall Plan aid was offered to the Soviet Union and its satellites as well, but the Soviets declined. Combined with the substantial efforts the states of western Europe made on their own behalf, the Marshall Plan was spectacularly successful.

The Written Record

MARSHALL COMMENCEMENT ADDRESS, HARVARD UNIVERSITY

In a commencement address delivered at Harvard University on June 5, 1947, General George Marshall, the U.S. secretary of state, put forth the argument for the European Recovery Program, better known as the Marshall Plan.

In considering the requirements for the rehabilitation of Europe, the physical loss of life, the visible destruction of cities, factories, mines, and railroads was correctly estimated, but it has become obvious during recent months that this visible destruction was probably less serious than the dislocation of the entire fabric of European economy. For the past 10 years conditions have been highly abnormal. The feverish preparation for war and the more feverish maintenance of the war effort engulfed all aspects of national economies. Machinery has fallen into disrepair or is entirely obsolete. Under the arbitrary and destructive Nazi rule, virtually every possible enterprise was geared into the German war machine. Long-standing commercial ties, private institutions, banks, insurance companies, and shipping companies disappeared, through loss of capital, absorption through nationalization, or by simple destruction. In many countries, confidence in the local currency has been severely shaken. The breakdown of the business structure of Europe during the war was complete. Recovery has been seriously retarded by the fact that two years after the close of hostilities a peace settlement with Germany and Austria has not been agreed upon. But even given a more prompt solution of these difficult problems, the rehabilitation of the economic structure of Europe quite evidently will require a much longer time and greater effort than had been foreseen. . . .

The truth of the matter is that Europe's requirements for the next three or four years of foreign food and other essential products—principally from America—are so much greater than her present ability to pay that she must have substantial additional help or face economic, social, and political deterioration of a very grave character. . . .

Aside from the demoralizing effect on the world at large and the possibilities of disturbances arising as a result of the desperation of the people concerned, the consequences to the economy of the United States should be apparent to all. It is logical that the United States should do whatever it is able to do to assist in the return of normal economic health in the world, without which there can be no political stability and no assured peace. . . . Any government that is willing to assist in the task of recovery will find full cooperation, I am sure, on the part of the United States Government. Any government which maneuvers to block the recovery of other countries cannot expect help from us. Furthermore, governments, political parties, or groups which seek to perpetuate human misery in order to profit therefrom politically or otherwise will encounter the opposition of the United States.

By means of diplomacy if possible and force if necessary, it became the policy of the United States to prevent the Soviet Union from extending its direct control, or its influence by proxy, beyond the limits it had consolidated in 1947. This policy of containment was foreshadowed in the Greek civil war. Greek communists, encouraged by the communist states of Albania, Yugoslavia, and Bulgaria, behind whom a Soviet hand could be perceived, tried to seize control of the government. Stalin concurrently pressured Turkey to allow the Soviet Navy unhindered passage through the straits leading from the Black Sea to the Mediterranean. In response, President Harry S. Truman proclaimed that countries facing the threat of communist aggression could count on help from the United States. Under this Truman Doctrine he sent American military aid to Greece and Turkey. The threat to the Turks receded, and by 1949, after severe fighting, the Greek government put down the communist uprising with the help of American advisers.

In 1948 the Soviets turned up the pressure on Berlin. The old capital of Germany, it will be recalled, lay deep in the Soviet zone of occupation, in which they had installed the satellite government of East Germany. The Western allies—the United States, Britain, and France—retained their own zones of occupation in Berlin. By shutting off the highways from the west, the Soviets sought to force the allies to abandon the city to them. The allies circumvented the blockade with a huge and daring airlift. Outwitted, the Soviets eventually relented and reopened the land routes. They did not, however, weaken in their resolve to drive the Western powers from the most important city in central Europe.

Alarmed by the relentless Soviet probing over Berlin, in 1949 the United States, France, and Britain consolidated their occupied sectors in a fledgling independent state, the Federal Republic of Germany, or West Germany. The West German capital was established at Bonn, a town ever to be characterized as "sleepy" by Western journalists. The same anxieties over Soviet intentions that gave birth to the Federal Republic of Germany also gave rise to the North Atlantic Treaty Organization (NATO), a standing military alliance including most of the nations of western Europe.

Inside NATO, the United States resembled an eight-hundred-pound gorilla, so disproportionately great was its power compared to that of its partners. By resorting to a kind of diplomatic jujitsu, however, weaker members of the alliance sometimes succeeded in getting what they wanted from their formidable friend. American reliance on France's steadfastness in pursuing its war in Indochina, for instance (see Chapter 2), gave the French room to maneuver in Europe, even when their perceived interests clashed with those of the United States. An American-backed proposal to create a European Defense Community (EDC) met stiff French resistance, for the EDC raised the specter of a newly armed West Germany, an alarming prospect to a France still struggling to recover from World War II. The Americans moderated their enthusiasm. German rearmament eventually took place, but only from 1955, and within the structure of NATO.

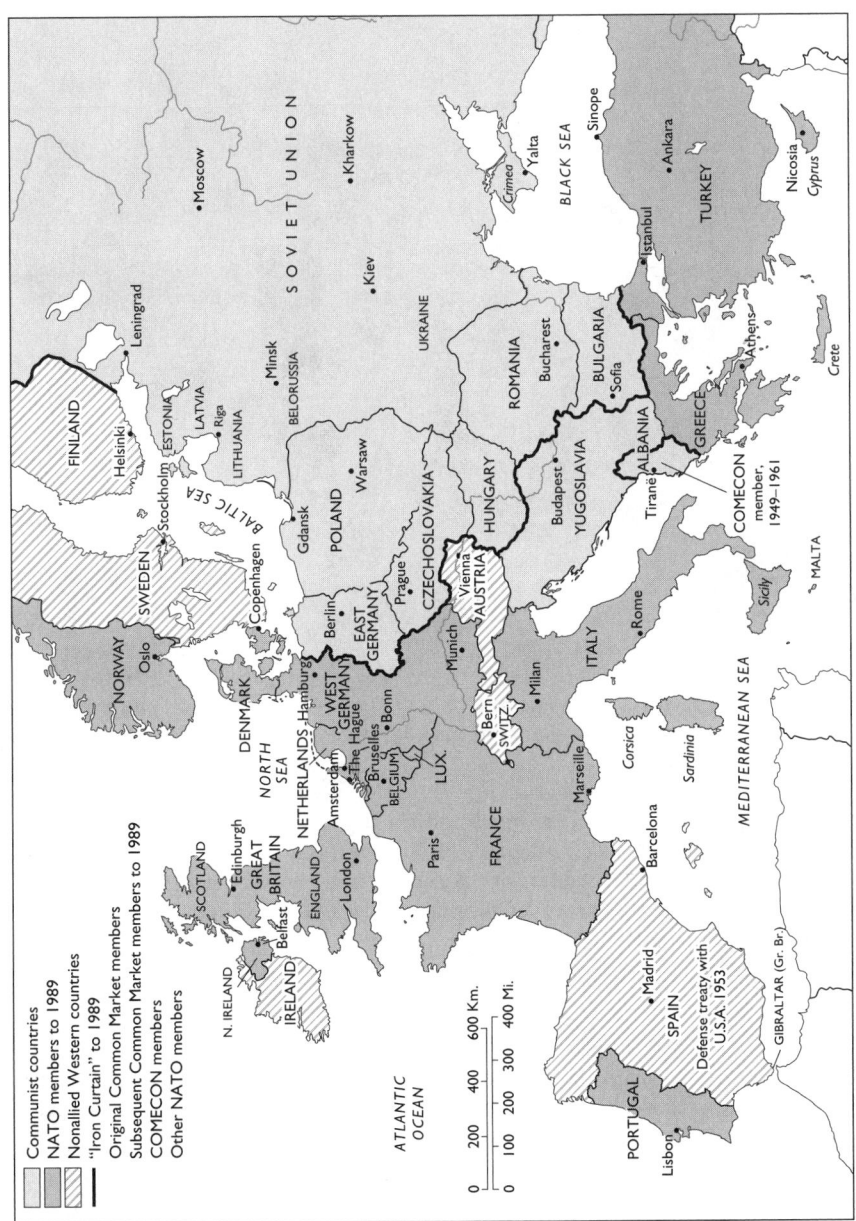

Military Alliance and Multinational Economic Groupings, 1949–1989.

Communist countries
NATO members to 1989
Nonallied Western countries
"Iron Curtain" to 1989
Original Common Market members
Subsequent Common Market members to 1989
COMECON members
Other NATO members

Berlin in ruins, an urban landscape characteristic of much of Germany at the end of World War II. With an eye toward damaging civilian morale as well as hitting military and industrial targets, Allied aircraft dropped millions of tons of bombs on German cities. The aerial bombardment reduced thousands of buildings to rubble and killed hundreds of thousands of Germans. It is not clear, however, that bombing had any greater effect on the Germans' will to fight than a similar German campaign had on British city-dwellers from the summer of 1940 on. In his book The Natural History of Destruction *German novelist W. G. Sebald comments on the odd silence that fell on this subject among Germans in the decades following the war.   (Getty Images.)*

Still, dependence was dependence. Once the Americans decided the war in Indochina was lost, as they did in 1954, the French could not go it alone. And once the United States intervened in 1956 in the Suez Affair, the concerted French, British, and Israeli operation against Egypt's Gamal Abdel Nasser, that adventure was doomed. After Suez, however, Charles de Gaulle aggressively pursued a line independent of the United States. Suez aside, Britain remained the generally loyal partner of its former colony. West Germany never ceased to forget how much it owed to the United States for its readmission to the club of respectable nations. Here a mixture of prudence, idealism, and self-interest worked to the mutual advantage of both parties. The leadership of West Germany believed their country needed the sponsorship of the Americans among their new friends in western Europe and American protection from their old enemy, the Soviet Union.

For their part, the Americans garrisoned in West Germany comprised the land forces that were the first line of defense against a Soviet invasion. In reality they were a trip wire, installed to guarantee that the Americans would not renege on their commitment to defend western Europe; they could only have slowed, not halted, the advance of huge Soviet armored divisions from the east. They also counted on a rearmed West Germany to assist in its own defense.

After the mid-1950s the American struggle with the Soviet Union shifted away from Europe. Successive American presidents never ceased reiterating their intention of standing by western Europe in the event of a Soviet attack. Nevertheless, they were circumspect to the point of inaction about pulling any European chestnuts out of the fires of decolonization. So great was American power in a bipolar world, however, that American policy continued to impinge on Europe even when American attention was focused on far distant regions of the world.

American foreign policy in the years following World War II was largely bipartisan. Democrats and Republicans generally agreed on the aims to be pursued: the reestablishment of liberal democracy and trade in western Europe, the containment of the Soviet Union within its borders, and a global engagement against the spread of communism, whether under the aegis of the Soviet Union, China, or another Asian power.

Such a threat appeared to materialize in June 1950, when communist North Korea invaded South Korea. The communist camp (the Soviet Union, China, and North Korea) may have thought the invasion would go unchallenged. At the behest of President Harry Truman, however, the United Nations sent troops to the defense of South Korea. Turkey, Holland, Belgium, Greece, and France all contributed small combat units. Under General Douglas MacArthur the largely American force halted the North Korean drive and pushed the enemy back beyond the 38th parallel, almost to the frontier with China. The government of the People's Republic of China found this intolerable, as it had repeatedly warned. Chinese troops joined the North Koreans in pushing the Americans southward again. By 1951 the line of battle had been stabilized roughly along the boundary established six years earlier between North and South Korea. After prolonged negotiations, an armistice was finally concluded in July 1953. After all the fighting the United States had managed to hold on to the devastated southern portion of the country; the communists had been driven back north, which they turned into a "hermit kingdom" isolated from the outside world. Neither side could call the Korean settlement a victory.

By the time the Korean War ended, Stalin had been dead more than three months. His heirs recognized that any attack that threatened the vital interests of the United States might touch off the disaster of nuclear war. Yet to relax the tension also put the Soviet Union at risk of losing its position as leader of the world communist movement. Balancing these risks remained the major foreign policy challenge to Stalin's successors until nearly the end of the Soviet regime.

As will be seen in Chapter 2, the exigencies of the Korean War drew the United States into supporting France's war in Indochina. At length France gave up its struggle to reestablish its colony in southeast Asia. A main feature of the peace accord negotiated in Geneva in 1954 was the creation of two Vietnams. A line drawn at the 17th parallel of latitude separated a communist north, under the leadership of Ho Chi Minh, from a noncommunist south, under the leadership of Catholic nationalist Ngo Dinh Diem. The peace settlement promised free elections within two years. Diem adeptly put down rival claimants to power, but he frittered away his limited opportunities for long-term success. Canceling the promised elections, he drew his immediate family around him and ruled despotically. In 1958 and 1959, guerrilla activity under the direction of a shadowy group calling itself the Viet Cong, or VC, backed by Hanoi from the outset, broke out in the countryside.

Having backed Diem as its man in South Vietnam, the United States stuck with him. In neighboring Laos, formerly part of French Indochina, a shadowy war unfolded between rebels supported by both North Vietnam and the Soviet Union and shifting, unstable, and corrupt government forces supported by the United States. Two bantamweight fighters traded jabs as their Soviet and American handlers crouched in opposite corners of the ring, hoping their man would deliver a knockout punch. Laos was a good example of the proxy wars the superpowers fought around the globe in the cold war era, far from the main arena of Europe. To the degree these conflicts reduced tensions in Europe, Europeans were the beneficiaries, a consequence of no solace to those caught up in the fighting.

Under the presidency of John F. Kennedy from 1961 to 1963, Diem continued to elude American pressures for reform. American military advisers entered the country in ever greater numbers. Buddhist-led protests against Diem's harsh and arbitrary rule increased. In November, only weeks before Kennedy was assassinated in Dallas, Diem and his brother were arrested and then murdered in a South Vietnamese army coup connived at by the CIA and high-ranking officials of the American government.

Lyndon Johnson, thrust into the U.S. presidency by Kennedy's assassination, declined the fleeting opportunity the tragedy gave him to reassess American policy in Vietnam. Instead, he substantially reinforced the number of American troops his predecessor had committed to the struggle and, in the guise of an aerial bombing campaign, took the offensive against North Vietnam. By such means, in a phrase that has stuck, Johnson "escalated" the war.

His administration made vigorous efforts to enlist European governments in the defense of South Vietnam, but to no avail. It was not that U.S. NATO allies opposed American policy—they were against the spread of Asian communism and sympathetic to Washington's attempt to preserve an independent South Vietnam. Nevertheless, they resisted Johnson's arm-twisting on the issue of sending combat troops. In the end, they did not share the American conviction that the struggle in Vietnam deeply mattered to Western security and were not eager to explain to a skeptical public why they had committed soldiers to a far-off war. By and large, however, they kept their opinions to themselves (and were encouraged by Washington not to make their misgivings known). Only Charles de Gaulle outspokenly criticized the American venture and periodically called for negotiations to end it. Although a handful of Asian nations, as well as Australia and New Zealand, contributed modest numbers of troops, the Vietnam War was America's war. Characterized early on by the American journalist David Halberstam as a "quagmire," it became America's disaster.

In the end, it was less the Vietnam War than the anti–Vietnam War movement that affected the history of Europe in the 1960s. Student activists in France, West Germany, and Italy took their cues in dress, demeanor, and gesture from their American counterparts and from each other; the channels of international cultural transmission were myriad, complex, reciprocal, and somewhat mysterious in their workings. The Vietnam War was not the only issue in the repertory of Europewide student protest; it was not the most important issue, in the long run. In France, for instance, it was a catalyst of protest in general, rallying French students to a movement embracing issues of far greater immediacy and importance to them than a distant war in Southeast Asia. One such issue was the overcrowding of French universities and the apparent indifference of French authorities to these conditions. There were many others.

Restlessness in the Soviet Bloc, 1948–1968

Meanwhile, despite the long shadow the Red Army cast over eastern Europe, the satellite states proved restive under Soviet domination. In 1948 the Soviets faced rebellion from Yugoslavia, hitherto the most pliant of all the new communist states of eastern Europe. Yugoslavia, created in the aftermath of World War I from remnants of the Habsburg and Ottoman empires, had overthrown a pro-German government in 1941. Throughout World War II it remained a scene of guerrilla warfare against the Germans and Italians. Two main groups battled the foreigners, each as hostile to the other as they were to the conventional forces they harassed. The Chetniks represented the Serb royalist and Orthodox dominion over the south-Slav kingdom; the Partisans were led by the Croatian Tito. With Soviet help the Partisans gained the upper hand against the Chetniks and won control of Yugoslavia in 1944.

Once in power the charismatic Tito established a communist government and abolished the Yugoslav monarchy. With a view to accommodating long-standing ethnic and religious tensions in the region, he organized Yugoslavia along federalist lines. For three years he assiduously adopted all the standard Soviet policies with respect to politics, the economy, and culture. He was also inclined, however, to pursue independent policies of his own. In June 1948, at the instigation of Moscow, Tito's regime was expelled from the Communist Information Bureau (Cominform), a collection of European communist parties bearing the Soviet seal of approval. The Soviet satellites broke their economic agreements with Yugoslavia, unloosed barrages of anti-Tito propaganda, and stirred up trouble along borders they shared with the new pariah.

Stalin believed he could bully the Yugoslavs into knuckling under. "I will shake my little finger," he said, "and there will be no more Tito."

The United States was quick to exploit Tito's fallout with Stalin. With an eye to deepening the wedge driven into the Soviet bloc, Washington offered aid to Yugoslavia, and Tito quickly accepted. Under his guidance, Yugoslav communism set its own course, rejecting the brutal, secretive, and highly centralized Stalinist model. Decentralization spread from the economy, where a modicum of worker participation in planning was encouraged, to local governments, to the central government in Belgrade, and finally to the Yugoslav Communist party itself. This national brand of communism was anathema to the Soviet regime, whose own system required strict adherence to rules laid down in Moscow and the unwavering faith of rank-and-file party members in the wisdom of the leadership. Alarmed that Titoism might be catching, the Soviets conducted a series of ferocious purges of "Titoists" in eastern Europe, cowing into submission anyone who might hope to try the Yugoslav experiment.

Differing with Moscow was bad; rebellion against Soviet rule was worse. In March 1953 Stalin died, casting the Soviet leadership into turmoil. Who would succeed the iron-handed dictator? In the interim, how secure was Moscow's control of the Soviet Empire? An unwelcome answer came in June, in the form of an uprising of workers in East Berlin. A strike over the government's plan to cut wages by as much as a third swelled into large street demonstrations. Demonstrators turned to rioting against the East German government, demanding free elections and the end of the Soviet occupation. In a pattern that repeated itself elsewhere in the Soviet bloc in coming years—in Poland, Hungary, Czechoslovakia, and Poland again—Soviet tanks rumbled through the streets. With the help of the local police, the rebellion was swiftly put down, but not before spreading throughout East Germany. Two hundred sixty-seven people were killed in the fighting, martial law was declared, thousands were arrested and imprisoned. Blame was affixed to "fascists," provocateurs, and outside agitators. In the aftermath of the revolt the regime proffered carrots, in the form of rescinding wage cuts and making concessions on a range of welfare issues. The badly frightened communist leadership also continued to wield the stick of repression. In the factories, for instance, it established networks of militiamen and stool pigeons expected, in the event of trouble, to act alongside Soviet forces. By such measures the regime sought to tighten its grip over 17 million East Germans.

The Soviet succession crisis was not resolved as swiftly as the East German rising was put down. At first the struggle for power produced a collective leadership, a solution that allowed ambitious and mistrustful men to keep an eye on each other—at the cost of nearly paralyzing the government. At length, however, Nikita Khrushchev outwitted and outmaneuvered his rivals to become first secretary of the Communist party and, eventually, premier. One of Khrushchev's first acts as party secretary was to seek to heal the breach with Tito. In May 1955 he went in person to Belgrade and publicly apologized for the quarrel. Relations between Tito and Moscow improved, although the Yugoslavs never abandoned their ties to the Western democracies. Khruschev even went so far as to declare that many prominent victims of the Titoist purges had been executed wrongly. But in making these admissions Khrushchev opened the door to new troubles.

In 1956 Khrushchev denounced Stalin and admitted to many past injustices in the Soviet Union. This proved far too strong a brew for the European satellites. Anticommunist riots by workers in Poznan, Poland, in June 1956 were followed by severe upheavals elsewhere in Poland. The uprising was conducted by one wing of the Communist party, led by Wladislaw Gomulka. Not even the presence in Warsaw of Khrushchev himself prevented Gomulka's rise to power, although at one moment the Soviets seem to have contemplated imposing their will by force. Yet because the new government in Poland was still communist, they allowed it to remain in power until 1970.

In Hungary, however, the upheaval went further. Starting as an anti-Stalinist movement within the Communist party, the Hungarian disturbance at first brought Imre Nagy into office as premier. But popular hatred of communism and the Soviets boiled over, and young men and women took up arms in Budapest in the hope of ousting the communists and taking Hungary out of the Soviet sphere. When Hungary denounced the Warsaw Pact, Khrushchev ordered full-fledged military action. In November 1956 Soviet tanks and troops swept back into Budapest and put down the revolution in blood and fire. A puppet government was installed and more than 150,000 Hungarians fled to the West.

The Hungarian uprising demonstrated that Khrushchev was unwilling to permit much deviation from the Soviet line and that he would use military power when that line was crossed. Perhaps most important, more definitively than the East German rising of 1953 or the Poznan riots of 1956, it demonstrated to other satellite states that they could not count on aid from the Western democracies in the face of Soviet resistance. The effect was to concede the impermeability of the Iron Curtain, putting an end to major probes across it by either side.

The eastern European satellites had been bound together in the Council for Mutual Economic Aid (Comecon), established in 1949, which took measures to standardize machinery and coordinate economic policies and issued blasts against western European efforts at economic cooperation through the Common Market. Yugoslavia never joined Comecon, and after 1958 it was not invited to send observers. In 1958–1959 Comecon called for a specialization plan in which the more developed countries would concentrate on heavy industry, and Romania in particular on the production of raw materials (chiefly food and oil). The Romanian government protested, pointing to its already considerable achievement in heavy industry.

Thus the Romanians, like the Yugoslavs, assumed a more independent position within the communist bloc. They increased their trade with the noncommunist world and remained neutral in the growing Soviet-Chinese quarrel. In 1964 the Soviets sanctioned Romania's continued efforts to build a steel industry. Soviet propaganda, however, called for integrating the lower Danube region—which would have meant taking territory from Romania—and denied that the Romanians had contributed to the Allied caused in World War II. The Romanians claimed full credit for their "liberation from fascism" and dared to demand the return of Bessarabia and northern Bukovina. Yugoslav-Romanian cooperation became an important part of Romanian policy. Largely owing to the balancing skill of the Romanian communist leaders, first Gheorghe Gheogiu-Dej, who was party secretary from 1952 to 1965, and then Nicolae Ceausescu, supported by the traditionally anti-Soviet sentiments of Romanians generally, the Romanians demonstrated a measure of independence in foreign and economic affairs.

In East Germany, the Soviet Union had created its most industrially productive European satellite, fully integrated into Comecon. Strategically East Germany was of great importance to the USSR; control over East Germany enabled the Soviets to keep Poland surrounded and to keep communist troops within easy reach of West Germany. Every year thousands of East Germans had been escaping into West Berlin, and the East German population had declined by 2 million between 1949 and 1961. Because West Berlin provided an example of prosperity and free democratic government that was more effective than any propaganda, Khrushchev was determined to get the Western powers out of Berlin. He threatened to sign a peace treaty with the puppet government of East Germany, which was not yet recognized by the West, to turn over to it all communications to Berlin, and to support it in any effort it might make to force the Western powers out. Western refusal to abandon agreements concluded during World War II led to a prolonged diplomatic crisis in 1959.

Western powers could not permit the Soviets to re-create the conditions that led to the airlift of 1948 or accept the suggestion that, once Western troops were removed, Berlin would become a "free city." Defenseless and surrounded by communist territory, Berlin and its 2 million citizens might soon be swallowed up. Moreover, the Soviet proposal for a confederation of East and West Germany aroused the gravest doubts. How could a state that was a full member of the Western coalition of NATO join with one that belonged to the Soviet coalition's Warsaw Pact? How could a state that stood for capitalist development federate with one completely communized? How could a parliamentary state governed by a multiparty system federate with a communist totalitarian state?

While the Berlin threat persisted, American President Dwight D. Eisenhower and Khrushchev agreed to exchange visits, and Khrushchev made a dramatic tour of the United States. But when the leaders of the two great powers met at a summit in Paris in May 1960, tensions were once again inflamed. A Soviet missile had brought down an American U-2, a lightweight, extremely fast spy plane that had been taking high-altitude photographs of Soviet territory from bases in Turkey and Pakistan. The Soviets had captured the pilot unharmed. After an initial denial, Eisenhower had to admit the truth of the charge: The incident ended both the summit meeting and the plans for his own visit to the Soviet Union.

When Eisenhower's successor, John F. Kennedy, met Khrushchev in Vienna (June 1961), Khrushchev insisted that his country would sign the treaty with East Germany before the end of the year. Tension mounted, and the number of refugees fleeing from East Berlin rose to a thousand a day. On August 13, East German forces cut all communications between East and West Berlin and began to build a wall to prevent further departures. Taken by surprise, the United States realized that it could not resort to arms to prevent the closing of East Germany's own border. The Berlin Wall became the infamous symbol of a government that had to imprison its own people to keep them from leaving. Escapes, recaptures, and shootings continued along the wall for nearly three decades, but the immediate crisis proved to be over. Khrushchev had backed away from unilateral cancellation of the Berlin treaties.

If the Soviet leadership was willing to swallow hard and accept—because it recognized it had little choice—Yugoslav and then Romanian demands for autonomy, its tolerance of deviation, to say nothing of disloyalty, had narrow limits. In its response to the East German, Hungarian, and Polish risings, as well as to the ceaseless flight westward of East Germans, it had shown itself capable of ruthless and decisive action. In Czechoslovakia in 1968 it faced another bout of restlessness with Soviet rule. Long the most Stalinist of the eastern European governments, the Czech regime was unpopular at home. Soviet exploitation and the rigidity of communist dogma had crippled the once flourishing Czech economy. Then in 1968 Alexander Dubcek, a Slovak communist trained in the Soviet Union, took over the Czech Communist party as first secretary. The Dubcek government freed the press from censorship; it appeared that the regime might even permit opposition political parties to exist. Some Czech army officers apparently favored revising the Warsaw Pact, which enabled the Soviets to hold military exercises in the territory of any member state.

However, the Czechs could not put through such a radical liberalization without alarming the Soviets and the East German government. In the spring and summer of 1968 the Soviets moved from first denouncing the Dubcek regime to intimidating and bullying it, and finally to armed intervention. Soviet and satellite tank divisions, more than 500,000 strong, swept into the country and met no active resistance. There was little bloodshed, but there was great shock. Those who had been arguing that the Soviets had outgrown the Stalinist repression of earlier years found themselves proved wrong, and the French and Italian Communist parties joined the Yugoslav and Romanian parties in condemning the invasion.

The return of Stalinism to Czechoslovakia was inexorable. Dubcek was ousted, and a grim purge of Czech intellectuals followed. The Soviets had been so alarmed by the Czech cultural, economic, and political ferment and its military and diplomatic implications that they were willing, at least temporarily, to sacrifice much of the international goodwill that they had been able to accumulate.

Did a Nuclear Balance Create a Nuclear Peace?

NATO, which combined in one military alliance the armies of nineteen countries, was incapable of putting into the field anything like the numbers of troops and conventional weapons available to the Red Army and posed at the door of western Europe. NATO military planners worried endlessly over how to keep the huge Soviet armored divisions from pouring westward from their barracks and through the so-called Fulda Gap, the shortest and easiest route from East Germany to the Rhine. They never came up with a good answer. Yet despite the huge imbalance in conventional forces between the NATO allies and the Soviet Union, the peace was kept in Europe until the Soviet Union was no more.

One reason for this may lie with Soviet intentions. It could be the Soviets never had the aggressive designs the Western democracies imputed to them. Perhaps, as they invariably insisted, their armored divisions were meant solely for the defense of the homeland. A more likely explanation for the long peace may rest with Soviet and American nuclear capabilities. For their part, the Americans compensated for NATO's inferiority in conventional forces by unfurling a nuclear umbrella over western Europe. Any deliberate move by the Red Army toward the area the umbrella covered was guaranteed to provoke an American nuclear response. The Soviets could not test American resolve without risking their own nuclear annihilation. This was precisely the point.

For some years this arrangement belonged to the realm of theory. Until the early 1950s the Americans had few nuclear weapons and the Soviets next to none. For a longer time, both sides had to rely on relatively slow and vulnerable bombers to deliver such weapons to targets. Then in the late 1950s, to the astonishment and consternation of the Americans, the Soviets succeeded in putting their nuclear weapons atop accurate long-range guided missiles. The United States quickly followed suit, and each side acquired a nuclear threat wholly credible to the other. Released from the realm of theory like a genie from its bottle, it was no longer merely a question of an American nuclear force shielding western Europe from Soviet conventional forces. The nuclear capabilities of both sides were roughly equivalent. Each side strove to maintain parity; each suspected its adversary of scheming to gain superiority. In the end, capabilities mattered more than intentions. In the 1960s the Soviet Strategic Rocket Forces became capable of wiping out every city in North America; slightly later, multiwarhead Soviet missiles gained the capacity to destroy American missiles and bombers on the ground, with enough missiles in reserve to launch a second strike if the Americans chose to retaliate. American nuclear capabilities were the mirror image of the Soviets'. The sheer power of the weapons themselves, one historian wrote, was "threat enough to keep the United States and its allies on edge for decades."

Linking nuclear weapons to rapid delivery systems created a great paradox. The balance of nuclear forces assured that each superpower could destroy the other several times over. This grim knowledge underlaid the doctrine of "mutually assured destruction," whose acronym happened to be MAD, a system of deterrence that proved robust enough to keep the peace. Each superpower, knowing it risked almost certain annihilation at the hands of the other, chose not to reach for the nuclear sword.

MAD rested on the premise that the offensive capacity of nuclear missiles would keep each superpower from launching a strike against the other. Neither side, the argument went, would risk a retaliatory strike that would mean the end of everything. Cold war international politics, however, were not as oddly rational as the realm of nuclear-weapons theory. Accidents might happen—for example, a radar operator might mistake a flight of geese for a flight of missiles—and on more than one occasion they almost did. The nuclear standoff was buttressed by the additional insurance of arms-control treaties. Second thoughts about MAD occurred in the form of proposals to establish missile-defense systems. Proponents tried to sell them as efforts to shore up MAD by reducing the risk of catastrophe inherent in accidental launches. In the view of some experts on both sides, however, these defensive systems were merely disguised attempts at gaining a first-strike capability. The side with a sound missile defense, they pointed out, could shoot first and then throw up a shield against a retaliatory strike. In 1972 the United States and the Soviet Union agreed to limit their anti-ballistic missile systems to token—meaning ineffectual—forces.

Although western Europe looked to the American nuclear umbrella for protection from the combined threat of Soviet nuclear and conventional forces, the United States was not the only Western nuclear power. Britain exploded its first thermonuclear device in 1953. By and large, the British nuclear weapons program piggybacked on the American one. France pursued a course independent of the United States. Conducting a first nuclear test in 1960, French officials explicitly justified their country's having its own *force de frappe*, or nuclear deterrent, on the ground that the United States might one day leave Europe in the lurch.

The nuclear arsenal of the United States dwarfed those of its French and British allies. Some western Europeans were glad of its protection; some regarded themselves as hostages to the U.S.-Soviet antagonism that justified the arsenal's existence; still others felt protected and held hostage at the same time. Peace activists, pacifists, anti-nuclear demonstrators, and intellectuals and politicians of longstanding anti-American tendencies occasionally coalesced on nuclear issues. For instance, they opposed installing American land-based missiles in Europe in response to Soviet advances in nuclear weaponry. Such moves, they charged, merely heightened tensions at the expense of the very Europeans they were meant to protect. It was also true, however, that the United States gave its own hostages to the nuclear standoff in the form of the thousands of American combat troops stationed in West Germany. The Americans were there to act as a trip wire, a guarantee that

Soviet aggression against western Europe, conventional or nuclear, would meet an immediate response from the United States.

Looking back from the early twenty-first century, it is hard to conceive of the high level of tension, anxiety, and fear generated by the nuclear standoff, the "balance of terror," as it was aptly called. In the end things did not go badly wrong. Except for frequent maneuvers in the field, the troops remained in their barracks; the missiles remained in their silos. Yet this outcome was far from certain. More than once between 1945 and the end of the Soviet Union, Europe appeared to edge near the brink of its third general war in little more than a half-century. Nowadays the nuclear balance of terror has been supplanted by other international worries, especially the specter of terrorism. In the late 1990s Britain reduced its nuclear arsenal to a handful of missiles carried aboard submarines, of which no more than one is ever at sea; France disarmed and dismantled its remaining land-based missiles; and the United States and Russia greatly reduced, by agreement, their nuclear-weapons stockpiles (true, large numbers of such weapons remained). In 1965, say, such a prospect would have been as unthinkable, and therefore as unforeseeable, as the sudden implosion of the Soviet Union itself.

In turn, in 1945 combining atomic bombs and guided missiles into a fearsome weapon was years in the future, an idea unknown beyond a small circle of researchers, not the least of whom were former German rocket scientists working in the secret laboratories of the United States and the Soviet Union. These German scientists were yet another prize the Americans and Russians competed for in the ruins of Berlin. Similar ruins, it will be recalled, stretched across Europe and into the western reaches of the Soviet Union. Millions of people lived atop these ruins. To them and to their luckier compatriots in regions relatively undamaged in the war, the immediate future looked scarcely less grim and uncertain than the immediate past had been. Survival, making do, getting along from day to day, were the preoccupation of the overwhelming majority of the population. Rebuilding or restoring shattered economies and political systems were urgent requirements in every nation that had been drawn into the war. In central Europe in the immediate postwar era, the Soviet Union sought to extend, by the creation of satellite states, its already considerable land-based empire. Meanwhile, pressures built to the breaking point against European rule in the overseas empires of Britain, France, and the Netherlands. Acquired over the course of centuries, these empires were lost in decades.

SUMMARY

Europe in the late summer of 1945 was a scene of desolation from the English Channel deep into the Soviet Union. The war's aerial and ground campaigns exacted a staggering loss of life among combatants, noncombatants, and domestic livestock. The bodily and psychic wounds borne by survivors, military and civilian alike, were incalculable. Entire cities had been reduced to rubble; in them legions of the homeless scrambled to survive. Millions were displaced from lands their families had lived on for generations. The railway network that had linked cities and countrysides across Europe was a thing of shreds and patches. The war had drained the treasuries of all the belligerent countries, putting banking and other financial institutions under almost unbearable pressure. The industrial sector of every national economy barely ticked over.

The biggest and most consequential geopolitical reality to emerge from the war was that Germany was no more and that the Red Army of the Soviet Union had raised the hammer-and-sickle flag over Berlin, the former German capital. Having advanced its military forces into central Europe, the Soviet government saw no reason to withdraw and many reasons to remain. For one thing, Soviet troops controlled a third of the former territory of its most feared and hated enemy. For another, its military position enabled the Soviet Union to shape the immediate political destinies of the lands wedged between itself and the easternmost advance of the Western allies. A buffer zone comprised of eastern Germany, Poland, Czechoslovakia, the Baltic states, Bulgaria, Romania, and Yugoslavia not only protected from assault the western frontiers of the Soviet Union but also established a bloc of compliant trading partners.

The alliance between the Soviet Union and the Western powers had at length accomplished the defeat of Nazi Germany. In the aftermath of war, it quickly crumbled. Over the years historians have differed over which side—if either—was to blame; they have disagreed over that most difficult of questions, the intentions of policy makers. Into the actions of Stalin and Truman and other major figures they have read a number of aims. Whatever its causes, the precipitate chill in relations that followed victory in Europe persisted for decades in the aptly named cold war. Europe jelled into eastern and western blocs—one dominated by the Soviet Union, the other by the United States. The military and political moves of one were countered by the moves of the other. Partly with the aim of reducing the perceived Soviet threat to western Europe, partly with a view to setting its most important trading partners on their feet, the United States established the Marshall Plan. Spurning such assistance, the Soviet Union strengthened economic ties with its own satellites. Bolstering economic recovery with a military shield, the United States and its allies established NATO. The Soviet Union responded with the Warsaw Pact. And so it went, through numerous crises over Berlin and other geopolitical hot spots around the world.

The United States liked to think of itself as Europe's great benefactor, freeing the continent from Nazi domination, getting it back on its feet economically, protecting it militarily from designs imputed to the Soviet Union. It failed to recognize, in the opinion of President de Gaulle and others, the degree to which these were self-serving actions. Europeans found American adventures elsewhere disquieting, and they feared being dragged into messes not of their own making. Opposition to the war in Vietnam became a catalyst of the French student revolt of 1968 and its sequels elsewhere in Europe.

Nuclear weapons cast the longest of shadows over the relationship between the superpowers and their allies. Despite occasional blustering over assisting in the liberation of eastern Europe from the communist yoke, neither the United States nor NATO ever lifted a finger, even when there were risings in such restive places as East Germany in 1953, Hungary in 1956, or Czechoslovakia in 1968. A chief reason that peace endured was that neither side was willing to risk a nuclear confrontation. Nuclear pressures and tensions increased—to say nothing of the risk of catastrophic accidents—as each side acquired ballistic missiles. Prudence prevailed over recklessness and no accidents occurred. How much the avoidance of nuclear war owed to wisdom, how much to historical contingency—another name for chance—remains hard to say.

TWO

The Loss of European Empire

The Vasco da Gama Era

In the spring of 1498 a squadron of vessels under the command of Vasco da Gama, a Portuguese explorer, arrived off the coast of India. A number of crew members went ashore, the first Europeans to reach Asia by sea. They opened what an Indian historian in 1953 called "the Vasco da Gama" era, a stretch of nearly five centuries in which European dominion over the non-European world slowly and sporadically grew and then precipitously declined. The five-hundredth anniversary of da Gama's landing in India was scorned in some quarters and celebrated in others, but when 1998 arrived not a single outpost remained of the European seaborne empires that had once stretched around the globe.

Da Gama's voyage announced a shift of preponderance in European power from the Mediterranean Sea to the north Atlantic. The major states in the contest for overseas empire over the next four centuries—Portugal, Spain, the Netherlands, France, and Britain—all had coastlines near or on the Atlantic Ocean. Large or small, all made the armed sailing ship the instrument of their expansion—first in trade, next in territory. Such a powerful and mobile weapons platform, unmatched elsewhere, enabled the Atlantic sea powers to overawe anyone with a mind to getting in their way. Soon they dominated the major sea routes of the world. They could sail anywhere that favorable winds would carry them. By such means they came to dominate world trade.

For a long time they were content to assure safe journeys for rich cargos, secure from the depredations of pirates and rival sea powers, if not from the great natural dangers of the oceans. Eventually they began acquiring control of territory not only at the ends of established trade routes but also in newly discovered lands. In many places, such as China and Africa, they maintained footholds, in the form of coastal trading stations; in others, such as the eastern seaboard of North America, with its salubrious climate, welcoming geography, and thinly scattered native population, they pushed into the interior.

The costs of the imperial adventure ran from war and disease through slavery, racism, exploitation, and plunder, to the corrupting effects of overlordship on rulers and subalterns alike. Imperialists liked to claim their system was beneficial if not benign. To non-Europeans, they said, European rule brought greater security, Western medicine, science and technology, improved public health, better public works, economic development, and enlightenment in general.

By 1915, near the outbreak of World War I, fewer than a dozen states controlled roughly a fourth of the earth's territory. By far the largest overseas empires were Britain's, which ran to more than 4 million square miles, and France's, which included more than 3.5 million. The Great War proved to be the high-water mark of the imperial tide. By the end of World War II, European overseas rule was under challenge nearly everywhere. Nothing weakened the hold of the European powers as much as the shock of war. This was especially true in Asia, where Japan scored a string of victories over Britain, France, the Netherlands, and the United States. The Japanese confirmed what Asian nationalists suspected: The Europeans were not invincible.

Nationalist challenges to European rule differed markedly. At one pole were Mohandas Gandhi and his followers, who pursued in India the tactics of nonviolent opposition to the continuance of British rule. Clustered at the other pole were nationalists prepared to end European rule by violence. The European response to these challenges fell into three patterns. In India, Britain at length acceded to nationalist demands. In the Netherlands East Indies (Indonesia), the Dutch briefly resisted and then abruptly agreed to withdraw. Alone among the European imperial powers, France fought two long, costly, bloody, and embittering wars to maintain French rule, first in Indochina, then in Algeria.

The French War in Indochina

When Japan overran Southeast Asia in 1941–1942, it found it convenient to leave the government of Vichy France nominally in charge of Indochina. In March 1945 the Japanese brushed aside the French in favor of ruling Indochina themselves, but the tide of the Pacific War had long since turned against them elsewhere. On September 2, 1945, the day Japanese officials signed the formal terms of surrender, the communist and nationalist leader Ho Chi Minh proclaimed the independence of Vietnam. In the hope of winning the backing of the United States, long-time champion of national self-determination, Ho modeled his proclamation after the Declaration of Independence.

To American officials, however, Ho seemed less a national liberator than a communist enslaver. Behind Ho they detected the sponsorship of Stalin and the specter of a rising Asian communism. The Americans' suspicions overwhelmed their fleeting sympathies, and Ho's hopes for help in heading off the return of the French were disappointed. Faced with widespread civil disorder in the weeks following the Japanese surrender, the British on-scene commander allowed a contingent of French troops to land in Saigon.

The Written Record

HO CHI MINH'S DECLARATION OF INDEPENDENCE

In an early bid for Vietnamese independence, Ho Chi Minh, leader of the Vietnamese Communist party, turned the principles of Western liberalism against the West. Quoting from the American Declaration of Independence and the French Declaration of the Rights of Man and the Citizen, both quintessential expressions of the Enlightenment, Ho called for the recognition of the independence of Vietnam. Thirty years and two wars later, independence was achieved.

"All men are created equal. They are endowed by their Creator with certain inalienable rights; among these are Life, Liberty, and the pursuit of Happiness."

This immortal statement was made in the Declaration of Independence of the United States of America in 1776. In a broader sense, this means: All the peoples on the earth are equal from birth, all the peoples have a right to live, to be happy and free.

The Declaration of the French Revolution made in 1791 on the Rights of Man and the Citizen also states: "All men are born free and with equal rights, and must always remain free and have equal rights."

Those are undeniable truths.

Nevertheless, for more than eighty years, the French imperialists, abusing the standard of Liberty, Equality, and Fraternity, have violated our Fatherland and oppressed our fellow citizens. They have acted contrary to the ideals of humanity and justice.

In the field of politics, they have deprived our people of every democratic liberty.

They have enforced inhuman laws; they have set up three distinct political regimes in the North, the Center, and the South of Vietnam in order to wreck our national unity and prevent our people from being united.

They have built more prisons than schools. They have mercilessly slain our patriots; they have drowned our uprisings in rivers of blood.

They have fettered public opinion; they have practised obscurantism against our people.

To weaken our race they have forced us to use opium and alcohol.

In the field of economics, they have fleeced us to the backbone, impoverished our people, and devastated our land.

They have robbed us of our rice fields, our mines, our forests, and our raw materials. They have monopolized the issuing of banknotes and the export trade.

They have invented numerous unjustifiable taxes and reduced our people, especially our peasantry, to a state of extreme poverty.

They have hampered the prospering of our national bourgeoisie; they have mercilessly exploited our workers.

In the autumn of 1940, when the Japanese Fascists violated Indochina's territory to establish new bases in their fight against the Allies, the French imperialists went down on their bended knees and handed over our country to them.

Thus, from that date, our people were subjected to the double yoke of the

French and the Japanese. Their sufferings and miseries increased. The result was that from the end of last year to the beginning of this year, from Quang Tri province to the North of Vietnam, more than two million of our fellow citizens died from starvation. On March 9, the French troops were disarmed by the Japanese. The French colonialists either fled or surrendered showing that not only were they incapable of "protecting" us, but that, in the span of five years, they had twice sold our country to the Japanese.

On several occasions before March 9, the Vietminh League urged the French to ally themselves with it against the Japanese. Instead of agreeing to this proposal, the French colonialists so intensified their terrorist activities against the Vietminh members that before fleeing they massacred a great number of our political prisoners detained at Yen Bay and Caobang.

Notwithstanding all this, our fellowcitizens have always manifested toward the French a tolerant and humane attitude. Even after the Japanese putsch of March 1945, the Vietminh League helped many Frenchmen to cross the frontier, rescued some of them from Japanese jails, and protected French lives and property.

From the autumn of 1940, our country had in fact ceased to be a French colony and had become a Japanese possession.

After the Japanese had surrendered to the Allies, our whole people rose to regain our national sovereignty and to found the Democratic Republic of Vietnam.

The truth is that we have wrested our independence from the Japanese and not from the French.

The French have fled, the Japanese have capitulated, Emperor Bao Dai has abdicated. Our people have broken the chains which for nearly a century have fettered them and have won independence for the Fatherland. Our people at the same time have overthrown the monarchic regime that has reigned supreme for dozens of centuries. In its place has been established the present Democratic Republic.

For these reasons, we, members of the Provisional Government, representing the whole Vietnamese people, declare that from now on we break off all relations of a colonial character with France; we repeal all the international obligation that France has so far subscribed to on behalf of Vietnam and we abolish all the special rights the French have unlawfully acquired in our Fatherland.

The whole Vietnamese people, animated by a common purpose, are determined to fight to the bitter end against any attempt by the French colonialists to reconquer their country.

We are convinced that the Allied nations, which at Tehran and San Francisco have acknowledged the principles of self-determination and equality of nations, will not refuse to acknowledge the independence of Vietnam.

A people who have courageously opposed French domination for more than eight years, a people who have fought side by side with the Allies against the Fascists during these last years, such a people must be free and independent.

For these reasons, we, members of the Provisional Government of the Democratic Republic of Vietnam, solemnly declare to the world that Vietnam has the right to be a free and independent country—and in fact is so already. The entire

> Vietnamese people are determined to mobilize all their physical and mental strength, to sacrifice their lives and property in order to safeguard their independence and liberty.
>
> Ho Chi Minh, "Declaration of Independence of the Democratic Republic of Vietnam," *Selected Writings* (Hanoi: Foreign Languages Publishing House, 1977), pp. 53–56.

The French had many reasons for seeking to reestablish themselves in Indochina. For one, French business interests were eager to recover their investments there. The Michelin Tire and Rubber Co., for instance, owned huge rubber plantations in Vietnam, and other French firms profited from deposits of manganese, bauxite, and other valuable minerals. Substantial offshore petroleum and natural gas reserves had scarcely been tapped.

The hope of regaining lost prestige probably outweighed the prospect of economic gain in the French decision to return. World War II left France humiliated by the defeat of 1940, divided by the German Occupation, and daunted by the tasks of recovery. Restoring the empire was seen as a way of restoring France to greatness. This ambition had a practical side. In World War I France drew on a vast reservoir of troops from the empire to help defend it against Germany. The defeat of 1940 occurred with such shocking speed that the Germans reached Paris before help from French colonial troops could arrive. Still, the conviction that France owed its security to its imperial holdings lingered on.

Where the Vietminh, the communist revolutionary movement led by Ho Chi Minh, saw one Vietnam stretching from north of Hanoi to south of Saigon, the French saw the three provinces (Cochinchina, Annam, and Tonkin) they had ruled since the late nineteenth century. In 1945 France had neither the military strength to reestablish itself in Indochina by force nor the political flexibility to bargain with the Vietminh over sharing power. French representatives negotiated agreements with the more pliable rulers of Cambodia and Laos, the other constituent parts of Indochina; they held sporadic talks with Vietnamese nationalist leaders, including Ho Chi Minh himself. These talks went nowhere and the French continued to do what they could with the meager military forces at hand. In March 1946 French envoys and Ho Chi Minh suddenly reached an accord allowing some fifteen thousand French troops to return to the region around Hanoi in exchange for French recognition of the Democratic Republic of Vietnam (DRV), a state ostensibly free yet within the French Union.

The March accord was the most hopeful moment in the last years of French Indochina. The signatories soon fell to quarreling over what they had agreed to. In December the agreement turned to ashes. A dispute over the collection of customs duties exploded into the French naval bombardment of Haiphong. As many as six thousand people died in the shelling. Henceforth a state of war existed between France and the DRV.

French military forces dominated the cities and towns of Vietnam, but they never succeeded in extending their control to the villages and forests. In some ways the struggle between the French and the Vietminh was a classic guerrilla war. The Vietminh conducted hit-and-run raids, melting away in the countryside and living among the peasants "like fish in water," to paraphrase Mao Zedong. The conflict also bore many features of conventional warfare. In the hope of luring the Vietminh into an untenable position, the French command in early 1954 sent a force of sixteen thousand to the valley of Dien Bien Phu, near the border with Laos. It was the French whose position proved untenable. They did not reckon with General Vo Nguyen Giap's ability to sustain a heavily armed force of his own in such a remote region. Dragging artillery pieces to the high ground surrounding the valley, the Vietnamese soon made Dien Bien Phu what the historian Bernard Fall called "hell in a very small place." Outgeneraled and outgunned, the French surrendered after a fifty-five-day siege. Rising opposition in France to the costs and casualties of the war transformed the battle from a tactical reverse to a major defeat.

Dien Bien Phu drove France to a negotiated settlement. At Geneva in July 1954 French negotiators reached an agreement handing the Vietnamese control of territory north of the 17th parallel and withdrawing French troops south of that line. The southern portion came under the leadership of the Catholic nationalist Ngo Dinh Diem, who had the backing of the United States. In 1956 the last French soldiers departed. By then, however, the United States had long since become the dominant Western force in South Vietnam. Some embittered French officials believed the Americans had lent them just enough support to keep from losing the war—for a time—and not enough support to help them win it.

The French War in Algeria

On November 1, 1954, a rebellion broke out against French rule in Algeria, home to roughly 1 million settlers of European origin. Living alongside them, virtually excluded from a share in either wealth or power, was an indigenous Arab and Berber population of some 9 million. When word of the rising flashed across the Mediterranean, French officials immediately emphasized that the rebellion would be dealt with as if it had taken place on the mainland—a signal to the settlers that they would not be abandoned. Announcing the commencement of "operations for the maintenance of order," it reinforced the troops already in North Africa. Only in 1999 did the French government concede these operations were a war in everything but name.

A group calling itself the Front de Libération Nationale (FLN), or National Liberation Front, claimed responsibility for the November 1 rising. The FLN was not the only expression of Algerian nationalism, but it was the most radical and the most ruthless.

To the French army, losing Indochina made preserving a French Algeria all the more vital. Algeria offered the Indochina hands a chance to redeem their sense of honor. They were convinced that the lessons of "revolutionary warfare" they had learned in Indochina could be applied against the rebellion in North Africa.

French military forces in Algeria reached 400,000 by mid-1956. Committing such a large force required calling up reservists and sending over draftees. Distributed across Algeria in packets, they guarded roads, schools, hospitals, power stations, and the like, seeking to deprive the rebels of targets, separate them from the Arab population, and protect the settlers. Meanwhile, a Strategic Reserve of some fifteen thousand professional soldiers hunted down the rebel bands.

Eager to lessen the pressure on these rural forces, in August 1956 the FLN leadership decided to launch a campaign of urban terrorism. In the Casbah, the Muslim quarter of Algiers, the FLN established small terrorist cells running to perhaps five thousand members in all. After September 1956 the number of terrorist shootings and bombings rose steadily. In January 1957 the French army intervened. Brushing aside the police and helping themselves to their records on terrorist activity, regiments of the 10th Parachute Division took down the terrorist network. Hauling in suspects by the truckload, the paratroopers tortured them into yielding the intelligence they needed to dismantle the terrorist cells. By September 1957 terrorist actions in Algiers had been reduced to one a month; the city had been made safe for the settlers.

The Battle of Algiers ended in a short-term French victory. Not only was the terrorist network in the principal city of Algeria destroyed; feeling the heat, the highest ranking leaders of the FLN fled the country for Tunisia, where they turned their attention from terrorism to diplomacy. In Algeria an embittered, isolated, and increasingly paranoid internal leadership fought on alone. In the long run, however, the Battle of Algiers proved costly to the French. The army's use of torture set off a firestorm of controversy on the mainland. The government's denials that such methods had been employed met with disbelief and undermined the moral high ground against terrorism. As the financial, human, and moral cost of keeping Algeria French mounted, doubts about the wisdom of such a policy increased.

The year 1957 was one of growing military success and deepening political crisis. While the 10th Parachute Division fought the Battle of Algiers, other French forces drastically reduced the infiltration of fighters, weapons, and supplies across Algeria's borders with Tunisia and Morocco. Nevertheless, the settlers' anxieties rose as the FLN's military capabilities declined. Their one sure ally was the French Army. Army activists, mainly Indochina veterans, did not see eye-to-eye with the settlers on everything, but they were just as determined to maintain French rule in Algeria. On May 13, 1958, the settler leadership, with the army's connivance, staged in Algiers a demonstration meant to dissuade the French government from negotiating with the FLN.

Acting in concert with military and civilian conspirators on the mainland, the settlers appealed to General Charles de Gaulle to return to power. In de Gaulle they saw not only the hero of resistance to the Germans but also a champion of empire. Against the looming prospect of military intervention

A Closer Look

FRANTZ FANON, *THE WRETCHED OF THE EARTH*

In his conviction that a writer must act as well as think, Frantz Fanon resembled his contemporary, the French novelist Albert Camus. Each participated in a resistance movement; each wrote philosophical essays. There the resemblance ends. They were on opposite sides in the Algerian War (it would be more accurate to say Camus was caught in the middle, between the European settlers and the indigenous community). Trained as a psychiatrist, the Martinique-born Fanon wrote *Black Skin, White Masks* while working as a clinician in Lyon, France. Joining the psychiatric staff of an Algerian hospital shortly before the outbreak of the revolt against French rule, in 1956 Fanon resigned to work with the rebels of the National Liberation Front. He continued to write for European publications sympathetic to the cause of Algerian independence. His frank advocacy of violence made *The Wretched of the Earth*, published on the eve of his death from leukemia in 1961, one of the most controversial as well as celebrated essays in the literature of anticolonialism.

The existence of an armed struggle shows that the people are decided to trust to violent methods only. He of whom they have never stopped saying that the only language he understands is that of force, decides to give utterance by force. In fact, as always, the settler has shown him the way he should take if he is to become free. The argument the native chooses has been furnished by the settler, and by an ironic turning of the tables it is the native who now affirms that the colonialist understands nothing but force. The colonial regime owes its legitimacy to force and at no time tries to hide this aspect of things. . . .

The violence of the colonial regime and the counter-violence of the native balance each other and respond to each other in an extraordinary reciprocal homogeneity. This reign of violence will be the more terrible in proportion to the size of the implantation from the mother country. The development of violence among the colonized people will be proportionate to the violence exercised by the threatened colonial regime. In the first phase of this insurrectional period, the home governments are the slaves of the settlers, and these settlers seek to intimidate the natives and their home governments at one and the same time. They use the same methods against both of them. . . . For the settlers, the alternative is not between Algérie algérienne and Algérie française but between an independent Algeria and a colonial Algeria, and anything else is mere talk or attempts at treason. The settler's logic is implacable and one is only staggered by the counter-logic visible in the behavior of the native insofar as one has not clearly understood beforehand the mechanisms of the settler's ideas. From the moment that the native has chosen the methods of counter-violence, police reprisals automatically call forth reprisals on the side of the nationalists. However, the results are not equivalent, for machine-gunning from airplanes and bombardments from the fleet go far beyond in horror and magnitude any answer the natives can make. This recurring terror de-mystifies once and for all the most estranged members of the colonized race. . . . Terror, counter-terror, violence, counter-violence: that is what observers bitterly record when they describe the circle of hate, which is so tenacious and so evident in Algeria.

In all armed struggles, there exists what we might call the point of no return. Almost always it is marked off by a huge and all-inclusive repression which engulfs all sectors of the colonized people. . . .

Today, national independence and the growth of national feeling in underdeveloped regions take on totally new aspects. In these regions, with the exception of certain spectacular advances, the different countries show the same absence of infrastructure. The mass of the people struggle against the same poverty, flounder about making the same gestures and with their shrunken bellies outline what has been called the geography of hunger. It is an underdeveloped world, a world inhuman in its poverty; but also it is a world without doctors, without engineers, and without administrators. Confronting this world, the European nations sprawl, ostentatiously opulent. This European opulence is literally scandalous, for it has been founded on slavery, it has been nourished with the blood of slaves and it comes directly from the soil and from the subsoil of that underdeveloped world. The well-being and the progress of Europe have been built up with the sweat and the dead bodies of Negroes, Arabs, Indians, and the yellow races. We have decided not to overlook this any longer. When a colonialist country, embarrassed by the claims for independence made by a colony, proclaims to the nationalist leaders: "If you wish for independence, take it, and go back to the Middle Ages," the newly independent people tend to acquiesce and to accept the challenge; in fact you may see colonialism withdrawing its capital and its technicians and setting up around the young State the apparatus of economic pressure. The apotheosis of independence is transformed into the curse of independence, and the colonial power through its immense resources of coercion condemns the young nation to regression. In plain words, the colonial power says: "Since you want independence, take it and starve." The nationalist leaders have no other choice but to turn to their people and ask from them a gigantic effort. A regime of austerity is imposed on these starving men; a disproportionate amount of work is required from their atrophied muscles. An autarkic regime is set up and each state, with the miserable resources it has in hand, tries to find an answer to the nation's great hunger and poverty. We see the mobilization of a people which toils to exhaustion in front of a suspicious and bloated Europe.

on the settlers' behalf, he was named the last prime minister of the French Fourth Republic.

Under the new Fifth Republic, tailor-made for de Gaulle, military pressure on the FLN increased. Following a plan devised by General Maurice Challe, the new French commander in Algeria, an enlarged General Reserve reverted to conventional warfare, employing air power, artillery, and extremely mobile helicopter-borne units in coordinated cross-country sweeps. France simultaneously embarked on a vast program of economic reform and development aimed at drawing the Muslim population into the making of a new Algeria.

In 1960 General Challe declared that "the rebels were practically defeated." Challe's claim still holds up. Less than two years later, however, Algeria had won independence. Essentially the FLN acquired by diplomacy what it could not win by force. Long-term historical trends were running against a French Algeria. The climate of international relations had grown increasingly inhospitable to old-style colonialism. Diminished in power and status, France could no longer ignore pressure from more powerful states. If the French expected the Soviet Union to be hostile to their Algerian policy, they did not count on the chilliness of the United States. Estranged from their old ally, they found themselves isolated in the United Nations, a forum generally sympathetic to the cause of national liberation from foreign rule. On this sympathy the FLN played with great skill.

Still, long-term trends alone did not decide the fate of French Algeria. Charles de Gaulle must be credited with steering France away from a potentially disastrous course. His intentions—what he hoped for as distinct from what he settled for—remain controversial. First he invited the rebels to put down their weapons and sit down at the negotiating table, an offer he characterized as an honorable "peace of the brave" and the FLN regarded as an invitation to surrender. Soon he began speaking of an "Algerian Algeria," without explaining what he meant. The settlers and army activists smelled a sellout. In April 1961 four generals who had held high commands in Algeria led a *putsch*—a military coup—against de Gaulle. Barely a handful of professional regiments followed them to ruin; the conscript army remained loyal to the regime.

Settler and army diehards banded together in the OAS, or Secret Army Organization, a terrorist mirror image of the FLN. Among its targets was de Gaulle himself, whom more than once it came close to assassinating.

De Gaulle was not to be deterred. "All my life," he had written in a famous passage of his war memoirs, "I have had a certain idea of France." The idea of France he wished to present to the world in 1961 was that of a generous nation freely granting independence to Algeria and closing a long chapter in its own history. Overseas empire, he said in one speech, was as obsolete as gaslights and horse-drawn carriages. Free of imperial burdens, a reinvigorated France could attend to its burgeoning domestic economy, its opportunities as the leader of a new Europe, and its responsibilities as a regional power exercising worldwide influence. On July 1, 1962, following months of arduous negotiations between de Gaulle's representatives and representatives of the FLN, Algeria gained its independence.

The end of French rule was messy. The settlers, believing they faced a perilous future in the new country, repatriated to France. Several thousand Muslims who had fought alongside the French army as auxiliaries, or harkis, also went to France. As many as sixty thousand harkis who stayed behind were put to death by the new authorities in retaliation for having served France. The terrorist OAS, bent on avenging its lost hopes, stepped up its shootings and bombings. Finally its campaign sputtered out.

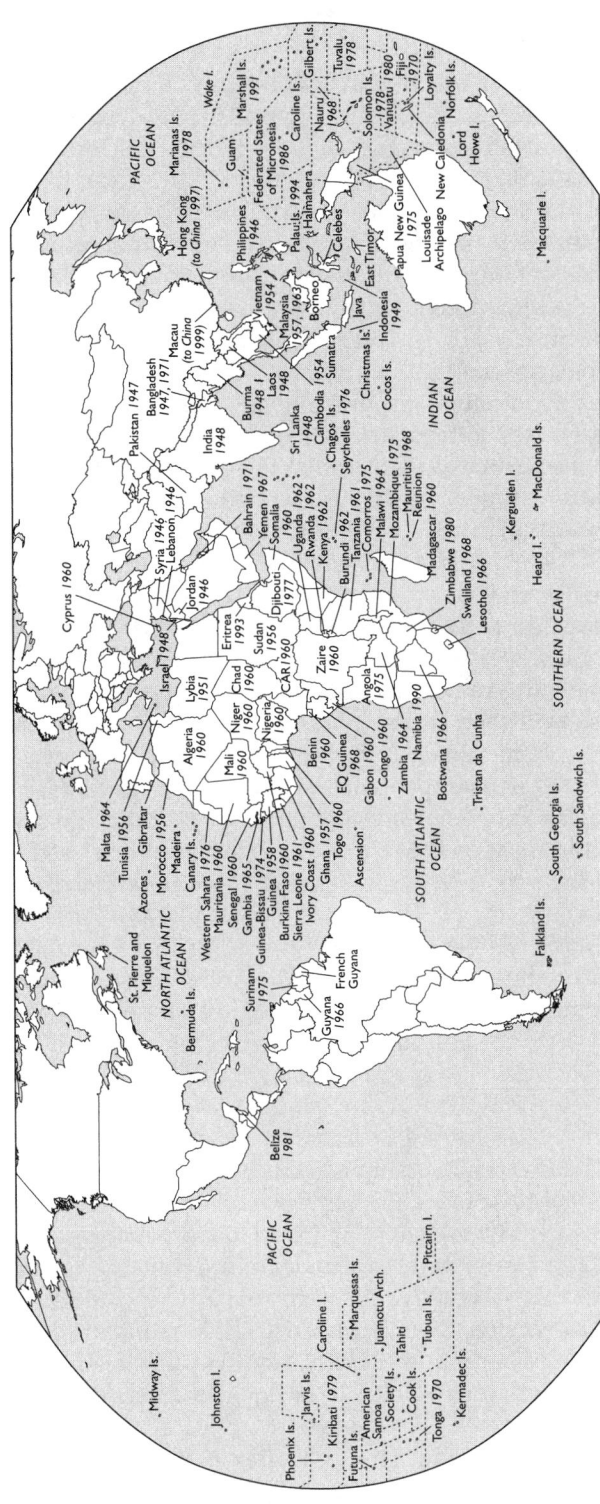

Decolonization, 1945–1998.

Britain Leaves India

Britain never claimed India was British in the thoroughgoing way France asserted Algeria was French. Although British rule over the Indian subcontinent dated from the eighteenth century, the Raj, as British sovereignty in India was called, had always been exercised indirectly, through native intermediaries of one kind or another. This did not necessarily mean that colonial rule was less harsh than elsewhere, but it did mean that British authority generally spoke in a native voice and was masked by a native face. Indirect rule became more pronounced after 1857, the year of the Indian Mutiny, a bloody uprising that nearly put an end to the Raj altogether. When World War II ended in 1945, no one doubted that Britain would soon be handing over power in India to the Indians; in the home island hardly anyone whom the government needed to take seriously opposed the idea. Still, the end of the Raj came sooner than expected, and at the cost of great violence and bloodshed and the partitioning of the subcontinent into two separate states.

In retrospect Indian independence appears to have come as no surprise because it had been prefigured in earlier events. In 1919, for instance, the Government of India Act accepted India as a nation in the making with a parliamentary government on the British model. Nevertheless, such expressions of intention have often been derailed by subsequent events. In India the great obstacle to realizing an Indian parliamentary government was less the faltering of British will than the mutual antagonism of the two great religious communities of Hinduism and Islam. A Hindu majority, wealthy and Western-oriented in its upper reaches, dominated a poor, backward, peasant Muslim minority. Muslim leaders feared that an Indian parliamentary government would mean perpetual rule by Hindu politicians exercising power on behalf of their coreligionaries, leaving Muslims worse off than they were under the Raj.

The Muslims were probably right to harbor these fears. Many a Hindu politician had no interest in promoting the welfare of Muslims, to say nothing of reaching out to them in a common struggle for independence. In his capacity to look beyond the Hindu community, as in nearly everything else about him, Mohandas Gandhi was a rare figure. The Western-educated Gandhi first gained prominence as a lawyer in South Africa, where he employed the tactics of nonviolent resistance in winning the easing of legal discrimination against Indians. Returning to India in the 1920s, he abandoned Western ways for the garb and guise of a Hindu mystic, but without shedding the political acumen that such a transformation, for all its deep sincerity, in fact revealed. He soon emerged as the principal leader of the National Congress Party. His colleagues in this largest Hindu party were, like Gandhi, members of a Western-educated elite; they had learned their nationalist ideals, as well as their ideas about liberty and equality, from Western teachers. In Congress's early years, though, they wanted to be equal partners of the British Raj, not free of it.

Meanwhile, Muhammad Ali Jinnah rose to prominence in the Muslim League, another all-India party. Like Gandhi, Jinnah was a Western-educated

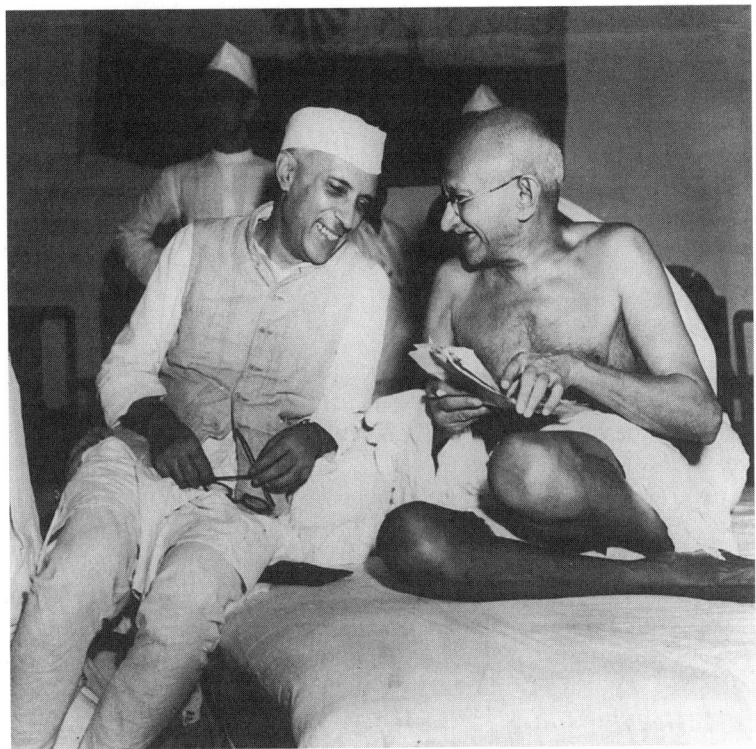

Jawaharlal Nehru, president of the Indian National Congress when this photograph was taken in 1946, shares a laugh with Mohandas Gandhi, the principal leader of the Congress Party from the 1920s on. Known as Mahatma (great soul) for his high standing as a Hindu spiritual leader as well as politician, Gandhi was the strategist and philosopher of nonviolent civil disobedience as the chief form of resistance to British rule. His practices were adopted by American civil rights leader Martin Luther King, Jr. In 1948 Gandhi was shot and killed by a Hindu fanatic who opposed his conciliatory attitude toward Muslims. Nehru was prime minister and minister of foreign affairs for many years after India gained independence. (Getty Images.)

lawyer; like Gandhi, Jinnah advocated Hindu-Muslim cooperation, at least in his early years as an activist. In practice, however, cooperation broke down when Congress turned its back on assurances it had made with respect to guaranteeing Muslims representation in an Indian parliament. In 1930 Jinnah angrily severed his ties with Congress and shortly assumed the leadership of the Muslim League. By 1940 he had traveled the road to separatism, declaring that "There are in India two nations" and demanding the creation of a separate Muslim state.

Britain took India into the war against Germany in 1939 without bothering to consult the Indian nationalist leadership. Jinnah swallowed this affront and supported the British war effort, enhancing the Muslim League's influence with British authorities. Huge numbers of Indians volunteered to serve in the British armed forces. The Congress party, at Gandhi's insistence, withheld its support from the war and mounted against the Raj an aggressive "Quit India" campaign, which the authorities swiftly rolled up. Once Japan attacked British holdings in Asia, the British government became more conciliatory toward Indian nationalism. Meanwhile, some nationalist politicians upped the ante by publicly favoring a Japanese victory in nearby Burma. Antagonism between Congress and the Muslim League intensified. The blast of war carried India beyond the autonomy the British government offered in the hope of shoring up its defenses against the Japanese onslaught. Vague assurances about handing over power sometime in the future had to be made into specific commitments.

By 1945 Indian independence was a foregone conclusion. The Labour party had a long anticolonial tradition, but the Indian question was not a top priority when the party came to power. A near-catastrophic deterioration in relations between the Muslim and Indian communities pushed independence to the fore. By March 1946 widespread Hindu-Muslim rioting threatened the breakdown of civil order. The Labour government offered India full independence. As the army and police began fracturing into rival Hindu and Muslim mobs, observers wondered whether the viceroy, the chief British official on the scene, would be able to keep control. The idea of a free India uniting the two great religious communities was lost.

Independence came at the cost of partition, accompanied by an enormous loss of life. In August 1947 a separate Muslim Pakistan was created from the northwestern and northeastern shoulders of the subcontinent, widely separated by a swath of Indian territory. The northeastern corner later became the state of Bangladesh. In the regions they dominated by force of numbers, Hindus and Muslims fell upon and massacred the minorities in their midst. Huge numbers of people were displaced. In 1948 Gandhi was murdered by a Hindu fanatic who regarded his concern for the Muslims as a betrayal. Jinnah, Gandhi's Muslim counterpart, died of tuberculosis the same year.

From the Raj the new India and Pakistan inherited large and well-trained civil services—already native-born, for the most part, long before independence. They were also the inheritors of roads, railways, and other institutions and services, although India fared better in this respect than Pakistan. Along with these material bequests the new rulers also drew on a Western political legacy combining British parliamentary politics, especially the practical side of organizing mass parties and running electoral campaigns, with Enlightenment ideals of democracy, nationalism, and secularism. No longer, however, as the historian J. M. Roberts pointed out, did Indian or Pakistani politicians have an alien ruler to blame when things went wrong. When the British withdrew in 1947 they left behind a subcontinent mired in economic and social distress. The new republic of India faced daunting problems.

The Netherlands Yields in Indonesia

The Netherlands neither withdrew from its colonial holdings in Asia as swiftly as Britain handed over power in India nor held on as tenaciously as

France did in Indochina. Instead, like France it tried to fight its way back into control; like Britain, it concluded it had no future in lands it had occupied for centuries. In reaching this conclusion it was helped along by pressure from the United Nations. From the perspective of the early twenty-first century it seems hardly credible that a country slightly less than twice the size of New Jersey once ruled the world's largest archipelago—more than seventeen thousand islands sprawling across the Pacific southeast of the Asian landmass. In the seventeenth century, however, when it established itself in the islands, the Netherlands was a great sea power, a leading imperial power, one of the richest countries in Europe, and Britain's formidable rival.

For the first two centuries of Dutch rule, Indonesia was immensely lucrative to Dutch merchants and traders. In the scramble for wealth the interests of Indonesians were largely ignored. Finally in the twentieth century, paternalism replaced indifference in Dutch treatment of the native population. When the Japanese swooped down from the north in 1942 they were greeted by some nationalists as a welcome alternative to the Dutch. Dutch rule for a time was broken completely. Having fled the Netherlands rather than deal with the German occupier, who assumed direct rule, the Dutch monarchy and government had no means of holding onto overseas territory; the Japanese interned the Dutch remaining in Indonesia in concentration camps. No Allied armies operated in Indonesia during the war. Nationalists led by Sukarno (like many of his countrymen, he used only a single name), including collaborators and noncollaborators alike, took advantage of the Japanese surrender, and the absence of Allied troops, to declare an Indonesian republic. The Dutch managed to negotiate their way back into the country.

The accord that allowed the Dutch back in, repeatedly violated by both sides, soon broke down completely. Fighting broke out when the Dutch threw their support to separatist groups seeking to wrest free of Sukarno's nationalists. A four-year war ensued, marked by sporadic and sometimes heavy and cruel fighting. The Dutch defeated the Indonesian nationalist forces and even managed to jail Sukarno. The cold war, however, gave the Indonesians the leverage they needed to oust the Dutch. The Soviet Union made itself Sukarno's champion in the United Nations. The Dutch had no such formidable ally. Only France, which had its own Asian entanglements, backed them in the UN. Both Britain and the United States feared that supporting the Netherlands' claim to Indochina would serve to drive other Asian nationalists into the Soviet embrace. Bowing to the inevitable, in 1949 the Dutch recognized the independence and sovereignty of the Republic of Indonesia.

Oil Transforms the Middle East

Europe's ties with the Middle East stretched back to the Macedonian warrior Alexander the Great, who subdued Egypt, Persia (Iran), and Mesopotamia (Iraq) on his way to India; and to the Roman Empire, which ruled much of the region for roughly two centuries. More than two thousand years of entanglements between Europe and the Middle East preceded the discovery of oil, at the turn of the twentieth century, in the lands bordering the Persian Gulf. Converting naval vessels from coal- to oil-fired boilers combined with the rise of the automobile industry to increase vastly the West's appetite for petroleum. The desire to control access to a reliable supply of the indispensable mineral grew along with the appetite.

Petroleum has dominated the relationship between Europe, the U.S., and the Middle East ever since the discovery of large reserves in Saudi Arabia, the small states along the Persian Gulf, and in Iraq and Iran. At the outset, European and American companies paid royalties to local governments in the expectation of pumping oil and natural gas out of the ground well into the future. They enlisted their governments, who had a strategic interest in keeping the oil flowing, to bully and cajole local governments into giving them preferential treatment. When governments showed minds of their own, they risked being overthrown, as in the case of the CIA-inspired coup against Mohammad Mossadegh, the popular prime minister of Iran, in 1953.

To jump ahead in the story, the tables were turned in 1960, when many of the oil-producing states, out from under the Western thumb, banded together to form the Organization of Petroleum Exporting Countries (OPEC). They quickly discovered they held a powerful new weapon in international diplomacy. They used the mechanism of oil pricing and the accompanying threat of increases both to cow Western industrial nations dependent on a continued flow of oil and to influence Western policies toward Israel.

The Creation of Israel

When the British withdrew their forces from Palestine in 1948, the Jews proclaimed the state of Israel and secured its recognition by the United Nations. The Arab nations declared the proclamation illegal and invaded the new state from all directions. Outnumbered but faced by an inefficient enemy, the Israelis won the war. A truce was patched together under the auspices of the United Nations in 1949. Israel secured more of Palestine than the UN had proposed, taking over the western part of Jerusalem, a city the UN had proposed to neutralize. The eastern part of the "old city" of Jerusalem, together with eastern Palestine, remained in the hands of the Arab state of Jordan.

During the 1948 war almost a million Palestinian Arabs fled from Israel to the surrounding Arab states. The United States organized a special agency that built camps and gave relief to the refugees and tried to arrange for their permanent resettlement. The Arab states, however, declined to absorb them, and many refugees regarded resettlement as an abandonment of their belief the Israelis would soon be pushed aside, allowing them to return to their homes.

The new state of Israel continued to admit as many Jewish immigrants as possible. The welding of Jews from many cultures into a single nationality was a formidable task. Working in a hostile environment, the Israelis depended on outside aid, especially from supporters in the United States.

The Suez Crisis

In 1952, less than four years after the Arab defeat in Palestine, revolution broke out in Egypt, where the corrupt monarchy was overthrown by a group of army officers led by Gamal Abdel Nasser. They established a republic, encouraged the emancipation of women, and pared down the role of the conservative religious courts. Only one party was tolerated, and elections were rigged. Regarding the West as not only colonialist but also pro-Israel, Nasser turned to the Soviets for aid. Czechoslovak and Soviet arms flowed into Egypt, and Soviet technicians followed.

Nasser's chief showpiece of revolutionary planning was to be a new high dam on the Nile at Aswan. He had counted on the United States to contribute to its construction, but in mid-1956, for political reasons, the United States changed its mind. Nasser retaliated by nationalizing the Suez Canal, formerly operated by a Franco-British company. He announced he would use Canal revenues to finance the Aswan dam. For several months, the new Egyptian management kept canal traffic running. In the meantime, the French and British governments secretly allied themselves with Israel.

In the fall of 1956 Israeli forces invaded Egyptian territory, and French and British troops landed at Suez. The Soviet Union threatened to defend Egypt by force. The United States, angry with Britain and France for cutting a secret deal with Israel, failed to support them. With the United States and the Soviet Union siding together, the United Nations condemned the British-French-Israeli attack. A United Nations peacekeeping force occupied the Egyptian-Israeli frontier. The Suez Canal, closed down by the Egyptians, reopened. European influence in the Middle East fell sharply.

Arab-Israeli Conflicts

After the Suez crisis, Nasser's economic policy was governed by the grim struggle to support a fast-growing population. In 1967 he demanded that the UN peacekeeping troops installed in 1956 be removed. UN Secretary U Thant complied. The Egyptians began a propaganda campaign against Israel and closed the Strait of Tiran, the only access by sea to the Israeli port of Elath. The Israelis then struck the first blow in a new war, destroying the Egyptian air force on the ground and also striking at the air forces of other Arab states. In six days they overran the Sinai peninsula; all of Palestine west of the Jordan River, including the Jordanian portion of Jerusalem; and the Golan Heights on their northern frontier with Syria, from which the Syrians had been launching raids for several years.

Israel's victory in the Six-Day War humiliated not only Nasser but also the Soviet Union, which had supplied much of the equipment the Egyptian Army abandoned as it retreated. The Soviets supported the Arab position, arguing their case in the United Nations, denouncing Israel, and rearming Egypt. Israeli armies remained in control of all the territory they had occupied. Had negotiations begun soon after the war, much of this territory could perhaps have been recovered, but as time passed the Israeli attitude hardened, and it became difficult for any Israeli government to give up any part of Jerusalem or the Golan Heights, whose possession ensured Israeli territory against Syrian attack.

For their part the Arabs, led by Nasser, refused to negotiate directly with the Israelis or to take any step that would recognize the existence of the state of Israel. Rearmed, the Egyptians proclaimed their intention of evening the score. Israel lived as an armed camp, its young men and women serving equally in the armed forces, ever alert for an attack.

In 1969 and 1970 tension again mounted in the Middle East. Arab Palestinians organized guerrilla attacks on Israeli or Israeli-occupied territory from Jordan, Syria, and Lebanon. The Lebanese government—precariously balanced between Christians and Muslims—was threatened by the Palestinian guerrillas and forced to concede Lebanese territory nearest the Israeli frontier. In the airports of Zurich, Athens, and Tel Aviv, terrorists attacked planes carrying Israelis.

At times the Palestinian Arab terrorist movement took on the aspects of a sovereign power, negotiating with the Chinese, compelling Nasser to modify his pronouncements, and demanding to be heard in the United Nations. In the autumn of 1970 terrorists hijacked four large airliners in a single day, holding the passengers hostage in Jordan and demanding the release of certain captives of their own. During the tense negotiations that followed, hostilities broke out between the Arab guerrillas and the Jordanian government. The Syrians intervened on the side of the guerrillas, and the threat of American intervention on the side of Jordan's King Hussein and of a Soviet response was suddenly very real. Jordanian successes, Syrian withdrawal, and American and Soviet restraint helped the critical moment pass.

The Scramble for Africa

European powers exploited sub-Saharan Africa for centuries from trading stations along the coastal perimeter. The most infamous example of exploitation was the Atlantic slave trade. The trade in slaves, which went on several hundred years, was the direct consequence of New World colonialism. On the backs of millions of black slaves were built the plantation economies of North and South America and the Caribbean. Tea and coffee drinkers in the home countries relied on slave labor for sugar; slaves cultivated the raw cotton that fueled the industrial revolution.

In the last quarter of the nineteenth century Europeans suddenly turned from exploiting the human capital of Africa to ruling Africa itself. Plunging into the interior, between 1875 and 1900 they divvied up nearly the entire continent. What provoked the "Scramble for Africa"? Was it greed, the all-purpose and often accurate explanation for European overseas expansion? There is not much evidence to suggest that European chancelleries were suddenly drawn deep into Africa by private, commercial interests. The usual civilizing and evangelizing motives have also been put forward, and perhaps they had something to do with it. A more compelling case has been made, however, for the theory that imperialism was the result of the partition of Africa, not the cause of it.

According to this theory, the Scramble for Africa was set off by diplomats as a function of their strategic interests elsewhere. Britain intervened in Egypt in 1882, for instance, to put down an indigenous rebellion against the khedive, a collaborationist ruler up to his neck in foreign debt. It was less the turbulence in Egypt that worried the British government, however, than the threat this turbulence posed to the Suez Canal, the lifeline to India, the heart of the British Empire. The British meant to leave Egypt promptly, once order was restored; they wound up staying until the early 1950s. Britain's military intervention upset its uneasy cooperative relationship in Egyptian affairs with France. The French began looking around for ways to counter the British move by acquiring African territories of their own. Other powers, including the recently unified Germany, eager to keep pace with their continental rivals, jumped in. The scramble for Africa was on.

Exploiting the Congo

One beneficiary of the Anglo-French rivalry in Africa—as an entrepreneur, not a head of state—was Leopold II, king of Belgium. The Egyptian affair undermined informal understandings that the lands of the Congo River basin would be left alone. When Otto von Bismarck, the German chancellor, in 1885 offered to mediate African disputes among the European powers, mainly Britain and France, Leopold saw his chance. Unsuccessful in earlier bids to acquire territory in the Congo region, he presented himself as the agreeable alternative to a clash between the great powers. In the guise of doing everyone a favor, he acquired a private Congo empire.

Thus began one of the darkest episodes in the history of European overseas empire. The African realm Leopold II ruled was one third as large as the United States and larger than all of western Europe. For all his royal ancestry, Leopold II was essentially a businessman on the model of an Andrew Carnegie or John D. Rockefeller: as big a risk-taker, just as ruthless, far more sinister in his methods and their consequences. By threat and by violence, the Belgian king intimidated the inhabitants of the Congo into working for him. He employed forced labor first in amassing ivory for a lucrative world market and then in supplying raw rubber to the burgeoning bicycle and automobile industries.

In dragooning workers into these and other enterprises and in other acts of harsh and exemplary discipline, Leopold II and his agents were responsible for the deaths of as many as 10 million people. There are many ways of interpreting Joseph Conrad's novel *Heart of Darkness*, the tale of an English sailor's journey up the Congo River and his encounter with the ivory trader Kurz, both the agent and the victim of imperial greed and megalomania; there have been many arguments over whether Conrad was a Victorian racist or not. Nevertheless, there can be no doubt, one historian recently insisted, that the novel presents an accurate and detailed description of conditions in the

Prime minister Patrice Lumumba of the newly independent Republic of the Congo (second from left) and aides with Dag Hammarskjold, UN secretary general. Their diplomatic smiles conceal tensions at the UN Security Council, where this photograph was taken in July 1960, over chaos in the Congo and a cold war confrontation over the Soviet shootdown of an American reconnaissance aircraft. Lumumba was assassinated in March 1961 following a coup d'état led by Joseph Mobutu, an affair in which the American CIA played a role. (Time Life Pictures/Getty Images.)

Congo at the moment its exploitation began. It depicts "the actual facts of the case," as Conrad himself put it. Leopold II died in 1909, after clearing more than a billion dollars in today's money, and the government of Belgium took over the administration of the Congo, but the practices he initiated continued well into the 1920s.

Violence Wracks the Congo

Independence came to the Congo in 1960, the same year British Prime Minister Harold Macmillan spoke of "the winds of change" overtaking the world.

Surprised by the suddenness with which native leaders took up the cry for self-rule, Belgian administrators had done almost nothing to prepare for it. The entire territory boasted fewer than thirty African university graduates. No Congolese officers were to be found in the army; no native engineers or other civilian experts were at hand to take over from the Belgians. Greatly compounding these liabilities, the cold war almost fatally compromised the transition to Congolese independence, leaving the new nation crippled from the start.

Soviet sponsorship of the new prime minister, the spellbinding Patrice Lumumba, was enough to make him suspect in American eyes. The United States supported rebels in the breakaway province of Katanga, whose colossal mineral wealth American, British, and Belgian mining firms were eager to get their hands on. The United Nations sent a peacekeeping force to restore order in the Congo and quell the Katangese rebellion. Amid scenes of anarchy, in 1961 Lumumba was assassinated, with Washington's connivance, by Belgian secret service agents. Soon the Americans wheeled out their own chosen successor, a Congolese army sergeant named Joseph Mobutu, who had a hand in planning Lumumba's murder. In 1965 Mobutu seized power in a coup d'état. With American backing he ruled until 1997, when he was overthrown in his turn. During his long reign the native-born despot out-plundered Leopold II. Wracked by instability and war from independence until today, the Congo Republic, as it is called after several name changes, remains trapped in the long shadow cast by the history of European misrule.

Peaceful Transitions from European Rule

At least to the degree they have escaped the violence that has attended the history of the Congo almost since the inception of European overlordship, most former European colonies have met a happier fate. Algeria apart, independence came peacefully to the majority of the new states of Africa. Between 1945 and the 1960s, the high era of decolonization, most citizens of the once-great empires greeted the loss of their overseas colonies with indifference. Colonies of white settlement, such as Algeria in the French case or Rhodesia (Zimbabwe) in the English, were exceptions. Even here, though, a belligerent nostalgia for empire, or solidarity with beleaguered white settlers, did not capture enough hearts in the home countries to keep governments from divesting themselves of overseas rule.

"They are the dust of empire," Charles de Gaulle is said to have remarked in the 1960s of the newly independent states of Africa. Whether the French president actually made the remark or not, it was consistent with his policy of firmly closing the door on an era in the history of France. The "Francophone bloc" was a French-speaking archipelago in an otherwise English-speaking sea. Still, such lingering affinities as these came at a much lower political, emotional, and financial cost than direct or even indirect rule. Even in the short run, the independence of former European dependencies in Asia and Africa brought Europe its own forms of independence. Free of the ramifying snares of colonial war and political discord, France in the decade of the 1960s experienced rates of economic growth approaching 10 percent a year. Britain's postcolonial growth rates did not reach such dramatic levels, but by the same decade the expense of empire had fallen off sharply.

"To govern is to choose," the French prime minister Pierre Mendes-France once remarked. Freeing their colonies freed the former imperial powers of Europe to choose other ways of spending their resources. To take the most obvious example, neither France nor Britain nor the Netherlands needed for homeland defense the large armies and navies they had required for maintaining their empires. By the end of the twentieth century defense budgets in France and Britain absorbed less than 3 percent of GDP and in the Netherlands less than 2 percent, a far smaller share than had been the case in imperial days. A compelling reason the British Labour government handed over power in India in 1947 was the need to pay for the new National Health Service. It could not simultaneously prop up the Raj and provide all British citizens with health care. It had to make a choice.

The end of empire also freed the former imperial powers of entanglements with respect to tariffs, trade agreements, subsidies, currency zones, and other forms of preferential treatment put in place in the hey-day of colonialism. Freed of these entanglements, and of the old rivalries of imperial foreign policy, the large states of Europe were able to give whole-hearted attention to the building of a European economic union.

SUMMARY

European dominion over territories and peoples overseas was acquired in the course of centuries and relinquished in the space of decades. Portugal, Spain, the Netherlands, Britain, France, and the latecomers Belgium, Germany, and Italy all had imperial ambitions. All sought a "place in the sun," as the thirst for acquisition was called; for a time Britain, the leading imperial power, boasted an empire on which the sun never set. As to the motives of their quest for overseas territory, many were professed and many ascribed; they included a desire to establish colonies of settlement, to monopolize raw materials, to trade in goods and in the sale of human beings, to spread religion and culture, to compete with rivals, to secure geopolitical advantages, and to ease tensions in Europe. Fitfully acquired, European possessions overseas often proved hard to retain. The wars of national liberation that came to Asia and Africa after 1945 broke out first in North and South America in the late eighteenth and early nineteeth centuries.

World War II weakened the hold on their territories of the remaining imperial powers, but they did not all respond in the same way to indigenous challenges to their rule. Britain performed a nearly headlong withdrawal from the Indian subcontinent. The Netherlands made a half-hearted attempt to reassert control over the Dutch East Indies, but soon the vast archipelago found independence as the state of Indonesia. Only France, of the major imperial powers, chose to resist, with force, nationalist demands for an end to French rule. Defeat in World War II may have made postwar French governments all the more determined to hold on in Indochina and Algeria. American governments encouraged the French to see resistance to Ho Chi Minh's demand for independence in Indochina as resistance to the spread of communism in Asia. Controlling the cities, the French never mastered the countryside. A sharp military reversal in the spring of 1954 sapped their will to continue the struggle. No sooner had France negotiated its withdrawal from Indochina than it faced a nationalist insurrection in Algeria. The presence of one million settlers of European origin virtually assured it would not leave its North African colony without a fight. Unable to assuage the settlers' fears of abandonment, the Fourth Republic gave way to the Fifth. Stepping up military pressure on the rebels, the new regime also undertook a program of sweeping reforms. In the end, however, the rebels' military setbacks did not keep them from achieving diplomatic victory and their aim of Algerian independence.

In the Middle East the aftermath of World War II saw the waning of European influence and the emergence of the new state of Israel. Arab nationalists championed the cause of Palestinians displaced to make room for the new Zionist homeland. Over the rival claims of Jews and Arabs to the same ancient places four wars ensued, followed by the ill-fated Israeli occupation of south Lebanon; a relentless campaign of anti-Israeli terrorism by radical Islamist groups; and two more-or-less spontaneous Palestinian uprisings, or intifadas.

Sub-Saharan Africa, last to fall under European dominion, was also last to experience the upwelling of nationalism. Partly because their resistance to national liberation movements elsewhere had gone badly, partly because their African holdings had long been more tenuous and less valuable to them than other overseas territories, the former imperial powers were more inclined to negotiate their withdrawal than to fight to stay on. For instance, France relinquished rule over its West African colonies with scarcely more than a rhetorical murmur against certain ungrateful nationalists. Britain chose to leave Kenya rather than endure a protracted guerrilla war. In the Congo, however, greed for riches and cold war politics conspired to send that former Belgian territory into near anarchy. South Africa's white-supremacist regime spent years deploying the laws of apartheid and the forces of repression against a persistent nationalist challenge. Finally it too surrendered rule of a land in which Dutch explorers had first set foot more than three centuries earlier.

Western Europe

Britain from Postwar Social Reform Through the Thatcher Revolution to Tony Blair's New Labour Party

In July 1945, just weeks after World War II ended in Europe, British voters turned Winston Churchill out of office. Churchill had embodied lion-hearted resistance to Nazi Germany. Sixty-five when he became prime minister in 1940, he had been in the public eye since his flamboyant youth. As a danger-seeking and slightly vainglorious cavalry officer serving on the frontiers of empire, he was a character right out of *Indiana Jones*. Like his father Randolph, who came crashing down from high office as a comparatively young man, Churchill entered politics early. His was a public life of great successes, great failures, and great errors of judgment. For instance, as first lord of the admiralty, the civilian head of the navy, he bore the chief responsibility for planning and executing the disastrous Dardanelles campaign of 1915. The Dardanelles would have ruined the career of many a politician. Like his contemporary Harry Houdini, however, Churchill made seemingly miraculous escapes from situations fraught with peril. Between the world wars he occupied a string of ministerial posts before falling out of office and out of favor in the Conservative party. In the eyes of his enemies an opinionated crank, to his smallish circle of admirers he was a Cassandra-like prophet, crying out from the wilderness against the Nazi menace. When Churchill's warnings came true, Parliament turned to him for leadership.

British voters turned away from Churchill and his party in 1945 not from ingratitude but because a majority of them favored an agenda of postwar social reform he opposed. The contrast in style, temperament, and outlook between Churchill and his successor Clement Atlee, an introspective middle-class lawyer, could scarcely have been greater. As leader of the Labour party, Atlee was committed to sweeping social reform in Britain and home rule for much of the British Empire.

The new government proceeded to take over, with compensation to the owners, the coal industry, railroads, and parts of commercial road transportation and began to nationalize the steel industry. Britain already had a well-developed system of social insurance; this was now capped by a system of socialized medical care for all who wished it. The educational system was partly reformed to make it more democratic and to lengthen the period of compulsory education.

When the Conservatives, with Churchill still at their head, were returned to power in 1951 and remained there for twelve years, they halted the nationalization of steel but otherwise kept intact the socialism of their opponents, including the national health plan. Thus a social revolution was achieved without bitter divisiveness between the parties.

In the postwar years the British were not able to keep up with the extraordinary pace of technological innovation. The British automobile industry, for example, which immediately after the war gained a large share of the world market, yielded the lead in the 1950s to the Germans, with their inexpensive, standardized light car, the Volkswagen Beetle. Furthermore, Britain was one of the last countries in Europe to develop a system of superhighways, completing its first modern highway only in 1969. The British were falling behind because they had been the first to industrialize and now their plants were the first to become outdated and inefficient. While British management and labor remained bound to traditional ways, the West Germans, buoyed by vast sums of money provided for their economic recovery by their former enemies, and especially by the United States, embarked on new paths.

Even in apparent prosperity, Britain remained in economic trouble. Continued pressure on the pound in the 1960s repeatedly required help from Britain's allies to maintain its value. This weakness of the pound signaled an unfavorable balance of trade in which the British were buying more from the rest of the world than they could sell. In the 1950s and 1960s, in what came to be called the "brain drain," some of Britain's most distinguished scientists and engineers left home to find higher pay and more modern laboratories in the United States, Canada, or Australia.

Under Harold Wilson, a shrewd politician often criticized for opportunism, the Labour party came to power in 1964 and governed until 1970. In 1966 Wilson froze wages and prices in an effort to restore balance between what the British spent and what they produced. In his own party, such measures were deeply unpopular and were regarded as exploiting the poor to support the rich. Wilson had to devalue the pound after heavy foreign pressure against it. Despite the unpopularity of his policies, by 1969 the deficits had disappeared and general prosperity continued, along with high taxes and rapid inflation. Prices were rising so fast that the gains from rising wages were largely illusory. The national health plan and education for working-class mothers had freed more women for an increasingly technical work force. But a spiral continued with only momentary breaks, regardless of the parry in office, and except for a period of prosperity and relative confidence in the late 1960s and early 1970s, Britain's decline in relation to its competitors continued.

Yet Britain in the 1960s was a far from gloomy place. Nowhere was this more apparent than in the exuberance and inventiveness of British popular

Portrait of a lady, 2000. Baroness Thatcher poses alongside her portrait at the National Portrait Gallery in London. Born a grocer's daughter, Margaret Thatcher rose to become leader of the Conservative Party, the first woman prime minister of Britain, the longest-serving prime minister since the early nineteenth century, and the first woman head of government of any European country. The champion of free-market economic policies, she presided over what allies and adversaries alike called a "revolution"—reducing the political clout of trade unions, reprivatizing key parts of the industrial sector, and dismantling some provisions of the welfare system. As assertive as any man who had held the job, she reveled in being called "the Iron Lady." (Time Life Pictures/Getty Images.)

culture. Beginning with the phenomenally popular Beatles—perhaps the most creative and certainly the most successful garage band of all time—England for a time set styles in clothing for young people in the West and in music for young people everywhere. Coming to prominence shortly after the Beatles, the Rolling Stones continued to exert great influence into the new millenium. The Beatles were working-class boys from the old industrial port city of Liverpool; lower-class, too, were many leading innovators in music and fashion. In their eagerness to assimilate the new popular culture, youths of the middle and upper classes helped weaken the class sentiment that had so long pervaded English society and thought.

In 1979 Margaret Thatcher—a grocer's daughter, as she never tired of pointing out—became prime minister of a Conservative government that she went on to lead for eleven years. The longest-serving British prime minister in the twentieth century, she was also perhaps the most revered and most reviled of postwar British leaders. An avid free marketer and a sworn enemy of trade unions, she came to office determined to curb union influence on the economy and politics, and she largely succeeded. Thatcherism, rather like its counterpart of Reaganism across the Atlantic, sought to reduce inflation by squeezing the money supply, sharply reducing government spending, and cutting taxes, especially on the rich. The declining output that had character-ized the economy throughout the postwar period was reversed; despite fits and starts along the way, economic growth has continued ever since. In 1982 a victory in war over Argentina, which had attempted to claim from Britain, by force, the south Atlantic Falkland Islands, sent Thatcher's popu-larity skyrocketing.

Thatcher's second government introduced changes aimed at dismantling aspects of the welfare state. Most notably, certain national industries in energy and telecommunications were privatized. Mrs. Thatcher's third gov-ernment, formed after the parliamentary elections of 1987, ran into increas-ing difficulties. Privatizing industry had been one thing; the prime minister's attempt to introduce market principles into the national health and education systems was quite another. Accusations that she and her party had no com-passion for the poor struck home; her antagonism to a common European currency and the cause of European integration fueled an internal party revolt against her; opposition to her attempt to impose a poll tax on votes intensified to riot, and in 1990 she resigned. After all the drama of the Thatcher era, John Major proved a colorless but effective successor. Smooth-ing the rough edges of Thatcherism, Major backed away from some of his predecessor's domestic policies and sharply moderated her opposition to European union, winning British ratification of the Treaty of European Union, or Maastricht Treaty, in 1993.

Meanwhile, conditions of life had greatly improved for most people. The Labour government had imposed heavy income taxes on the well-to-do and burdensome death duties on the rich, using the income thus obtained to redistribute goods and services to the poor. An increasing number of new universities offered young people of all classes educational opportunities that had previously been available only to the upper and upper-middle classes.

In the postwar years race became a serious issue in Britain for the first time. Indians, Pakistanis, West Indians, and Africans—Commonwealth subjects with British passports—left poor conditions at home and migrated freely to Britain in large numbers to take jobs in factories, public transportation, and hospitals. Despite its liberal and antiracist protestations, the Wilson government was forced to curtail immigration sharply. Some Conservative politicians predicted bloody race riots (which, in fact, occurred in 1981) unless black immigration was halted, and some extremists proposed that nonwhites already in Britain be deported.

Closely related to the race issue at home was the question of official British relations with southern Africa, to which the Labour government refused to sell arms because of the apartheid policies of the South African regime from the late 1940s. Brought gradually into place from 1948 to the late 1960s, apartheid laws (the term means "apartness") led to separate tracks of development for whites, blacks, coloureds—persons deemed of mixed race—and Asians in a complex and highly expensive system of segregation by race. Relations deteriorated quickly after South African police fired upon a mass demonstration at Sharpeville in 1960, killing many black Africans. In 1961, under pressure from the prime ministers of Canada and India with Britain's approval, the rigidly racist government of South Africa withdrew from the Commonwealth.

To this strain was added a major challenge to British authority when the white-dominated government in Southern Rhodesia, unwilling to accept a constitution that provided for full black participation in legislation, unilaterally declared Rhodesia independent of Great Britain, citing the American colonies in 1776 as a precedent. This move led to the imposition of sanctions by the United Nations and years of delicate negotiations punctuated by civil war, until a cease-fire, a constitution, and elections were ultimately accepted by all parties, and the Thatcher government declared Rhodesia independent, as Zimbabwe, in 1980.

Perhaps most persistently debilitating to British security, however, was the Irish problem, long quiescent, which arose again in the late 1960s. In Ulster (the northern counties that were still part of the United Kingdom), the Catholics generally formed a depressed class and were the first to lose their jobs in bad times. They were inflamed by the insistence of Protestant extremists (the Orangemen) of publicly celebrating the anniversaries of the victories of William III in the 1690s that had ensured English domination over the region. Marching provocatively through Catholic districts, the Orangemen in the summer of 1969 precipitated disorders that began in Londonderry and spread to Belfast and other areas. The regular police were accused by Catholics of being mere tools of the Protestant oppressor and had to be disarmed. The British Army then intervened to keep order.

The government of the Irish Republic, the independent southern counties, suggested that the United Nations be given responsibility for the problem, a suggestion unacceptable to both the Northern Irish and British governments. Extremists of the south, the Irish Republican Army (IRA), who had always claimed the northern counties as part of a united Ireland, now revived their terroristic activities. But the IRA itself was split between a relatively moderate wing and the Provisionals (Provos), anarchists dedicated to nearly indiscriminate bombing. The level of fighting steadily escalated in Northern Ireland. In 1972 the British suspended the Northern Irish parliament and governed the province directly. In 1981 a group of prisoners, insisting that they not be treated as common criminals but as political prisoners, resorted to hunger strikes; although ten prisoners died, the British government continued to refuse political status to people they viewed as terrorists.

In early 1995 there at last appeared the prospect of an enduring cease-fire. Following more than two years of arduous negotiations, in 1998 the Good Friday agreement, the work of the American George Mitchell, former Senate majority leader, established the framework of a peace process between the Loyalists, chiefly the Protestant Ulster Unionists, and the Republicans, chiefly Sinn Fein, political wing of the IRA. Violence, and provocations short of violence, continued to flare up on both sides; the peace process faltered from time to time. The chief long-term obstacle to a final settlement was the Unionists' refusal to share power with the Republicans unless the IRA proved its willingness to disarm. For their part, the Republicans refused to give up their weapons until the Unionists provided better evidence of their own good faith.

Eighteen years of Conservative party rule in England ended in 1997 with the landslide victory of a rejuvenated Labour party led by Tony Blair, at forty-three the youngest British prime minister since the Napoleonic Wars. Assuming his party's leadership in 1994, Blair reinforced his recent predecessor's efforts to detach Labour from its socialist past. By abandoning a long commitment to worker ownership of the means of production—made manifest in various nationalization schemes—and loosening the party's old links with trade unions, Blair pushed what he called "New Labour" toward the political center. Continuing to move slowly on British adoption of the European Union's currency, the euro, he nevertheless worked to improve Britain's ties with fellow EU members; he became a committed advocate of peace in Northern Ireland and of a more active role for NATO in European affairs. His party's victory in the 2001 election won him a second term as prime minister. From within the left of his own party he faced criticism for aggressively aligning Britain with the aims of American foreign policy, especially the war on terrorism. At home the Labour party faced the great challenge of reforming Britain's public services, widely seen as dilapidated and unresponsive, especially in health care and rail transport, where a 1995 scheme of privatization went badly awry.

France from Defeat in World War II to Leadership of the European Union

Defeat by the Germans, brutal German occupation and economic exploitation, the spectacle of French collaboration with the enemy—all this was followed by a liberation that, despite the part played in it by the Fighting French and the French Resistance movement, was clearly the work of American, British, and Soviet arms. Compounding this, since the early nineteenth century France had not kept pace with the leading industrial nations in production, finance, or population growth. Only a rising birth rate gave cause for optimism. Hundreds of thousands of French men and women decided to have children—a clear sign of the recovery that lay ahead. The arrival of nearly a million refugees from the colonial war in Algeria in 1962–1963 and the influx of almost 4 million foreign workers made France, already a cosmopolitan nation, even more so, and assured the nation a labor supply on which to base its rapid industrial expansion.

The French government-in-exile, led by General de Gaulle, had easily reestablished in liberated France the old republican forms of government, called the Fourth Republic. But after de Gaulle temporarily retired from politics in 1946, the Fourth Republic began to look like the Third. Cabinets lasted on average only a few months; to the old splinter parties was added a Communist party of renewed strength, openly dedicated to revolutionary change. After nine years of war, Indochina was lost in 1954; in the same year rebellion broke out against the French in Algeria; Morocco and Tunisia were both lost in 1956, and the crisis deepened.

In 1958 de Gaulle took power again. A plebiscite confirmed a new constitution. The constitution of the new Fifth Republic provided for a president to be elected for a seven-year term by direct popular vote. An absolute majority was required, and, if not achieved in a first election, was to be obtained in a runoff between the two candidates with the most votes. Elected outright in 1958, de Gaulle was reelected to a second term in 1965 in such a runoff. Under the new constitution the French president appointed the premier, who could dissolve the legislature and order new elections at any time after the first year. Thus the new constitution gave the executive more power, the legislature much less.

De Gaulle's enemies soon called him a dictator, the personification of French haughtiness and superiority. He was obstinate, opinionated, and authoritarian; yet he was also consistent, clear, capable, and utterly committed to creating a stable and progressive French state. He intended that France be taken seriously in world affairs. To this end he fought to keep Britain out of the Common Market, worked to prevent American dominance in Europe, and sought to establish a creditable French military presence. He did not want to see France bled by further colonial wars, and though he believed strongly in the unity of all French-speaking peoples (seeking even to establish a separate cultural mission to the French-speaking people of Quebec), he nonetheless worked out a settlement making Algeria independent in 1962.

Starting with Marshall Plan aid in 1947, great economic and social changes began in France. A full-scale reorientation of the economy was undertaken in accordance with the practices of modern industry. Helped by foreign investment, especially American, France began to experience a real boom. Prosperity meant that for the first time the French, by the hundreds of thousands, bought cars, television sets, and record players; that they traveled in ever growing numbers; that they experienced fearful traffic jams; and that those who found the new ways unsettling blamed all the changes on the Americans. Those who feared that France would adopt the new British-American culture emphasized the continuity, unity, complexity, and alleged purity of the French language and looked for their own cultural influences to offset Americanization and "Coca-Colanization."

De Gaulle retained a strong dislike of the Anglo-Saxons. The thought of such supranational bodies as the Common Market and NATO that could rob France of sovereignty even to a small degree was uncomfortable, and talk of a United States of Europe was totally unacceptable. He spoke instead of *Europe des patries*, a "Europe of fatherlands," in which France would take the lead. But to do this France must have its own atomic weapon. Therefore de Gaulle refused to join the United States, Great Britain, and the Soviet Union in a treaty barring atomic tests, and France continued to test nuclear weapons in the atmosphere, exploding its first hydrogen bomb in 1968. Vigorously opposed to communism at home, de Gaulle nonetheless came to terms with the Soviet Union; the Soviets, he argued, no longer represented the threat to the general peace that they had represented in the 1950s. In balancing the scales against the industrial and military power of the United States and Britain, France needed friends. To South America, to Canada, to Poland, and to Romania, de Gaulle carried his message that France would be the leader of Europe.

In the spring of 1968, however, while de Gaulle was in Romania, Paris erupted. The French universities had been ignored by the regime in a period when the young throughout western Europe were bursting with resentment against "the machine civilization" of the cold war society. Students in Paris occupied university buildings, fought the police, and eventually drew a reluctant Communist party into the battle in order that it not lose the support of the French workers, who had already begun to strike in sympathy with the students. De Gaulle returned to Paris, assured himself of army support, proposed a referendum, which he was obliged to abandon in favor of new elections, and then won a great victory at the polls, obtaining a larger majority in the legislature than before. His new minister of education, acknowledging the legitimacy of many of the grievances of the students, pushed through the legislature a reform bill decentralizing the educational system. De Gaulle now staked his political future on the issue of regional reform in a public referendum—and lost. As he had done before, he withdrew into private life. In the 1969 elections the Gaullists were returned to office with a substantial majority, and Georges Pompidou became president of France.

France now entered more readily into competition rather than confrontation with its former allies. To make the French more competitive, the franc was devalued. The veto against Britain's entry into the Common Market was abandoned, and, without rejoining NATO, France began more formal cooperation with it. An economic recession began in 1973, however, and public confidence wavered. France returned to governments that could administer programs only with the help of complex coalitions, as the aristocratic Valéry Giscard d'Estaing became president. Fearful of the left, and ultimately beset by political scandal, Giscard did not press the social reforms his platform had promised. From 1972 to 1977 the Socialist and Communist parties formed a common front to oppose the right and center parties, but the communists withdrew in 1977.

In 1981 an able Socialist party regular who had worked to broaden the socialist base by weakening the communists, their traditional enemies, won the presidential election. This man, François Mitterrand, was a bundle of contradictions. Starting out in public life as an official of the collaborationist Vichy regime, he became a leader of the Resistance, a statesman but also a schemer and fixer in the rough-and-tumble of French politics, an austere intellectual but also a self-indulgent pleasure-seeker, a champion of democracy and civil rights but also an abuser of the considerable powers of the French presidency, tolerant of, and probably a participant in, the political corruption of his time. Engineering a "union of the left," he led the socialists to power for the first time in a generation. Mitterrand took a strongly anti-Soviet stance over the Soviet Union's invasion of Afghanistan, which had begun in December 1979. He declared himself committed to a mixed-enterprise economy and to cooperation with the Americans in their efforts to renew disarmament talks while seeking to base a nuclear missile force within Europe. In 1986 France began a graduated process of industrial privatization, achieved by 1993, and in 1995, Mitterrand retired.

Mitterrand was succeeded in the presidency by Jacques Chirac, long-time Gaullist mayor of Paris. Shortly after his election in May 1995 Chirac became the first president—or high official of any kind, for that matter—to accept the French state's responsibility, under the Vichy regime, for the arrest and deportation of seventy-six thousand Jews to Germany. Following Chirac's example, other French leaders came forward to end fifty years of silence and evasions over French collaboration with the German occupier during World War II.

France's two-headed executive power, which under the constitution of the Fifth Republic provided for a president as head of state and a prime minister as head of government, made governance awkward when the two incumbents belonged to different parties that held sharply different views on questions of policy. This is just what happened during the five years that Chirac's first presidency coincided with the Socialist Lionel Jospin's term as prime minister. As leader of the leftist majority that controlled the National Assembly following the elections of 1997, Jospin cut the work week to thirty-five hours, helped settle two serious strikes, and pursued policies displeasing to Chirac and his conservative allies. Chirac and Jospin faced each other in the presidential election of 2002. Five years in office had given Jospin the political liabilities that always come with governing; a string of municipal corruption scandals running through Chirac's time as mayor of Paris cast a shadow over his presidential campaign. Jean Marie Le Pen, a veteran right-wing nationalist rabble-rouser, won nearly 20 percent of the vote in the first round of the election, eliminating Jospin, who failed to come up with enough votes to continue into the second round. Chirac won handily, and a center-right coalition won a majority of the seats in the National Assembly, enabling Chirac to name as prime minister a far more congenial conservative.

France was one of the first countries to face the problem of large-scale immigration from former colonies, followed by substantial new immigration from politically unstable, repressive, or poverty-stricken states. At first France accepted Muslim immigrants from North Africa and French-speaking blacks from sub-Saharan Africa, but by the 1990s public opinion was turning against the influx of immigrants, many of whom were in fact refugees. In 1993 France restricted entry and passed laws making it possible to expel foreigners more easily. In the meantime the same problem—that of international "boat people"—became serious in the United States, to which thousands of Cubans and Haitians were fleeing. Germany, attractive to workers from the Balkans and Turkey, experienced anti-immigrant rioting. Britain had long since closed its doors to much Commonwealth immigration, especially South Asian and West Indian. France thus joined other Western nations in turning to more restrictive policies in the face of a worldwide problem that no one nation could solve and that calls for action from the United Nations barely seemed to touch.

Germany from Disunion to Reunification

The West German postwar recovery was the most remarkable of all. The wartime destruction of much of Germany's industrial plant had paradoxically proved beneficial; the new plant was built with the latest technological equipment. The Allied High Commission gradually abolished control over German industry, save for atomic energy and certain military restrictions. It provided economic aid and scaled down prewar German debts. By the early 1950s West Germany had a favorable balance of trade and a rate of industrial growth as high as 10 percent a year.

The West German gross national product rose from $23 billion in 1950 to $103 billion in 1964, with no serious monetary inflation. This prosperity was spread though all classes of society. The working class in West Germany had begun to enjoy affluence; new buildings rose everywhere, while superhighways grew overcrowded and had to be widened and extended. The economic miracle attracted population into West Germany from southern Europe and drew other Germans out of East Germany into the Federal Republic. East Germany thus had a net loss in population as West Germany boomed. By the late 1960s the German birth rate had fallen, however, and in the 1980s the population had stabilized at 62 million. This made for a highly industrialized, close-knit, urban nation.

The independent West German state had a constitution that provided for a legislature whose lower house represented the people directly and whose upper house represented the states (*Länder*). The president, elected by a special assembly for a five-year term, was largely a ceremonial figure. Real executive leadership was vested in the chancellor, a prime minister dependent on a parliamentary majority. Under the firm leadership of Konrad Adenauer, the Christian Democrats held power until 1961. A Rhineland Catholic, former mayor of Cologne, conservative, pro-French, and democratic, Adenauer was forced to retire only because of age and continued to wield enough influence to weaken his successor, Ludwig Erhard, a Protestant and professional economist, who remained in office for five more years.

Germany had been rather successfully "de-Nazified"—a requirement stipulated by the Allied High Commission. As a result of the Nuremburg trials in 1946, seventy-four major Nazi leaders were convicted of war crimes. In general, lower-level Nazis were required only to demonstrate that they fully accepted the new democratic government; to have dismissed all civil servants who had held posts under the Nazi regime would have crippled any administrative recovery. Some Nazis who had escaped to other parts of the world, notably South America, continued to be hunted and, if captured, tried for war crimes.

The major political question remained that of an eventual reunion with communist-dominated East Germany. Neither Germany recognized the other diplomatically. After years during which the East Germans, attracted by better living conditions in West Germany, crossed the border by the tens of thousands, the East German government in August 1961 began building a wall between two parts of Berlin. Though on special holidays families in West Berlin were allowed to cross into East Berlin briefly to visit relatives and friends, the wall stood as the visible symbol of a divided Germany.

As a consequence of the cold war, the Americans, British, and French permitted the West Germans to rearm early in the 1950s and to join NATO. Military conscription was introduced in 1955, and by 1970 West Germany had developed a sizable modern military. Access to the atomic bomb was not included in this rearmament. Even so, and despite low-key political leadership, the spectacle of a rearmed Germany caused much concern—in the Soviet bloc, in Britain, and among Jewish voters in all nations.

Chancellor Erhard's government fell in 1966, when a small disciplined party, the Free Democrats, in coalition with which the Christian Democrats were ruling, refused to support his proposals for higher taxes. The Christian Democrats now proposed a "grand coalition" with their chief opponents, the Social Democrats. The very popular mayor of West Berlin, Willy Brandt, became vice chancellor and foreign minister. This grand coalition commanded popular support, and it lasted until the elections of 1969.

In these elections Brandt, a Social Democrat, became chancellor and formed a coalition in his turn with the Free Democrats. Brandt moved slowly and cautiously to open discussions with the East Germans. The chief stumbling block was Soviet fear of West Germany. It gradually became apparent that a treaty between West Germany and the Soviet Union in which both renounced the use of force would be one of the necessary preliminaries. In the summer of 1970 Brandt reached agreement with the Soviets on the text of such a treaty. It recognized all existing European frontiers, which Germans and Soviets agreed never to try to alter by force, leaving open future negotiations. The second step was an agreement with Poland, which Brandt concluded during 1970. Brandt's *Ostpolitik*, or Eastern policy, culminated in a treaty with Czechoslovakia and in the entry of both Germanies into the

An unidentified man takes a hammer to the Berlin Wall, defining symbol and structure of the cold war. Erected in early August 1961 to staunch the exodus of East Germans to West Germany, the wall was dismantled—a demolition project accompanied by joyous celebrations—in the days following November 10, 1989. On that date the soon-to-be-defunct East German government lifted travel and emigration restrictions on its people. Divided throughout the cold war, Germany was reunified in 1990. (Getty Images.)

United Nations in 1973. A form of détente with the Soviet bloc was nearly achieved when in 1974 Brandt resigned upon the discovery that one of his closest assistants had been an East German spy, a discovery that renewed German fears of the designs of the Soviet bloc.

The 1970s also dimmed the West German economic miracle. While the German inflation rate, roughly 6 percent in 1975, was mild compared to the rest of Europe, and the growth rate continued at over 5 percent, unemployment began to climb. German social services were among the best in the world, and German per capita income had surpassed that of the nations that had defeated Germany in World War II, but a deep-seated memory of the inflation that had destroyed the democratic hopes of Weimar made the Germans cautious and insecure. Waves of terrorism further disconcerted the German leadership. Only Brandt, and after 1974 Helmut Schmidt, had seemed to provide the vigorous leadership the Germans had enjoyed under Adenauer.

Together with other nations in the West, Germany often appeared to lack able new leaders with dramatic solutions to the nation's problems. Although the electorate recognized that the range of dramatic new solutions was severely limited by the constraints of superpower confrontation and an eroding economy, they nonetheless hoped for a renewal of vigor at the top. Politics in the Federal Republic became fragmented when the grand coalition broke up, with powerful leaders emerging on the basis of strong local support. In 1982 the Christian Democrats, led by Helmut Kohl, won a landslide victory.

West Germany's economic growth, though slowed, remained prodigious, and Chancellor Kohl felt emboldened to pursue a more independent course in international affairs. While he kept West Germany in NATO, he forced the removal of American nuclear missiles that were deployed on German soil and intended for Soviet targets, and he called for negotiations with the Soviet Union on reducing short-range missiles, causing a rift with both Britain and the United States. Faced with protests at home, soaring social costs, and signs of a resurgence from the political right, Kohl moved to take advantage of the unexpected and overwhelming changes in eastern Europe and the Soviet Union. Soon the unthinkable was being thought on both sides of the rapidly crumbling Iron Curtain, and with communist leadership abandoned in East Germany, reunification appeared possible.

For forty-five years the "German Question"—how to deal with an economically powerful and energetic country dominating the heart of Europe— had been answered by keeping Germany divided. Whatever lip service they paid to the idea of a reunified Germany, many European leaders did not truly want to see one. They recognized that a country with 80 million people controlling 40 percent of European industrial production could well dominate the European Union. Chancellor Kohl moved quickly and adroitly, however, and in October 1990 one of the richest capitalist nations absorbed the former East Germany, a communist country near insolvency and psychologically demoralized after forty-five years of totalitarian rule. In December the first parliament for all of Germany since before the outbreak of World War II was elected. The new nation took the title Federal Republic of Germany. In terms of wealth, to be sure, the disparities between western and eastern Germany were at first enormous. Nor were they quickly overcome. Many residents of the former East Germany did not gladly surrender the security the communist state, for all its stifling restrictions, had afforded them; many formerly West Germans did not easily give up the habit of regarding the easterners as docile and unenterprising yokels.

Many a dire prediction accompanied German reunification, but none materialized. In 1999 the German capital was moved from the sleepy western town of Bonn to Berlin, the great historic city to the east. It may take another generation for the easterners to feel at home in a capitalist society and for westerners to welcome them. But fears that a new Germany would revert to the aggrandizing habits of the old prewar Germany and embark on a new search for living space appeared groundless. Chancellor Kohl's huge gamble on reunification succeeded beyond anyone's expectations. Success helped keep him in power for sixteen years, the longest term of any chancellor in postwar (west) German history. Germany's economic doldrums after 1995 took their toll, and in 1998 Kohl's ruling coalition of Christian Democrats and Free Democrats was ousted by an alliance, led by Gerhard Schröder, of left-leaning Social Democrats and Greens leaning further left. Germans voted Kohl (along with Einstein, Luther, and Goethe) one of the top ten "Greatest

Germans" of all time; soon after, he came under investigation for his part in handling an illegal party slush fund. In early 2000, refusing to speak of the allegations against him, he resigned the chairmanship of his party, his towering reputation at least temporarily in ruins.

Italy Pursues Political Stability

Unlike Germany, Italy was in turmoil for much of its postwar period. In 1946 a plebiscite showed 54 percent of the voters in favor of a republic, which was therefore established. Some monarchists and fascists remained, but neither group influenced parliamentary politics to any great extent. A strong Christian Democratic party (a Catholic party with a relatively liberal program) held power under a succession of leaders, with support from other groups. The government broke up large landed estates in the south to redistribute the land. A very strong Communist party, with which the larger faction of the socialists was allied, offered a persistent challenge. In the early 1960s a series of complicated negotiations began a process called the *apertura à sinistra*, the "opening to the left," in which the Christian Democrats won over some socialist support.

Italy's economic growth between 1953 and 1966 was so remarkable that the Italians, too, spoke of an economic miracle. As in France, this growth was achieved with some government ownership and with much government regulation and planning. Membership in the Common Market gave Italian enterprise opportunities that it had never had before. The grave problems of southern Italy, Sardinia, and Sicily were attacked by programs of investments, by providing jobs in the north or in Germany or Switzerland for the surplus workers of the south, and by old-age pensions. In the Italian balance of payments, an income of about $1 billion annually from tourists proved enormously important. Italian fashions became popular throughout the world, further bolstering both the economy and the national sense of well-being. The Italian motion picture industry began to rival that of France and ultimately overtook the immediate postwar leader, Britain.

By the late 1960s Italian political stability began to crumble in part due to severe internal political strains within the Christian Democratic party, and in part due to the uncertainty of the party's relationship with its supposed partners, the socialists. In part it was also due to the inflation that Italy was perhaps less able to bear than were the advanced industrial nations. Strikes occurred sporadically and unpredictably, and 1969 was marked by mass strikes.

The Italian bureaucracy was marked by no-show jobs, scandal, corruption, and pettiness. Economic mismanagement became evident in the 1970s. The Italian inflation rate soared; nearly 2 million Italians were unemployed. By 1974 Italy had a huge trade deficit and had to turn to the International Monetary Fund and to West Germany for credit. The government was unable to restrain demands for wage increases, which ran at 30 percent annually, spurring further inflation in prices and overburdening the middle class. The

Mafia, a centuries-old alliance of secret criminal societies organized along feudal lines and particularly powerful in Sicily, began to show itself overtly in southern Italy. Terrorists openly attacked judges, teachers, journalists, and police officers in the streets. In 1978 one group, the Red Brigade, kidnapped former premier Aldo Moro and murdered him after the Italian government refused to negotiate his release. The universities were in chaos; students throughout the nation went on frequent and prolonged strikes, so that the ablest sought their education in other countries. Of all the nations of western Europe, Italy's experiment with liberal democracy seemed most clearly on trial.

During this time the large Italian Communist party increased in size and organizing skills. In 1976 the communists polled 35 percent of the popular vote for the Chamber of Deputies. Led by Enrico Berlinguer, the communists declared their desire to enter into a coalition government with their former enemies and promised to abide by the constitution and to keep Italy in NATO. The United States doubted the sincerity of these promises and supported those Italian leaders best able to block Berlinguer's move toward power. But by entering into what it called a "historic compromise," the Communist party won a new middle-class following. In 1978 the Communist party was granted equality with other parties in shaping government policy when it promised to support a national unity government. Ministries continued to change hands with bewildering rapidity in Italy; the entire cabinet resigned in 1981 when it was revealed that many officials were members of an illegal and secret Masonic lodge.

Scandals in banking and politics, the kidnapping of public officials, instability in leadership, and recurrent social unrest continued to plague Italy throughout the 1980s and 1990s. When Silvio Berlusconi, a right-wing media billionaire and the richest man in Italy, became prime minister once again in 2001 (he had briefly headed a government in 1994), he faced four criminal trials. Three cases were dismissed; one charge of allegedly bribing a judge remained but seemed unlikely to be tried.

The Vatican Faces the Winds of Change

In the eye of the hurricane, one force for continuity seemed clear. The pope, based in the Vatican City, in the heart of Rome, began to assert bold new initiatives in the political sphere, while holding to traditional positions on doctrinal church affairs. The feeling that Pope Pius XII had not done enough to forestall World War II or to assist beleaguered Jews within the Nazi-controlled nations persisted, and after the war he and his successors sought to take clear positions on world affairs.

These positions were defined in the context of substantial changes within the church itself. The most extensive changes were initiated by Pope John XXIII, who in 1959 called the twenty-first Ecumenical Council of the church, in a tradition begun by Constantine the Great in the fourth century. Known as Vatican II, this council continued to meet under his successor, Pope Paul VI. The council made many changes in the liturgy, encouraged celebrations of Mass in vernacular languages, and opened up relations with many other denominations.

The church continued to be identified in many parts of the world with the forces of conservatism—especially in its opposition to birth control and to women clergy and its insistence on priestly celibacy—but it was also associated with the forces of reform. Innovative church leaders in Central and North America and activist bishops in Africa and Asia urged the church to face the statistical fact that most Catholics apparently practiced some form of birth control (80 percent in the United States, according to one survey), argued that the church should be a force for land reforms that would benefit the peasants, and held that the nature of the church service needed further change if the younger generation were to be retrained. The church continued to emphasize the sacredness of life and the essential dignity of every human person, giving Catholics a basis for opposing abortion, euthanasia, and the death penalty, positions many eagerly embraced.

These trends continued under a dynamic new pope, John Paul II, elected in 1978 as the youngest pope since 1846 and the first non-Italian pope since the sixteenth century. A Pole, Karol Wojtyla, former archbishop of Kracow and one of the most intellectually able and energetic men ever to hold the office, allied himself with the church's most conservative tendencies. He made extensive visits all over the world and took strong positions against military aggression, terrorism, and abortion. Of particular concern to this Polish pope was the government suppression of the Polish solidarity movement in 1981–1982. Seriously wounded in an assassination attempt in Rome in 1981, he recovered to resume his role as itinerant shepherd of his worldwide flock of Catholics, including many visits to his native Poland. Despite the debilitating effects of Parkinson's disease, he kept up his world travels throughout the 1990s. Unbudging in its opposition to birth control, no matter what the practices of its faithful might be, the Vatican also remained adamantly opposed to the ordination of women into the priesthood; it continued to insist on priestly celibacy. Early in the new century the Catholic church in the United States faced a crisis of unprecedented proportions over allegations of the widespread sexual abuse of women and children by priests, abuse the church hierarchy was charged with covering up.

The Low Countries, Spain, and Greece

The Low Countries shared both the general European prosperity and its problems. In Belgium, which enjoyed great material well-being, the chronic difficulties between the minority French-speaking Walloons and the majority Dutch-speaking Flemings remained unresolved. The Netherlands at first enjoyed prosperity and stability, though there, too, student unrest, terrorist outbreaks, and serious environmental pollution created persistent problems. Mass emigration from Indonesia and Suriname, which became independent in 1975, revealed racial prejudices for the first time within the Netherlands.

A political scandal over the business activities of Queen Juliana, which contributed to her abdication in favor of her daughter Beatrix, challenged even the monarchy. In the 1990s the Netherlands had one of the best-performing economies in Europe and some of the most liberal social policies in the world, including toleration of such soft drugs as cannabis and legalization of euthanasia. As in other European countries, social and political tensions over the immigration of non-Europeans rose in the new century. The Netherlands took on increasing importance in the world system of justice. The site of the Balkan war-crimes tribunal, it became the home of the International Criminal Court.

Spain under the dictatorship of Francisco Franco, who led a successful rebellion and war against the legal Spanish Republic between 1936 and 1938, had taken major steps toward modernization and a few mild measures to relax political tyranny. Low wages and bitter government opposition to the Basques, a people of mysterious origins inhabiting the borderlands between northern Spain and southwestern France, prevented full economic or political stability. Five languages were accorded formal recognition: Spanish, Catalan, Basque, Galician (a Portuguese dialect), and Valencian (a Spanish dialect). Franco arranged that after his death the monarchy would be restored under Price Juan Carlos, grandson of Alfonso XIII, and in 1975 Juan Carlos became king. The actual government remained in the hands of political parties, since Juan Carlos was a constitutional monarch. Still, it was Juan Carlos who presided over the dissolution of many of Franco's institutions.

The first free elections since the Spanish Civil War took place in 1976, returning moderates and democratic socialists to office. As Spain turned from agriculture to industry, and as tourism grew larger in its balance of payments, the need for stability became paramount. To this end Spain attempted in 1982 to come to a peaceful settlement with Britain over a longstanding dispute concerning ownership of Gibraltar, and the Spanish government granted substantial home rule to Catalonia and the Basque lands in 1980.

Under the Socialist government of Felipe Gonzalez, Spain joined both NATO and the European Community (now the European Union), effectively ending the country's long isolation from the rest of Europe. José Maria Aznar, Gonzalez's more conservative successor, continued to spur economic growth, steadily closing the income gap between the average Spaniard and the average European. A peaceful resolution of the Basque separatist problem, however, still looked beyond reach.

Although still the poorest country in the European Union, in the 1990s Greece made rapid strides in economic growth and some progress in resolving long-standing territorial disputes with Turkey in the Aegean Sea. In 2002, the government made several arrests of members of November 17, a left-wing terrorist group that had operated with impunity since 1975, when it murdered the CIA station chief in Athens.

Norwegians, Danes, Swedes, Icelanders, and Finns: Similarity and Difference Among the Scandinavians

Scandinavia remained a bloc of stability. At first glance the Scandinavian or Nordic countries—Norway, Denmark, and Sweden in the center, Iceland and

Finland on the wings—seemed remarkably similar. For much of their history, several were grouped together under a common rule. The languages of Norway, Denmark, and Sweden were similar enough to permit speakers of one to understand speakers of the two others (if they could all speak to each other, they could speak with very few outsiders, so all shared the same dedication to English as a lingua franca). All had in common a Lutheran religious heritage, which gave them a similar moral outlook even as practicing Lutherans faded to a small minority of the population. All five Scandinavian countries were to a high degree ethnically homogeneous, compared with other European countries. Their dedication to equality made the proportion of women in parliaments and governments higher in Scandinavia than anywhere else in the world. In their decades-long commitment to the welfare state was their push for equality made manifest, especially in the three central countries of Norway, Denmark, and Sweden. Their cradle-to-grave social-welfare programs made for extremely high taxes, with rates in one case exceeding 60 percent of annual earnings.

Scandinavians themselves insisted their countries were not as similar as they looked to outsiders, and they had plenty of evidence to make the case. Their economies were strikingly dissimilar. Only Sweden had a broad industrial base. Icelanders continued to make most of their living from fishing. Norway probably relied too much on offshore oil production. Finland, in the 1990s the Nordics' greatest economic success, had turned from timber to high-tech electronics, particularly the production of cell phones, in which it was a world leader. Denmark continued to rely on a network of small- and medium-sized firms producing food and furniture. In the 1990s all the Nordics sought to reduce their enormous welfare budgets, but in different ways and with varying degrees of success. The Danes curbed what voters had come to regard as excessive spending; the Swedes were most reluctant to abandon any part of a welfare system that perhaps they could no longer afford; the rest of the Scandinavian countries seemed more determined than the Swedes to reform their welfare states. Some of the northern countries were more interested in abandoning the armed neutralities or go-it-alone military defenses they had maintained for most of the twentieth century in favor of common security arrangements. All had different attitudes toward the European Union (EU). The Finns most eagerly embraced it; the Swedes were the most undecided about joining the monetary union that was a feature of membership; the Danes opted for the EU but against the euro, for the time being; the Norwegians were the least interested of all.

Toward a European Union

Often the maps in our heads do not square with maps on paper. These imaginary maps are shaped more by political and cultural considerations than by the realities of geography and topography. A trick question in Western civilization courses taught a generation and more ago was: Which city is farther east, Prague or Vienna? The answer, of course, is Vienna. Under the influence of a cold war mentality, however, students often said Prague, the capital of a communist state, and not Vienna, the capital of a noncommunist one. Yet Prague was behind the Iron Curtain, a boundary both figurative and literal, for only forty-one years of its long history. In the eighteenth century it was the most cosmopolitan of European cities, a frequent stop on the itinerary of the child prodigy Wolfgang Mozart and site of the premiere of his operatic masterpiece *Don Giovanni*.

Now "Europe" has become not only the name of the region extending roughly from the British isles to the Ural mountains but also an allusive or elliptical reference to the EU. The EU is potentially the most important and far-reaching development in the history of Europe since 1945. Unifying Europe is an ancient ambition, formerly achieved by means of the sword. Such European conquerors as Alexander the Great and the Romans fixed most of their expansionist (unifying) attentions east and south of Europe proper. In the ninth century c.e., however, the Frankish King Charlemagne briefly unified a fair portion of Europe. The two most famous sword-bearing unifiers were Napoleon I and Hitler. Their attempts at unification, despite their brevity—Napoleon's empire lasted eleven years from its proclamation in 1804, Hitler's barely seven, if its beginning is counted from his takeover of Austria in 1938—were enormously consequential. Both killed millions of people; both rearranged the political map of Europe; both had cultural, social, and economic effects that continue to work themselves out.

Having lived through the searing experience of Hitler's Europe, the early architects of the European Union were determined to constrain the nation-state's capacities as an engine of war. Turning the ambitions of Hitler and Napoleon upside down, they were bent on unifying Europe to keep Europeans from going to war with each other again. The best way to accomplish a lasting peace, they believed, was to vest certain historic responsibilities of the nation-state in a supranational organization. The founders were practical men, masters of the humdrum, and they started out modestly. Not all of them were committed to the lofty goal of political unification (nor are their successors in our day), but most had a good eye for the lowest common denominators of agreement and progress. These resided in the economic and financial benefits to be derived from supranational agencies. The name "European Union" came into official use only in 1992. The EU's precursors date from the aftermath of World War II.

A first precursor, and the first set of letters in the alphabet soup characteristic of supranationalism, was the Organization for European Economic Cooperation, or OEEC, established in 1948. The OEEC was set up to administer the Marshall Plan. "It would be neither fitting nor efficacious for this [U.S.] government to undertake to draw up unilaterally a program designed to place Europe on its feet economically," General Marshall said in a speech at Harvard University on June 5, 1947. "This is the business of the Europeans. The initiative, I think, must come from Europe." The Europeans took Marshall at his word. Among other things, the OEEC lowered internal tariffs and trade barriers among recipient states (it is important to remember that the Marshall Plan required Europeans to match American funds dollar for dollar

THE SCHUMAN DECLARATION

On May 9, 1950, Robert Schuman, the French foreign minister, announced a plan for the pooling of European coal and steel resources. A moderate Catholic politician, Schuman put forward a proposal drafted by his long-time associate and fellow party member, Jean Monnet. The Schuman Declaration outlined the ideas and ambitions that propelled the formation of the European Coal and Steel Community (ECSC), the first step on the road to the creation of the EU. The Declaration's shrewd mix of idealism and national self-interest, hopes for Franco-German reconciliation, and espousal of step-by-step methods was characteristic of the French approach to European union and widely shared among other western European states.

World peace cannot be safeguarded without the making of creative efforts proportionate to the dangers which threaten it.

The contribution which an organized and living Europe can bring to civilization is indispensable to the maintenance of peaceful relations. In taking upon herself for more than 20 years the role of champion of a united Europe, France has always had as her essential aim the service of peace. A united Europe was not achieved and we had war.

Europe will not be made all at once, or according to a single plan. It will be built through concrete achievements which first create a de facto solidarity. The coming together of the nations of Europe requires the elimination of the age-old opposition of France and Germany. Any action taken must in the first place concern these two countries.

With this aim in view, the French Government proposes that action be taken immediately on one limited but decisive point:

It proposes that Franco-German production of coal and steel as a whole be placed under a common High Authority, within the framework of an organization open to the participation of the other countries of Europe. The pooling of coal and steel production should immediately provide for the setting up of common foundations for economic development as a first step in the federation of Europe, and will change the destinies of those regions which have long been devoted to the manufacture of munitions of war, of which they have been the most constant victims.

The solidarity in production thus established will make it plain that any war between France and Germany becomes not merely unthinkable, but materially impossible. The setting up of this powerful productive unit, open to all countries willing to take part and bound ultimately to provide all the member countries with the basic elements of industrial production on the same terms, will lay a true foundation for their economic unification.

This production will be offered to the world as a whole without distinction or exception, with the aim of contributing to raising living standards and to promoting peaceful achievements. In this way, there will be realized simply and speedily that fusion of interest which is indispensable to the establishment of a common economic system; it may be the leaven from which may grow a wider and deeper community between countries long opposed to one another by sanguinary divisions.

By pooling basic production and by instituting a new High Authority, whose decisions will bind France, Germany and other member countries, this proposal will lead to the realization of the first concrete foundation of a European federation indispensable to the preservation of peace.

with their own money; it was not at all the giveaway it has often been portrayed to be). It spurred the transfer of credits and trade.

A second EU precursor was the North Atlantic Treaty Organization
(NATO). Devised to provide for the common defense of Western Europe
(and, with the addition of Turkey in 1952, to threaten the Soviet flank), NATO
was a supremely integrationist alliance, requiring frequent, standing consul-
tations among defense and foreign ministers and their staffs; collaboration
among the officer corps of the constituent armed forces; and the conduct of
joint military exercises. Calculating defense budgets to meet the needs of
NATO as well as those of each member's national armed forces was an exercise in employing domestic economic and financial means to serve supranational political ends.

A third precursor was the European Coal and Steel Community (ECSC),
founded in 1951. The ECSC served national and private as well as public,
supranational interests. Pooling the coal and steel resources of France, West
Germany, Italy, the Netherlands, Belgium, and Luxembourg, it established a
common market in the two resources that still drove the industrial economies
of the day. Here the foundations of a much broader market could readily be
perceived. Not incidentally, pooling resources gave France access, at lower
cost, to West Germany's higher-quality coal deposits. By ignoring Britain
(and its still vast coal deposits), which anyway preferred to stand aloof from
the continent, the ECSC also established a precedent for setting France and
West Germany against their cross-Channel neighbor.

The fourth precursor, the European Economic Community (EEC), established in 1958, not only added to the foundations laid down by other fore-
runners but also provided much of the scaffolding, bricks, and mortar of
which the EU was eventually constructed. The Treaty of Rome, as the founding document of the EEC was called, aimed to end all trade restrictions
among the member states of Belgium, France, Italy, Luxembourg, the Netherlands, and West Germany. It sought to create a true market in common, and
Common Market quickly came into common usage as a name preferable to
the sodden acronyms dear to bureaucrats. The Common Market was
endowed with a central authority powerful enough to coerce as well as cajole
in matters of economic, monetary, labor, and agricultural policy.

Britons found the Common Market both threatening and enticing: threatening because, absent British membership, it promised to turn Britain's special economic ties with its former colonies, and its isolation from the continent,
into pronounced disadvantages; enticing because membership promised to
extend to Britain the trade advantages enjoyed by its founding members.
Britons' national ambivalence persists, reflecting the history of a country that
belongs to Europe yet has long taken its distance from it.

In 1958 Britain proposed expanding the Common Market into a transatlantic free trade area, including itself. France promptly vetoed this idea, moving Britain to found, in 1960, a rival European Free Trade Association (EFTA),
to which it welcomed European nations not belonging to the Common Market. Nevertheless, in 1962 Britain once again applied to join the Common

Market, only to have French President Charles de Gaulle slam the door against it. De Gaulle was already on record as wanting no truck with those who promoted the Common Market as a step in the long march toward European political union. His vision of the Common Market was that of a *Europe des patries,*—a Europe of nations—at most a loose confederation of which France would assume the lead. De Gaulle used France's veto power over important Common Market decisions to get what he wanted. Suspicious of Britain's close ties to the Americans, he also regarded British imports of relatively low-priced Commonwealth agricultural products as a threat to France's large group of inefficient family farmers. So in 1963, and again in 1967, he barred the door to British entry.

Thanks in large part to de Gaulle's obstinacy and force of will, the EEC, to revert for a moment to its official name, was deflected from the path of political integration championed by the early postwar enthusiasts. It turned in a federalist direction. In 1967 the Common Market, the Coal and Steel Community, and Euratom (established by the Treaty of Rome as an agency to oversee members' nuclear research and development programs) were merged into the European Community (EC). Vested with taxing and judicial power, the EC, in the guise of its Court of Justice in Luxembourg, smallest of the member states, did not hesitate to act on the principle that community law superseded national law. Customs duties and a tiny value-added tax provided the EC with its own operating income. In 1979 the European Parliament, yet another creation of the Treaty of Rome, began returning its membership by the direct election of citizens instead of national parliaments. True, it remained largely a sounding board for the discussion of Common Market issues, not a genuine legislative body. Beyond the coal and steel community, supranational agencies for the regulation and coordination of industry did not arise, except in the air and space industries. One paradoxical example of such an agency, given de Gaulle's chilly suspicion of Britain, was the Anglo-French Concorde supersonic jet project.

De Gaulle's withdrawal from the scene in 1970 opened the way for an expansion of the EC, a move facilitated also by the federalist turn its structure had taken. In 1973 Britain was finally admitted, at the cost of reducing its ties both to the United States and the Commonwealth. Admission left the British public divided, first over the wisdom of joining at all and second over whether Britain ought to join the movement to adopt a common currency. "Euroskeptics," as doubters were called, at first resided mainly in the Labour party, but many Conservatives arrived at this position as time went on.

Expansion of the EC came at the cost of increasing heterogeneity. In 1975 Ireland and Denmark joined. By 1986, Greece, Spain, and Portugal had also been admitted, bringing the membership to twelve and extending the EC's reach beyond its western European origins. In the meantime, the industrial prowess of the EC grew apace. By the 1970s the Common Market was an industrial power of the first rank and the largest free-trade area in the world. In little more than a generation, the countries represented in the EC recovered from the penury and devastation left in the wake of World War II; by 1975 it had emerged as a direct competitor of the United States. Five years earlier the United States incurred a trade deficit with the EC of over $10 billion, an imbalance that threatened to become permanent.

Yet old habits of mind died hard. It was hard for Americans to get over the image of Europeans as their poor cousins, transatlantic relatives who assuredly deserved assistance but were also targets of the condescension that often accompanies acts of largesse. Among the Europeans such attitudes bred resentment. By the mid-1970s the momentarily poor had grown immensely rich. Able to compete on an equal footing with the Americans, when the Europeans felt shoved, they pushed back. The United States and the EC became embroiled in acrimonious trade disputes over everything from chickens to consumer electronics.

SUMMARY

Rallying his countrymen against Hitler, Winston Churchill avowed, "If we can stand up to him, all Europe may be freed and the life of the world may move forward into broad sunlit uplands." Churchill was a warrior, not a prophet. His speeches were meant to fortify his listeners for the struggle just ahead, not to peer into a distant future. Europe was freed in 1945, but broad sunlit uplands were so far beyond the horizon that few Europeans could be confident of reaching them. Britain turned to long promised social reforms. A national health service extended free medical care to all Britons. Other reforms broadened access to education and spread a social safety net under the entire British population. Across Europe the benevolent state, guarantor of health, welfare, unemployment, and pension benefits, supplanted the night-watchman state.

For all its achievements in social reform, neither the postwar Labour government nor its Labour and Conservative successors succeeded in lifting Britain from the economic doldrums in which it had been cast by the Great Depression and the war. Margaret Thatcher proposed free-market solutions to Britain's problems. In the 1980s she privatized industry, deregulated with a vengeance, brought the trade unions to heel, and, coincidentally or not, oversaw a period of sustained economic growth. Eventually, however, her overweening self-confidence cost her the Conservative party leadership. In 1997 the Labour party finally returned to power under the aegis of Tony Blair, who had jettisoned his party's longstanding socialist agenda in favor of a slightly-left-of-center reform program. At considerable risk to his popularity at home, Blair unhesitatingly reinforced Britain's "special relationship" with the United States.

At length the French Fourth Republic foundered on the adamantine rock of decolonization. Unable to find a satisfactory resolution of the Algerian War, it gave way to the Fifth Republic. Charles de Gaulle, for whom the new republic was tailor-made, found a way out of Algeria and presided over a period of economic growth and political stability unprecedented in France's twentieth-century history. His successors, including Jacques Chirac, first elected president in 1995, pursued the aggressively independent foreign policy and cautiously reformist domestic policies that were the twin pillars of Gaullism.

Western anxiety over Soviet aims led to the rearmament of a newly established West Germany. The German Federal Republic turned in a remarkable performance in economic growth for most of the 1950s and 1960s. Meanwhile, the East German economy languished under the inefficiencies of central planning. Western political leaders paid lip service to the idea of German reunification but were not disappointed when years went by and it did not happen. To their surprise, a unified Germany arose from the sudden collapse of communism in central Europe.

Unable to keep West Germany disarmed, France sought to make it a partner in the building of a European Union. Proponents of the plan believed that there was no better way to reconcile with an old enemy than to embrace it in a bear hug of mutual obligations and responsibilities. The visionaries behind this scheme started out modestly, with proposals for establishing a common market among six nations of western Europe. Even in the late 1940s, however, they dreamed of a day when customs barriers would be dismantled throughout Europe and perhaps even a degree of political unification accomplished.

FOUR

The Collapse of Communism in Central and Eastern Europe and the Soviet Union

The Decline of Marxist Ideology

When Stalin died in March 1953, he was succeeded as premier by his close associate Georgi Malenkov. The post of first secretary of the Communist party, however, went to Nikita Khrushchev. The Soviet Politburo thus made clear that no one person would immediately inherit all of Stalin's power. Soon the regime began to denounce the "cult of personality" (Stalin's despotic one-man rule) and proclaimed a "collegial" system (government by committee). The dreaded chief of the secret police, Presidium member Lavrenti Beria, was executed for treason. At a party congress early in 1956 Khrushchev denounced Stalin, emotionally detailing the acts of cruelty for which the late dictator was responsible. As details of the speech leaked out to the Soviet public, there was some distress at the smashing of the idol they had worshiped for so long, but the widespread disorder that some observers predicted failed to materialize. Abroad, however, the speech produced turmoil in the Soviet satellites in Europe and so gave Khrushchev's opponents at home an opportunity to unite against his policies. Within the Presidium they had a majority, but Khrushchev was able to rally to his support the Central Committee of the Communist party. Although he promoted change, he also made clear he would not brook dissent. When in 1956 Hungary rose against Soviet rule, he sent tanks into the streets of Budapest to suppress the rebellion. Khrushchev emerged from these tests in 1957 with his powers immeasurably enhanced.

Already in his sixties, Khrushchev could hardly hope for a quarter-century of dictatorship such as Stalin had known. Moreover, in making himself supreme he had deprived himself of some of the instruments available to

Communist Eastern Europe, 1949–1989.

Stalin. After 1953 he had released millions of captives from prisons and slave-labor camps. Almost everyone in the Soviet Union had a relative or friend now freed. Within a year or two Soviet society at every level except at the very top of the bureaucracy had absorbed these sufferers from tyranny. The secret police no longer enjoyed independent power in the state, a power that might challenge the party or the army; Khrushchev himself had emotionally denounced police terror. It was still possible to prosecute people by terrorist means, but Stalin's mass terror as a system of government had disappeared.

The Written Record

NIKITA KHRUSHCHEV'S SPEECH TO THE TWENTIETH PARTY CONGRESS

Speaking on February 25, 1956, to a closed session of the Twentieth Party Congress of the Soviet Union, Nikita Khrushchev, party secretary and Soviet premier, denounced the crimes of Stalin. Khrushchev's speech was an attempt to wipe the slate clean and set the Soviet Union on a new course. As many of his listeners had been willing participants or at best passive accomplices in Stalin's conduct of affairs (these accomplices included Khrushchev himself), the premier was taking a large and potentially dangerous chance. For eight years (1956–1964) Khrushchev put his distinctive stamp on the Soviet leadership, until he was removed by a powerful faction in the Soviet Politburo. Not until 1985, in the person of Mikhail Gorbachev, did a similarly energetic, creative, and provocative leader emerge from the stolid ranks of Soviet officialdom.

We have to consider seriously and analyze correctly [the crimes of the Stalin era] in order that we may preclude any possibility of a repetition in any form whatever of what took place during the life of Stalin, who absolutely did not tolerate collegiality in leadership and in work, and who practiced brutal violence, not only toward everything which opposed him, but also toward that which seemed to his capricious and despotic character, contrary to his concepts.

Stalin acted not through persuasion, explanation, and patient cooperation with people, but by imposing his concepts and demanding absolute submission to his opinion. Whoever opposed this concept or tried to prove his viewpoint, and the correctness of his position, was doomed to removal from the leading collective and to subsequent moral and physical annihilation. This was especially true during the period following the XVIIth Party Congress (1934)....

Stalin originated the concept enemy of the people. This term automatically rendered it unnecessary that the ideological errors of a man or men engaged in a controversy be proven; this term made possible the usage of the most cruel repression, violating all norms of revolutionary legality, against anyone who in any way disagreed with Stalin, against those who were only suspected of hostile intent, against those who had bad reputations. This concept, enemy of the people, actually eliminated the possibility of any kind of ideological fight or the making of one's views known on this or that issue, even those of a practical character.... The only proof of guilt used, against all norms of current legal science, was the confession of the accused himself; and, as subsequent probing proved, confessions were acquired through physical pressures against the accused.

This led to the glaring violations of revolutionary legality, and to the fact that many entirely innocent persons, who in the past had defended the Party line, became victims....

The Commission [of Inquiry] has become acquainted with a large quantity of materials in the NKVD archives.... It became apparent that many Party, Soviet and economic activists who were branded in 1937–1938 as enemies were actually never enemies, spies, wreckers, etc., but were always honest Communists; they were only so stigmatized, and often, no longer able to bear barbaric tortures, they charged themselves with all kinds of grave and unlikely crimes. . . .

Lenin used severe methods only in the most necessary cases, when the exploiting classes were still in existence and were vigorously opposing the revolution, when the struggle for survival was decidedly assuming the sharpest forms, even including a civil war.

Stalin, on the other hand, used extreme methods and mass repression at a time when the revolution was already victorious, when the Soviet state was strengthened, when the exploiting classes were already liquidated and Socialist relations were rooted solidly in all phases of national economy, when our Party was politically consolidated and had strengthened itself both numerically and ideologically. It is clear that here Stalin showed in a whole series of cases his intolerance, his brutality and his abuse of power. Instead of proving his political correctness and mobilizing the masses, he often chose the path of repression and physical annihilation, not only against actual enemies, but also against individuals who had not committed any crimes against the Party and the Soviet government. . . .

At long last Khrushchev's reforms offended too many powerful Soviet constituencies; military and foreign-policy elites had been both alarmed by Khrushchev's adventurism in installing Soviet offensive missiles in Cuba in 1962 and humiliated by the apparent climb-down of his acceding to the American demand to remove them. In October 1964 Khrushchev was removed from power and succeeded by two members of the Presidium. Leonid Brezhnev, one of the engineers of his removal, replaced him as first secretary of the Central Committee of the Communist party; Alexis Kosygin became premier. Both were "Khrushchev men." The two, but especially Brezhnev, provided the Soviet government with stability until Brezhnev became increasingly ill. By the early 1980s, he was virtually a figurehead. Khrushchev was denounced for his failures in agricultural policy, for departures from conventional wisdom on foreign affairs, and for "commandism"—rule by fiat. He was not, however, executed, and no large-scale purge followed his removal.

The Soviet Union's most spectacular achievements in the Khrushchev years occurred in space. The Soviets successfully launched the first earth satellite (*Sputnik*, 1957) and first reached the moon with a rocket (1959). The first manned orbital flight by Yuri Gagarin, in April 1961, was followed in less than a month by the first American flight, by Alan B. Shepard, Jr., and in February 1962 by the first American orbit, by John H. Glenn, Jr. By the mid-1960s the United States had caught up in most aspects of space technology, and American landings of manned space vehicles on the moon in 1969 and after overshadowed Soviet accomplishments in space.

Policy makers in both the United States and the Soviet Union convinced themselves that in terms of cold war prestige, the extravagant costs of the

A Budapest street scene in the aftermath of the Soviet suppression of the Hungarian uprising of 1956. The turretless Russian tank in the left foreground suggests the intense violence of the brief struggle between Soviet forces and Hungarian rebels. Similar uprisings against Soviet rule occurred in East Germany, Czechoslovakia, and Poland.   (Getty Images.)

space race were worth it. In the 1970s both nations cut back on their space programs, placing greater emphasis on satellites for monitoring the activities of other nations. Russia set a new space endurance record of 438 days in 1996, and continued into the mid-1990s the joint flights the United States and the Soviet Union had initiated in the mid-1970s.

If achievements in space caused the international reputation of the Soviet Union to soar, agriculture presented Soviet planners with apparently insoluble problems. In 1953 Khrushchev had embarked on a crash program to plow under more than 100 million acres of prairie in the Urals region, Kazakhstan, and Siberia. Drought and poor planning and performance led to a clear failure by 1963. By the following year, the number of collective farms was down to about 40,000 from an original 250,000 and the average size of the new units was far larger. Soviet economic performance continued to fail to meet its goals. The Soviet standard of living remained low by Western measurements, and by the mid-1970s general stagnation set in, characterized by crop failures and chronic crises and the need to purchase grain from abroad.

The Soviet Thaw

De-Stalinization extended to arts and letters the same partial relaxation that occurred in other fields. Two outstanding Soviet composers with followings in the West, Aram Khachaturian and Dmitri Shostakovich, spoke out for boldness, and in mid-1954 Ilia Ehrenburg, veteran propagandist for the regime, hailed the relaxation of coercive measures over artists in *The Thaw*, which gave a name to the entire period. Boris Pasternak took advantage of the "thaw" to offer for publication *Dr. Zhivago*, his novel about a doctor who, through all the agonies of World War I and the Russian Revolution, affirmed the freedom of the human soul. Accepted for publication in the Soviet Union, the novel was also sent to Italy to be published. Then the Soviet censors changed their minds and also forced Pasternak to ask that the manuscript in Italy be returned to him. The Italian publisher refused, and versions in Russian, Italian, English, and other languages appeared abroad, arousing great admiration. In 1958 the Nobel Prize Committee offered Pasternak the prize for literature and he accepted. But Pasternak's fellow writers reviled him as a traitor, and the government threatened him with exile if he accepted the prize. As a patriotic Soviet, he then declined it. Pasternak's Jewish origins, his intellectualism, and his proclamation of individualism had offended Khrushchev, making it impossible to publish *Dr. Zhivago* in the land in which it was written.

But the spirit of individualism found more vigorous expression among the younger poets and novelists who had grown up since World War II. A young Ukrainian poet, Yvgeny Yevtushenko, denounced Soviet anti-Semitism in his *Babi Yar* (the name of the ravine near Kiev in which the Nazis, with the help of the Soviets, had massacred thousands of Jews). When Yevtushenko recited his verses, the halls were crowded with eager, excited, contentious young people.

The Pasternak affair had shown the limits of the new freedom; the case of Alexander Solzhenitsyn was even more instructive to the new readership. A former army officer, Solzhenitsyn had been interned for eight years in a forced labor camp. When he published his autobiographical novel *One Day in the Life of Ivan Denisovich* in 1963, he described for the first time in print the camps of which all Soviets knew but did not speak. Solzhenitsyn was immediately attacked for being concerned with "marginal aspects" of Soviet life, and the censor refused to pass his next important novel, *The First Circle*. After his expulsion from the Soviet Union in 1974, his best-known work, *The Gulag Archipelago*, revealed extensive knowledge of the Terror and the great camps of Siberia. In 1970, to the embarrassment of Soviet leaders, Solzhenitsyn was awarded the Nobel Prize for Literature.

In 1968 the repression of young writers fed a dissident movement that continued to grow thereafter. Soviet citizens accused their own government of violating the human rights provisions of the Helsinki accords of 1975. A Nobel prize physicist, Andrei Sakharov, joined the dissidents, and in the late 1970s and early 1980s the Soviet leadership attacked those who sought to crit-

icize cultural policy, or to emigrate to Israel, or to speak favorably of the out-
cast Solzhenitsyn. Taking up residence in rural Vermont, Solzhenitsyn continued to espouse not only the anticommunist views that had earned him
admiration in the West, but also the mystical, Russian Orthodox, authoritarian themes that made him, for a democracy, a somewhat awkward hero. In
1994 he ended his exile and returned to Russia.

Despite the reversion to repression in literature, film, and art, the communist bloc was no longer monolithic, for the Soviet leaders were unable to prevent a drift toward polycentrism (the existence of independent centers of
power in the satellites). Warsaw Pact members remained more uniformly
aligned than those in NATO, but nonetheless cracks began to appear in the
Iron Curtain. As long as the satellite countries pursued a foreign policy in
common with the Soviet Union, they gained some freedom to make their
own economic decisions. Hungary and Romania struck out on paths of their
own—Hungary toward a consumer economy, and both countries toward
heavier industry, tourism, and trade with the West. Although the Soviet
Union crushed liberalization in Czechoslovakia in 1968, it had to accept a
declaration by Communist parties in 1976 that there could be several separate paths to the socialist state. This loosening of the Soviet hold was only
marginal, however, as events in Poland made clear. The Polish Solidarity
movement, an independent labor-led movement under the leadership of
Lech Walesa, challenged both the Polish Communist party and the hegemony of the Soviet Union. Under pressure from Moscow, the Polish army
suspended Solidarity and took control of Poland in 1981. Nonetheless, the
movement survived underground, and in 1989 Poland was permitted its first
free election in forty years.

The Soviet Quagmire in Afghanistan

At the end of the 1970s, the same decade the United States withdrew from
Vietnam, the Soviet Union stepped into a quagmire in Afghanistan. Writers
have noted the striking similarities between the American experience in Vietnam and the Soviet experience in Afghanistan. Each began with a tentative,
incremental escalation; each outside power wagered—or simply hoped—its
indigenous client had better prospects of success than proved to be the case.
Each war lasted far longer than almost anyone expected; each ended as a dismal and demoralizing failure.

There were also important differences between the two episodes. Afghanistan is five times the size of Vietnam; its gigantic mountains and arid terrain
made it a battleground quite unlike Vietnam's rain forests and rice paddies.
The Americans committed a force of over 500,000 to Vietnam; Soviet troops in
Afghanistan numbered 90,000 to 120,000 at most. Reaching back to the nineteenth-century struggle for mastery among the great powers of Europe, Russian interest in Afghanistan was far older than American interest in Vietnam.

Since the 1830s Afghanistan had been part of the Great Game, as the rivalry
between Britain and Russia in central and south Asia was called. Russia's

relentless expansion eastward provoked British fears of Russian encroachment on India's Northwest Frontier Province, on which Afghanistan abutted. Tensions over this contested borderland eased at the beginning of the twentieth century, when Britain and Russia were drawn together by mutual apprehension over Germany's ambitions. Nevertheless, the end of Tsarist Russia in 1917 and British India in 1947 did not end Russian—now Soviet—interest in affairs in Afghanistan, neighbor to such Soviet republics of central Asia as Turkmenistan, Uzbekistan, and Tajikistan.

In April 1978 a coterie of Soviet-trained Afghan army officers mounted a coup d'état against their government. They proclaimed the Democratic Republic of Afghanistan (DRA), yet another in the Soviet Union's lengthy list of client states. Outside Kabul, the capital, the new regime soon proved to have little popular support. No central authority had ever been strong enough to bring to heel the tribes, clans, and factions, many at odds with each other, that comprised the population of Afghanistan. Local leaders seized on abundant opportunities to make warlords of themselves, offering goods, services, and protection in exchange for the loyalty, gratitude, and muscle of as many armed men as they could muster from their neighborhoods. Two forces that transcended local and regional differences, Islam and xenophobia, together proved the undoing of the Soviet experiment in Afghanistan.

The Marxist army officers' seizure of power in Kabul met with resistance in the provinces. Local groups of mujahedeen, or Islamist guerrilla fighters, formed along tribal lines and harassed the civil and military representatives of the central government. Alarmed by the client DRA's increasingly precarious grip on power, on Christmas Eve 1979 the Soviet government sent its own military forces into Afghanistan. Its models for intervention were Hungary in 1956 and Czechoslovakia in 1968, when the Red Army had successfully put down challenges to client governments in those restive states. But Afghanistan was not central Europe.

The Soviet invasion began with ruthless efficiency. Soviet agents killed the president and replaced him with their own man. Things soon went awry. The Soviet 40th Army found itself arrayed against hundreds of guerrilla groups. Countless small-scale, local encounters grew into a nationwide resistance. The cold war came to Afghanistan with a vengeance. To the United States the mujahedeen looked to be promising allies in the struggle against the rival. Under the aegis of the CIA, covert American aid was funneled to the Afghan guerrillas via Pakistan, whose Inter-Service Intelligence agency (ISI) ladled it out. Assistance to the mujahedeen also poured in from western Europe (Britain, France, and Italy), the Middle East (Egypt, Saudi Arabia, and the United Arab Emirates), and Asia (China). Soviet Kalashnikov assault rifles, the famous AK-47s, weapon of choice of guerrillas the world over, came into the hands of mujahedeen for use against their similarly armed adversaries.

If the United States remained the mujahedeens' biggest covert supplier of money and advanced weapons, the Pakistani ISI insisted on playing the chief role in directing the conduct of military operations in Afghanistan. Absorbed in the task of weakening their Soviet adversary, the Americans swallowed their misgivings about the ISI's agenda or chose to minimize its significance. Inside the ISI, promoting the Islamic fundamentalism of such guerrilla chieftains as Gulbuddin Hekmatyar and others took precedence over defeating the Soviets, and it distributed its American-supplied largesse accordingly. The chief long-range aim of Hekmatyar and others was an Islamist revolution in Afghanistan, an ambition the Americans played down, to their later cost.

With respect to the Soviet Union the Americans got what they wanted. Their covert support for the mujahedeen aggravated the Soviet 40th Army's worsening position in Afghanistan. Soviet forces were faring poorly against the guerrillas before U.S. assistance began. Then such advanced weapons as shoulder-fired Stinger anti-aircraft missiles came into the hands of these fighters, who used them effectively against Soviet helicopters. Their adversaries' chief tactical advantage over the mujahedeen—greater speed of maneuver—deteriorated along with their morale.

The poor morale of the Soviet forces in Afghanistan, composed mainly of conscripts, spread home like a virus, infecting troops who faced the prospect of being sent there as well as the families and friends of returning soldiers and circles far beyond the military. Nothing like the vocal opposition to the Vietnam War arose in Soviet society, but disaffection and discouragement with the Afghan War were deep and widespread.

By 1985, before American assistance to the mujahedeen began arriving in substantial amounts, the Soviet government, now led by the reformer Mikhail Gorbachev, began having second thoughts about the invasion. These doubts soon hardened into a decision to withdraw. The battle of Soviet conventional forces against the Afghan guerrillas not only seemed unwinnable; it had also come to illustrate much that was wrong in Soviet society. It was not only a distraction from reform; it was also an impediment to it. On February 15, 1989—late in the life of the Soviet Union, as it turned out—the last Soviet troops pulled out of Afghanistan, abandoning the government they had propped up for more than a decade and leaving the country in grave disorder. As the editors of a Russian General Staff study of the war pointed out, "The problems so apparent in the wartime army soon became a microcosm for the latent problems afflicting Soviet society in general. The messages of doubt were military, political, ethnic and social. In the end they were corrosive and destructive."

The Gorbachev Era

After years of ill health, Brezhnev died in late 1982. With the selection of Yuri Andropov as his successor the Soviet Union seemed prepared to renew the rivalry with the other superpower and to adopt stern measures against dissidence in the Soviet bloc. Andropov had presided over the crushing of Hungary in 1956; he had been head of the Committee for State Security (KGB) from 1967 to 1982 and demonstrated a willingness to silence dissent. In early 1984, however, he died and was succeeded by Konstantin Chernenko, a colorless party hack. Already sick when he assumed office, Chernenko lasted only a year, dying in February 1985. His death appeared to set the Soviet Union on another course.

Mikhail S. Gorbachev, a much younger man, took over leadership of the party. Tough, resolute, and Westernized, Gorbachev embarked in 1985 on a dangerous, highly delicate modernization of the Soviet state, and though he challenged neither the party nor the military directly, it was clear that he favored a more open society. He allowed dissidents who had been exiled to Siberia and elsewhere to return home, he called for extensive industrial and agricultural reforms, and he moved to extricate the nation from the costly war in which it was mired in Afghanistan. In 1989 the last Soviet troops were withdrawn. Severely criticized in the West for not quickly disclosing the nature and extent of a disastrous nuclear accident at Chernobyl in April 1986, the Soviet Union appeared to have decided upon the course of openness, with most newspaper, radio, and television censorship abolished; protestors permitted to gather freely in Soviet cities; and Marxism largely expunged from school curriculums.

Observers debated whether Mikhail Gorbachev was leading the Soviet Union into liberalizing reform or simply riding the back of a tiger unleashed by a declining Soviet economy. Decades of failed production schedules, declining harvests, and inefficient management had made Russia and most of the socialist republics ripe for change. Gorbachev's energy and sense of urgency, his frequent trips to the West, and his relative youthfulness made him especially attractive from abroad.

In April 1985, Gorbachev announced a series of reforms intended to reshape the economy, calling the process *perestroika* (restructuring). Without sweeping reforms, he recognized, the Soviet Union was probably finished. He was taking a huge gamble, and in the end *perestroika* probably accelerated the outcome it was meant to ward off, undermining the planned economy, destroying loyalty to socialism, and discrediting the Communist party. The discrediting of the party pulled the rug out from under the Union, and the one force holding it together: Gorbachev. Despite enormous popularity in the West and genuinely major concessions with respect to issues of arms control (in part recognized by the award of the Nobel Peace Prize in 1990), Gorbachev was walking a tightrope. In July 1989, with conservatives openly concerned that the Communist party would lose control, Gorbachev repudiated the Brezhnev Doctrine, the policy of combating so-called antisocialist forces within the Soviet pact, which infers the Solidarity of the Warsaw Pact, and made numerous important changes in the party leadership. In November, in an attempt to retain moderate conservative support, he published a manifesto declaring that Marxism would be revived under his leadership, to show a "humane socialist" face.

In 1990 Gorbachev was able to persuade the Communist party's Central Committee to end the party's constitutionally guaranteed monopoly on power, a move that alienated conservative communists. In March elections voters in the Russian, Ukrainian, and Byelorussian republics forced the pace of democratization. Local government in several cities, including Moscow and Leningrad, came into the hands of even more insistent reformers. Under Boris Yeltsin, elected president in 1990, the Russian Republic declared its independence, and twelve other republics followed suit; Yeltsin then announced a "five-hundred-day" program for transition to open markets, and Gorbachev was forced to accept it. Still Gorbachev held on. He moved first to conciliate those who wished to break up the Soviet Union, promising to consider readjustments in the distribution of powers between Moscow and the republics. Then he tilted toward the hard-liners, putting soldiers on the streets of Soviet cities and reinstituting forms of censorship.

The Collapse of Communism in the Soviet Bloc

The collapse of Soviet-inspired regimes in central and eastern Europe was as sudden as it was unexpected. In April 1989 an accord between factions in Poland had promised free elections, and in August Tadeusz Mazowiecki, a solidarity lieutenant of Lech Walesa, the first noncommunist head of an Eastern bloc nation, was elected prime minister. In Hungary, *glasnost* was warmly embraced, and the Hungarian parliament legalized freedom of assembly, speech, and association. In October 1989 the Communist party formally dissolved. In November police in Czechoslovakia brutally repressed a large antigovernment protest, but demonstrators turned out in ever larger numbers, demanding free elections. The "Velvet Revolution" succeeded. On November 24, 1989, the entire Communist party leadership resigned, and in December the first cabinet without a Communist majority in more than forty years took power. Vaclav Havel, a major leader of the Velvet Revolution, was named president. A playwright and former dissident who had spent more than a decade in and out of communist prisons, Havel epitomized resistance to the old and now discredited regime. Even isolated Albania, as repressive a communist dictatorship as there was, loosened its grip on civil society.

The transition from communist dictatorship went far less smoothly in East Germany and Romania. In October 1989 Erich Honecker, longtime East German party leader, faced mounting demonstrations, a faltering economy, and charges of widespread party corruption. Gorbachev made clear the Soviet army would not lift a finger in support of the regime. Feeling abandoned, Honecker resigned. His successors had neither the will nor the heart to use force against street demonstrations; nor could they be certain their orders to repress the demonstrators would be obeyed. East Germany opened its border with Czechoslovakia, and thousands of East Germans poured through it. On November 9 the government agreed to issue exit visas, and in the midst of joyful celebrations, the last of the infamous Berlin Wall came down. Parliament revoked a constitutional clause assuring the Communist party a leading role in the nation, and the new premier promised free elections and a multiparty system. The chancellor of West Germany, Helmut Kohl, called for a confederation of the two Germanys and in March 1990, a slate that supported Kohl won the elections.

A Closer Look

VACLAV HAVEL'S "THE POWER OF THE POWERLESS"

The playwright Vaclav Havel was a leading dissident during the last two decades of communist rule in Czechoslovakia. The son of a well-off Prague building contractor, Havel was denied admission to the university because of his bourgeois origins. Working as a taxi driver and at other odd jobs writers take to support themselves, Havel found himself unable to get his early plays past the state censor. A few were produced, to great acclaim, in the West. Regarded as a suspicious character by the communist regime, Havel fell under the almost constant surveillance of the secret police; he was in and out of prison on various charges. In sum, he was labeled a threat to the state. In 1977, following the arrest for subversive activity of a rock band called Plastic People of the Universe, Havel and his fellow dissidents issued "Charter 77," a manifesto calling for the sweeping reform of Czechoslovak state and society. "The Power of the Powerless," written a year later, is typical of Havel's critiques of an enfeebled totalitarianism. Its opening sentence is a sardonic echo of the opening sentence of Karl Marx's and Friedrich Engels's famous 1848 "Communist Manifesto." A leading member of the "Velvet Revolution" of 1989, Havel became the first president of the democratic Czech Republic.

A specter is haunting Europe: the specter of what in the West is called "dissent." This specter has not appeared out of thin air. It is a natural and inevitable consequence of the present historical phase of the system it is haunting. It was born at a time when this system, for a thousand reasons, can no longer base itself on the unadulterated, brutal, and arbitrary application of power, eliminating all expressions of nonconformity. What is more, the system has become so ossified politically that there is practically no way for such nonconformity to be implemented within its official structures.

Who are these so-called dissidents? Where does their point of view come from, and what importance does it have? What is the real significance of the "independent initiatives" in which "dissidents" collaborate, and what real chances do such initiatives have of success? Is it appropriate to refer to "dissidents" as an opposition? If so, what exactly is such an opposition within the framework of this system? What does it do? What role does it play in society? What are its hopes and on what are they based? Is it within the power of the "dissidents"—as a category of subcitizen outside the power establishment—to have any influence at all on society and the social system? Can they actually change anything?

I think that an examination of these questions—an examination of the potential of the "powerless"—can only begin with an examination of the nature of power in the circumstances in which these powerless people operate.

The manager of a fruit-and-vegetable shop places in his window, among the onions and carrots, the slogan: "Workers of the world, unite!" Why does he do it? What is he trying to communicate to the world? Is he genuinely enthusiastic about the idea of unity among the workers of the world? Is his enthusiasm so great that he feels an irrepressible impulse to acquaint the public with his ideals? Has he really given more than a moment's thought to how such a unification might occur and what it would mean? . . . He put [the sign] into the window simply because it has been done that way for years, because everyone does it, and because that is the way it has to be. . . .

[T]he real meaning of the greengrocer's slogan has nothing to do with what the text of the slogan actually says. Even so, this real meaning is quite clear and generally comprehensible because the code is so familiar: the greengrocer declares his loyalty . . . in the only way the regime is capable of hearing; that is, by accepting the prescribed *ritual,* by accepting appearances as reality, by accepting the given rules of the game. In doing so, however, he has himself become a player in the game, thus making it possible for the game to go on, for it to exist in the first place. . . .

Let us now imagine that one day something in our greengrocer snaps and he stops putting the slogans merely to ingratiate himself. He stops voting in elections he knows are a farce. He begins to say what he really thinks at political meetings. . . . He rejects the ritual and breaks the rules of the game. He discovers once more his suppressed identity and dignity. . . .

. . . He has shown everyone that it *is* possible to live within the truth. Living within the lie can constitute the system only if it is universal. The principle must embrace and permeate everything. There are no terms whatsoever on which it can coexist with living within the truth, and therefore everyone who steps out of line *denies it in principle and threatens it in its entirety. . . .*

And since all genuine problems and matters of critical importance are hidden beneath a thick crust of lies, it is never quite clear when the proverbial last straw will fall, or what that straw will be. This . . . is why the regime prosecutes, almost as a reflex action preventively, even the most modest attempts to live within the truth.

. . . [T]he crust presented by the life of lies is made of strange stuff. As long as it seals off hermetically the entire society, it appears to be made of stone. But the moment someone breaks through in one place, when one person cries out, "The emperor is naked!"—when a single person breaks the rules of the game, this exposing it as a game—everything suddenly appears in another light and the whole crust seems then to be made of a tissue on the point of tearing and disintegrating uncontrollably.

From Havel, Vaclav. "The Power of the Powerless." As reproduced in *Open Letters,* trans. Paul Wilson, ed. Paul Wilson (New York: Alfred A. Knopf, 1991), pp. 127, 132, 136, 146–147, 213–214.

Nicolae Ceausescu, Romania's president since 1967, had taken his distance from the Soviet Union, but his own rule had become increasingly repressive. All industry had been put under state ownership, state farms owned nearly all of the arable land, and conservative Marxist economic policies had crushed individual initiative. Pollution was widespread and health problems severe. Inspired by protesters elsewhere, a large group assembled in the city of Timisoara; on December 16, 1989, at Ceausescu's command, his hated security forces opened fire on the demonstrators and buried hundreds in

President Ronald Reagan and Premier Mikhail Gorbachev synchronize their watches. Shortly after coming to office in 1981, Reagan proclaimed the Soviet Union the "evil empire." Gorbachev assumed power in 1985 intending to strengthen the Soviet Union by means of sweeping internal reforms. Each leader saw it in his own interest to agree to significant reductions in nuclear arms. Reagan's admirers credited his defense buildup with accelerating the demise of a Soviet Union too enfeebled economically to respond in kind. Gorbachev's detractors charged him with fatally weakening the Soviet state by encouraging demands that a communist regime could never satisfy. Such are the vagaries of history, always open to reinterpretation and surprise.   (Getty Images.)

mass graves. Protests spread rapidly, and the Romanian army joined in the rebellion rather than cooperate with the security forces. On December 22 a group calling itself the Council of National Salvation overthrew the government, and the next day, following a trial for genocide, Ceausescu and his wife were condemned to death and executed by a firing squad.

The End of the Soviet Union

The final collapse of communism in the Soviet Union came rapidly and dramatically. On August 19, 1991, communist hard-liners attempted a coup d'état. Seizing control of the press and television, they claimed that Gorbachev was ill (he was actually on vacation in the Crimea) and installed the vice president in his place. President Yeltsin denounced the coup, called for a general strike, and rallied the Russian people, who barricaded the Russian Parliament. Massive protests in Moscow and Leningrad, worldwide denunciation of the coup leaders, and declarations of noncompliance in several of the Soviet republics brought the coup toppling down, and on August 21 Gorbachev returned to Moscow. By then Yeltsin had demonstrated his popularity and courage to the world and had emerged as the dominant political leader. Three days later Gorbachev resigned as head of the Soviet Communist party, disbanded its leadership, and in effect ended communism's seventy-four-year reign.

Reform had begun first in the Soviet Union, Gorbachev's denunciation of Stalin had freed the satellite states to criticize communist rule, and in the space of eighteen months all of eastern Europe had outpaced the Soviet Union in dismantling communism. In December 1989, Lithuania declared its intention to reestablish its independence; Latvia and Estonia, the other two Baltic states, followed suit. The collapse of a monolithic communist bloc placed further pressures upon the Soviet Union to change. Formerly communist nations struggled to create free market economies despite their lack of experience and the absence of a suitable infrastructure.

Russia, the biggest of the former communist economies, inherited a huge, inefficient, obsolescent industrial system. The central planning that characterized the Soviet system fell away, leaving virtually nothing in its place save an equally characteristic black market—a vast illicit underground of goods and services. Russian reformers, led by young men appointed by President Yeltsin and abetted by Western enthusiasts, rushed to build a market economy on these ruins. They acted in the absence of the liberal institutions that make Western markets work—especially the independent law courts and government regulations that impose order, restraint, and reasonably fair dealing on capitalism. In these circumstances the former Soviet elites, augmented by a handful of newcomers, helped themselves to the vast state-owned wealth of the former Soviet Union. These oligarchs, as they were called, established a rapacious and unfettered capitalism. The new state's officials were so weak and passive that they could not enforce such laws as were on the books. A new kleptocracy, or rule by thieves, replaced the old bureaucracy, the rule of central planners.

The oligarchs amassed fortunes by simply helping themselves to real and industrial property and energy reserves formerly in the public domain. Some of the less wily and adroit were ruined when the ruble collapsed in 1998. Aided by strong-arm tactics and the employment of private security forces indistinguishable from criminal gangs, a new group of tycoons succeeded the oligarchs of the Yeltsin era. Instead of outright looting, they paid taxes to the state and lip service to the legal system. Buying up whole sectors of the economy, a handful of business groups brought a huge percentage of Russia's wealth under their control. In the face of this concentration and in the absence of a state able to enforce the rule of law, small businesses struggled to survive. For all the ruthlessness of the tycoons, Russia's economy in the new century was smaller than that of the Netherlands.

The hardships of Russia and the other members of the former Soviet Union in the post–cold war era received ample attention in the Western press. Less noticed were themes of relative good fortune. Unlike the bloody and protracted breakup of the overseas empires of the West, for instance, the dismantling of the Soviet land empire came about peacefully. That the transition from communist dependencies of Moscow to independent states would occur with little or no violence was by no means a foregone conclusion in 1989.

The Disintegration of Yugoslavia

In contrast to the Soviet Empire, Yugoslavia died a violent death. A coroner's verdict might have been death by virulent ethnic nationalism. Tito, it will be recalled, had encouraged and enforced a live-and-let-live policy among Yugoslavia's ethnic groups. He passed from the scene in 1980, however, and his death coincided with a pronounced decline in the country's economic fortunes. Day-to-day hardship and fear of a deeply uncertain future combined with disillusionment with communism to create among Yugoslavia's diverse peoples an atmosphere of mutual suspicion and distrust. All it took to make for serious trouble was a demagogue capable of exploiting these ethnic tensions. Not one demagogue but two soon emerged: Franjo Tudjman, president of Croatia, and Slobodan Milosevic, elected president of Yugoslavia in 1989.

A Serb and former communist official, Milosevic saw in Serbian nationalism a means of enhancing his own power. Leaving nothing to chance, he worked to inflame his fellow Serbs' already pronounced sense of grievance. To them he announced his aim of creating an ethnically pure "greater Serbia" from Yugoslavia's independent republics. At his instigation brutal fighting broke out in Croatia in 1991 and in Bosnia, which had a large Muslim population, in 1992. Meanwhile Serbia and Montenegro declared themselves the Federal Republic of Yugoslavia. Supplied by Serbia, Bosnian Serbs shelled Bosnian cities, especially Sarajevo. More than six thousand civilians died in the course of a two-year siege. Serb forces turned to "ethnic cleansing"—the systematic massacre, removal, rape, and imprisonment of Muslims and other non-Serbs. Europe had not witnessed genocide on such a scale since the Nazi campaigns of World War II. Alternating hand-wringing with diplomatic protests, sanctions, and the ineffective deployment of peace-keeping forces, NATO and the UN looked on. Finally in July 1995 the Bosnian Serbs overreached themselves. In the UN-designated "safe-haven" of Srebrenica they slaughtered more than seven thousand Muslim men and boys. Following a NATO bombardment of Serb positions and severe Bosnian Serb losses to Croatian forces in western Bosnia, Milosevic abandoned his erstwhile protégés and came to the bargaining table, signing a peace agreement at Dayton in late 1995.

Milosevic not only rode out a campaign of street demonstrations seeking his ouster but was reelected president in 1997. Soon, however, rebellion broke out in the overwhelmingly Muslim province of Kosovo. Guerrillas impatient with a nonviolent campaign to restore autonomy to the province took to killing Serbian policemen and other agents of the Yugoslav state. Milosevic embarked on another campaign of brutal repression. When a conference outside Paris in early 1999 failed to find a satisfactory means of protecting the Kosovars from the continuing depredations of Yugoslav police and paramilitary forces, NATO undertook a bombing campaign against Yugoslavia, going to war for the first time in its fifty-year history. In response, Milosevic stepped up an ethnic-cleansing campaign that drove more than a million Muslim Kosovars into neighboring Albania and killed thousands more. Seventy-seven days of bombing finally undermined Milosevic; his abandonment by the Russians, the Serbs' brother Slavs, left him no choice but to capitulate to allied demands. In June 1999 the vanguard of a large peacekeeping force entered Kosovo. Milosevic's presidency did not long survive the Kosovo debacle. In September 2000 he was defeated in a presidential election by the constitutional lawyer Vojislav Kostunica, ceding power only after popular protests in Belgrade and the countryside. Indicted for war crimes in 1999, in April 2001 he was arrested on charges of abuse of power and corruption. In June 2001 Milosevic was sent to the United Nations International War Crimes Tribunal in The Hague to stand trial as a war criminal.

SUMMARY

The Soviet Union, feared by Western governing elites for its intentions toward Western Europe, its influence in the non-European world, its military might, and its industrial potential, proved in the long run unable to live up either to its reputation in the West or the expectations it had encouraged among the Soviet people. Achieving early and spectacular success in the so-called space race with the United States, it did not perform well as a long-distance runner, eventually ceding to the Americans the victory represented by the landings on the moon. Nor was its earthbound performance more rewarding. The command economy, allocating goods and services by means of central planning, never performed even adequately; beyond the circle of the privileged Soviet elite, consumers scrambled to make do in a society of perpetual shortages. Obsessed with national security and especially fearful of falling behind the United States, the Soviet leadership poured far more into military spending than the system could afford. Mikhail Gorbachev's heroic efforts to reform the system faltered, and then failed. The communist regimes of eastern Europe went first—peaceably, except for Romania. The Soviet Union then imploded. From Poland to Central Asia, across the vast expanse of the former Soviet empire, successor regimes struggled, with markedly varied success, with the novelties of market economies and genuine to quasi-democratic polities.

FIVE

Arts and Sciences

The twentieth century was a century of great revolutions not only in politics and society but in science as well. These scientific revolutions overturned what Thomas Kuhn called "normal science," or the long-established way of doing things, and established new paradigms. Inquiries in physics, and especially in biology, profoundly altered our understanding of the physical universe and of life on earth. Meanwhile, the arts experimented with the new as they continued to draw on tradition.

The Revolution in Physics

The twentieth century was a century of revolutions, but none had a greater claim to changing the world than the revolution in physics. No one better exemplified the revolution than Albert Einstein. No scientist was better known to the public. In his time his fame exceeded that of any politician, athlete, or celebrity. His great achievement as a theoretical physicist was to make radical revisions in the Newtonian world-machine, the mechanistic model of the universe that had been accepted for more than two centuries.

Many nineteenth-century scientists were convinced that light moved in waves and was transmitted through the ether, which supposedly filled outer space. If the ether existed, then it would itself be moved by the motion of the earth, and a beam of light directed *against* its current would travel with a velocity less than that of a beam directed *with* its current. Experiments of the 1880s, however, showed that light traveled at 186,284 miles per second, whether it was moving with or against the hypothetical current. The ether was discredited.

In 1905, at the age of twenty-six, Einstein published a paper asserting that since the speed of light is a constant unaffected by the earth's motion, it must also be unaffected by all the other bodies in the universe. This unvarying velocity of light is a law of nature, Einstein continued, and other laws of nature are the same for all uniformly moving systems. This was Einstein's special theory of relativity, which had many disconcerting corollaries. In particular, it undermined the idea of absolute space and absolute time and made both space and time relative to the velocity of the system in which they were moving. Thus space and time are not absolutes but are relative to the observer.

Einstein equated not only space and time but also mass and energy. His famous formula $E = mc^2$ means that the energy in an object equals its mass multiplied by the square of the velocity of light. A very small object may contain tremendous potential energy. Such an object, for example, can emit radiation for thousands of years or discharge it all in one explosion.

The problem of mass also involved Einstein in a review of the Newtonian concept of a universe held together by the force of gravity—the attraction of bodies to other bodies over vast distances. Einstein soon concluded that the gravity—that is, the weight—of an object had nothing to do with its attraction to other objects. Galileo had demonstrated that both light and heavy bodies fell from the leaning tower in Pisa at the same speed.

Einstein proposed that it would be more useful to extend the concept of the *magnetic field*, in which certain bodies behaved in a certain pattern. Einstein did not penetrate the mystery of what holds the universe together, but he did suggest a more convincing way of looking at it. This was the essence of his general theory of relativity (1916), which stated that the laws of nature are the same for all systems, regardless of their state of motion.

Einstein's fame ultimately came to rest on a heart-breaking paradox. From his post at the Institute for Advanced Study, in Princeton, which he joined in 1933, Einstein grew increasingly alarmed by Germany's aggressive designs in Europe. A life-long pacifist but also an ardent anti-Nazi, in 1939 he momentarily put his pacifism aside to urge President Franklin D. Roosevelt to launch an inquiry into the feasibility of making an atomic bomb. The secret Manhattan Project produced such a bomb. The most horrendous weapon ever devised, the atomic bomb ended World War II, established the foundation of the epochal military and diplomatic standoff between the United States and the Soviet Union, and ushered in the era that is the subject of this book. Its mushroom-cloud signature endowed the cold war generations with a symbol of dread.

No one could have regretted all this more than Einstein. The Manhattan Project and its consequences exemplified the workings of applied science and the vagaries of history. Einstein had written Roosevelt about atomic-bomb research with an eye to countering Nazi Germany. The only two bombs ever employed were the ones dropped on Japan on the orders of President Truman. Still, the breakthroughs establishing that such bombs might be feasible were the work of Einstein the theoretical physicist. The Manhattan Project's discovery of a way to unlock, in one tremendous explosion, the potential energy in uranium rested on the insights expressed in $E = mc^2$.

The Manhattan Project not only represented science successfully applied to a prodigiously difficult problem. In its size, complexity, and expense—spending billions on intricate projects carried out by thousands of researchers at many widely scattered sites—it also foreshadowed the Big Science of the second half of the twentieth century and beyond. The wherewithal required to conduct basic research in physics, chemistry, biology, and medicine—among which the frontiers have grown increasingly blurred—tends to put it beyond the reach of all but deep-pocketed governments, private foundations, and large corporations, which sponsor work both in their own laboratories and in universities.

Research in experimental physics, for instance, has been concentrated in very large organizations dedicated to the study of very small things. Typical examples are the American Fermilab, named after the great Italian physicist Enrico Fermi and established in 1967, and the Centre Européenne de Recherche Nucléaire (CERN), founded in 1954. Fermilab and CERN are typical of Big Science, too, in their healthy appetites for funding, political influence, ambition, and sense of rivalry in their realm of basic research. Both conduct research into particle physics, "the branch of physics concerned with the properties, relationships, and interactions of subatomic particles." Both employ huge accelerators to investigate these subatomic particles. Fermilab boasts of being "the world's highest-energy physics laboratory." CERN claims to be "the world's largest particle physics laboratory." Although CERN, like Fermilab, is proud of being a leading site of truly international research projects, it also does not hesitate to emphasize its European-ness, to see itself almost as a research arm of the European Union.

In the exploration of space, a friendlier rivalry between Europe and the United States replaced the old cold war rivalry between the United States and the Soviet Union. Space exploration combined the noblest aspirations of science and spectacular feats of technology with the grimmer and more down-to-earth ambitions of achieving military superiority and winning international prestige over an adversary. The Soviets took the early lead in an almost frantic space race between the superpowers, putting into orbit in 1957 a beeping, basketball-sized sphere called *Sputnik*. Their edge over the United States in rocketry also enabled the Soviets to send into space in 1961 the first human, the cosmonaut Yuri Gargarin. To a public fascinated with space exploration as well as worried by early Soviet successes, President John F. Kennedy vowed to put an astronaut on the moon by the end of the 1960s. In 1969 Neil Armstrong made "a giant leap for mankind" by setting foot on the moon's surface.

Having cheered on their astronauts and cosmonauts much as they cheered on their athletes in the Olympic games, the Americans lost interest in the competition in space and the Soviets dropped out. The American National Aeronautics and Space Administration (NASA) turned to a hugely expensive space-shuttle project. Derided as a technological stunt ornamented with scientific experiments, the shuttle program was punctuated by tragic accidents. In 1986 and again in 2003 shuttles exploded in flight, the first shortly after liftoff, the second on reentering the atmosphere, killing the astronauts on board. The Soviets and their Russian successors limited themselves to relatively long-term habitation of earth-orbiting space platforms.

Many scientists thought unmanned spacecraft promised a far greater scientific payoff than manned ones. In their running debate with proponents of human space flight they could point to the example of *Voyager 1*. Launched in 1977, by the end of 2003 *Voyager* had flown to the edge of the solar system, the equivalent of 8.5 billion miles. Daily the small and sturdy vessel sent back measurements and other data as it (and its companion, *Voyager 2*) passed by Jupiter, Saturn, Uranus, and Neptune and approached a "region where the Sun's influence ends and the dark recesses of interstellar space begin."

Closer to home, Mars became an interplanetary object of international attention. The European Space Agency (ESA), founded in 1973, emerged by the end of the twentieth century as a major force in space exploration. As ESA liked to emphasize, not all its fifteen members belonged to the European Union; nor did all members of the EU belong to ESA. Still, ESA's ties with the EU were extremely close, and it kept an eye on promoting European economic interests as well as advancing science.

At the end of 2003 NASA and ESA spacecraft converged on Mars. Orbiting the Red Planet, ESA's *Mars Express* launched the piggyback probe *Beagle 2*, named after the vessel in which Charles Darwin made his great voyage of discovery. Shortly afterward, NASA landed, in rapid succession, two Mars "rovers"—*Spirit* and *Opportunity*. *Beagle 2* made not a beep after landing, but *Mars Express*'s remote sensors continued to transmit data on signs of previous life. On the surface the two NASA rovers performed similar investigations. If relations between ESA and NASA were cordial, they barely concealed their eagerness, common to all scientific research, to establish claims of precedence in discovery.

Although *Voyager 1* verged on leaving the solar system after journeying more than a quarter-century, the most powerful instrument of deep-space exploration remained the earthbound big telescope. Such instruments, like accelerators and other tools of particle physics, have always been enormously expensive. The bigger a reflecting telescope's mirror, the more light it gathers and the farther it can "see" in space (and time). For nearly a half-century the two-hundred-inch Hale telescope atop Mt. Palomar, in California, remained the largest. A bigger mirror was likely to sag under its own weight. Technological advances of the 1990s made it possible to build thinner and therefore larger mirrors. In 1993 twin ten-meter telescopes, each a mosaic of thirty-six hexagonal mirrors instead of a single glass slab, were installed on Mauna Kea, in Hawaii. The race to build ever larger telescopes was on. At the beginning of the twenty-first century the most ambitious of several projects was that of the European Southern Observatory (ESO), like ESA a consortium of members and nonmembers of the European Union, which proposed to construct a hundred-meter OWL (OverWhelmingly Large) telescope at its site atop a Chilean mountain.

What do astronomers expect to see with a telescope wider than a football field is long? Planets beyond our solar system, of which more than one hundred have been discovered in the last decade, are a high priority. Its huge light-gathering capacity should enable OWL to peer into the time galaxies were forming, 10 billion years ago. "With such a telescope," one leading astronomer has remarked, "you can for the first time really trace the connections between the first seconds of the Big Bang and the formation of life in the universe."

The Revolution in Biology

In late February 1953 Francis Crick met his research colleague James Watson at a pub near Cambridge University and announced, as Watson later recalled, that "we had found the secret of life." Crick was making a light-hearted reference to their work on DNA. Yet the fact was that he was substantially correct. By 1952 it was recognized that DNA alone was the only substance capable of storing all the information required to create a living being. In April 1953 Watson and Crick published in *Nature*, a leading British research journal, an article disclosing the structure of DNA. They explained how it looked and how it worked. Their research paper announced the most important discovery in biology in a century and opened the scientific frontier of the next century.

The discovery of the structure of DNA is as much a tale of rivalry and ambition as of disinterested scientific inquiry. Watson and Crick were experimenting in Cambridge University's Cavendish Laboratory with physical models of DNA. Despite their sharply contrasting personalities—Crick was confident and self-assured, Watson gawky yet brash—their research skills and intuitions marvelously complemented each other. In the meantime two other researchers, Maurice Wilkins and Rosemary Franklin, were working on DNA at King's College, London. Their working relationship was not a happy one. At King's Franklin took the lead in attacking the secrets of DNA by means of x-ray crystallography. This technique—the use of x-rays to create images of crystallized solids—suggested that DNA had a helical or twisted structure. Wilkins showed Watson Franklin's x-rays, apparently without her knowledge or consent. Seeing these remarkable x-rays prompted Watson's Aha! or Eureka! moment. In Franklin's work he had seen the evidence he and Crick needed to establish the structure of DNA as a double helix, a twisting ladder. The two uprights of the ladder are made of deoxyribose, a sugar. Pairings of "bases"—the DNA alphabet of A, T, G and C (for the chemicals adenine, thymine, guanine, and cytosine) act as rungs. In this structure inhere the mechanisms of both encoding and replication, enabling DNA to reproduce itself without changing its structure.

Watson recounted the discovery of the double helix in a bestselling—and disquieting—1968 book of the same name. *The Double Helix* conveys the excitement and exuberance of important scientific research and acknowledges Franklin's key contribution, but it also disparages her manner and appearance. In 1962 Wilkins, Watson, and Crick shared a Nobel prize for the discovery of DNA; Franklin had died in 1958, at the age of thirty-seven, of ovarian cancer. Nobel prizes are not awarded posthumously.

If the discovery of the structure of DNA was essentially the work of two pairs of researchers, one pair complementing each other brilliantly, the other not, the next great leap forward in biology was the work of large, rival teams.

James D. Watson, the co-discoverer of DNA, shown in 1957 with a molecular model of the
revolutionary discovery he and his colleague, Francis Crick, made in 1953. In his best-seller,
The Double Helix: A Personal Account of the Discovery of DNA *(New York, 1964),*
Watson recounted the rivalries, passions, and inspired guesswork that characterize high-
stakes scientific research.   (Time Life Pictures/Getty Images.)

In 1985 Robert Sinsheimer, chancellor of the University of California, Santa
Cruz, gathered together some leading biological researchers to discuss a proposal to unravel the sequence of the human genome. Such a task required
deciphering a string of 3 billion As, Ts, Cs, and Gs. Sinsheimer's gathering
concluded they were not up to it. In the larger community of biologists, skepticism ran high. Such a huge goal-driven project ran counter to the longstanding practices of biological research, in which investigators pursued
their own studies in small labs. Sequencing the human genome seemed to
require money and personnel on the scale of the Manhattan Project. Funding
of such magnitude would rob other worthy inquiries of support. Even worse,
in the view of some skeptics, the project might be construed as a stunt of little or no value, since much DNA code is "junk" without purpose or function.
If it were not a waste of time, others charged, unraveling the human genome
might prove to be dangerous.

From such unpromising beginnings sprang the Human Genome Project (HGP). In 1986 the U.S. Department of Energy (DOE) underwrote a pilot project. Over the years the DOE's national laboratories had concentrated on research in the physical sciences, including the development of nuclear weapons. The DOE's sponsorship of biological research made some biologists uneasy. In it they saw a scheme for giving work to underemployed bomb makers. Their worries eased when in 1988 the Human Genome Project received the endorsement of a panel of the National Research Council (NRC), an arm of the prestigious National Academy of Sciences, an authoritative and independent voice in American science and science policy. The NRC panel also proposed a plan of attack. Instead of plunging directly into the sequencing of the human genome, which in the current state of knowledge no one actually knew how to do, researchers should first try the less daunting task of constructing maps of human chromosomes. Such an approach promised to speed the discovery of disease-causing genes, thereby offering immediate medical payoffs. In the NRC's emphasis on the practical benefits that might accrue from basic research, the politics of publicly funded Big Science were at work. Resolving a long-simmering controversy over research tactics, the NRC recommended analyzing the genomes of simple organisms—yeast, the roundworm, the mouse—as a run-up to the human genome.

Also in 1988 the National Institutes of Health (NIH), the federal agency where biologists felt most at home, wrested control of the Human Genome Project from the less congenial DOE. James Watson was named to head it, bringing to the project his prestige in the scientific community, his public celebrity, and his gift for phrase-making. The goal of the HGP, Watson announced, was "to find out what being human is." The project's first breakthrough, however, was finding out what being a roundworm was.

In 1991 Craig Venter, who ran a large NIH lab, proposed a major shift in strategy. The project, he declared, should concentrate on finding disease genes and leave sequencing for later. Watson, who saw behind this demand an attempt to cash in on disinterested scientific research, was dead set against Venter's approach. He resigned. Soon Venter also left NIH to head the privately funded but nonprofit Institute for Genomic Research (TIGR). In 1998 Venter founded the for-profit Celera Genomics.

Between NIH and Celera Genomics the race to sequence the human genome was on. Different underlying philosophies, different sources of funding, different techniques, and different aims sharpened the competition. Disinterested, tax-supported, technically conservative in method, obliged to put their findings into the public domain, the NIH group battled the entrepreneurial Celera Genomics researchers—venture capital–supported, bold to the point of recklessness in method, obliged to give their financial backers something for their money. Hard feelings between the two teams of racers quickly intensified. One prominent scientist remarked that had the more intemperate of the antagonists been his own children, he would have given them a time-out.

Venter's challenge goaded the NIH team into a major change in philosophy. Francis Collins, who had succeeded James Watson as project leader, had long insisted on sequencing the human genome, "the book of life," as everyone had taken to calling it, to an accuracy of 99.99 percent. Determined not to be overtaken by Celera, however, Collins announced his team would produce a "rough draft" covering 90 percent of the genome. Each side attacked the other in the press, touting its own approach, disparaging the other's.

In private, however, some of the leading participants worked to bring about a cease-fire. Why not agree to declare the race a tie, allowing both sides to share in the glory? Venter and Collins, the two principals, agreed to publish their rough drafts simultaneously. In June 2000 President Bill Clinton and Tony Blair, the British prime minister, announced that both Celera and the Human Genome Project had produced a rough draft of all the DNA in a human cell.

As one of the leaders of the HGP put it, sequencing a genome, or producing a full list of all a creature's genes, was like chemists discovering the periodic table of the elements. The table gave chemists a list of the building blocks of their science. From the information in the periodic table chemists derived knowledge. Similarly, the genome is information—"the book of life." The rough draft is a reference genome describing organizational and structural properties invariant across the human species. Biologists must turn this information into knowledge, and they have only just begun. The human genome sequence, the HGP announced, "will serve as a basis for research and discovery throughout this century and beyond. It will have diverse practical applications and a profound impact upon how we view ourselves and our place in the tapestry of life around us." In February 2001 Celera Genomics and the Human Genome Project, the two teams led by Craig Venter and Francis Collins, respectively, published the sequence of the human genome.

The post-genomic era began. Sequencing the human genome was largely an Anglo-American enterprise, but Europe was eager to exploit the accomplishment in both basic and applied (especially biomedical) research. U.S. dominance, and the U.S. ability to attract European researchers to American laboratories—the so-called brain drain—rested only in part on the willingness of the U.S. government and private agencies to lavish huge amounts of money on research. It also derived from the character of American science as a large, open, comparatively unfettered single market, driven by competition and handsomely rewarding success.

This not-so-secret formula was not lost on Europeans. The European Union (EU), which is discussed at greater length in Chapter 6, took the lead in promoting post-genomic research. The EU's precursors had since the late 1940s been preoccupied with creating a single customs union, or common market. Dismantling the barriers to trade came to serve as a model for dismantling barriers to a Europe-wide area of scientific research. A March 2002 press release laid down the EU's goal for research in the post-genomic era: "asking scientists from industry and academia to conduct research at the cutting edge of science in a selected number of fields and giving them sufficient means to achieve critical mass and world-class excellence."

This announcement masked the paradoxical reality that the European Commission, the driving engine of the EU, was itself a huge, multinational, polyglot bureaucracy making do on a small budget and an unwieldy policy-making apparatus. Still, EU science officials recognized that the challenge to be faced was the United States, where public and private spending in post-genomic research was $6 billion annually and rising. European spending was only a fraction of this sum. Chief among the EU's efforts to meet the American challenge were multimillion-euro grants to such innovative agencies as the European Molecular Biology Laboratory, founded in 1974 (and dreamed of in a 1962 meeting that included James Watson and the great Hungarian-born physicist and biophysicist, Leo Szilard).

Among the practical applications of the sequencing of the human genome is finding genes linked to disease, of which thirty have already been identified and associated with breast cancer, muscle disease, deafness, and blindness. Breakthroughs in discovering DNA sequences underlying cardiovascular disease, diabetes, and arthritis are expected soon. Once understanding is achieved, effective new therapies are likely to follow. In the longer run, post-sequencing explorations will deepen understanding of complex living systems and produce applications ranging from human health to global climate change. Biology is poised to become the foremost science of the twenty-first century.

Modern and Postmodern Architecture

The birth of modernist architecture was a tale of two cities: Chicago in the 1890s and Weimar, Germany, in the 1920s. In Chicago Louis Sullivan announced that "form follows function." Rejecting earlier styles, he and like-minded architects drew on steel, concrete, and glass, the materials of an advanced industrial age, to reshape the skyline of downtown Chicago. Featuring thin curtain walls resting on slender piers, their tall buildings enclosed volumes of open space. In Weimar the Bauhaus, led by Walter Gropius and Ludwig Mies van der Rohe, aimed to unite the arts and crafts. First in Weimar and then in Dessau, to which they repaired in the 1920s, Bauhaus architects took the modernism of Sullivan and his associates in a sparer, even austere, direction. Their buildings were characterized by an aggressive simplicity and severe geometry of form. By turning their backs on historical precedents they offended the sensibilities of cultural conservatives. The Nazis considered the modernists a threat to "German" styles and traditions, and when the party won a majority on the Dessau town council in 1931, they closed the Bauhaus down.

Already dubbed "the International style" by the Museum of Modern Art in 1932, after World War II modernist architecture became the dominant form in cities around the world. For years it served as a virtual template for skyscrapers. In New York City, especially, thanks in part to the influence of such Ger-

A Closer Look

JOSEPH ROTH ON SKYSCRAPERS

The skyscraper was not only a favored form of modernist architects but also an expression of the technological achievements and urban aspirations of the twentieth century. Writing in 1922 the Austrian novelist, essayist, and newspaper reporter Joseph Roth celebrated the skyscraper. His celebration takes on ironic overtones in the aftermath of the 9/11 attack on the World Trade Center.

Whenever I look at pictures of New York, I am filled with awe at the omnipotence of human technology. In this next stage of its development, civilization will have the opportunity to draw nearer to the old notions of culture.

When the steam locomotive was first invented, the poets moaned about the defilement of nature; the imagination predicted terrifying dystopias: whole tracts of the world devoid of grass and trees, rivers dried up, plants withered, butterflies poisoned. They didn't understand that every new development constitutes a mysterious circle, in which the beginning and end touch and become identical.

Because the invention of the airplane was not a declaration of war on winged creatures, quite the opposite: It was fraternization between man and eagle. The earliest miner did not barge his way sacrilegiously into the depths, he returned home to the womb of Mother Nature. What may have the appearance of a war against the elements is in fact union with the elements: man and nature becoming one. There is freedom in skyscrapers as much as on mountaintops.

The long-desired fulfillment of some of the profoundest wishes of Earth: to overcome shortage of space by elevation and conquest of vertical space. Exploitation of every dimension: exaltation, visible from outside, that also communicates itself to the spirit within.

It is impossible for the proximity of clouds to have no effect on human beings. The view out of the window, taking in the full boundlessness of the horizon, works on both heart and soul. The lungs take in the air of heaven. Clouds wander past the brows of mortal man as previously only around the brows of Olympians.

I can see the skyscraper: a slender, floating construction on its broad pediment, noble and delicate in its lines, whose white and gray sets itself apart from the blue sky. Strong and safe in its assembly, it matches a natural mountain for strength.

Ten thousand people daily flow in and out of it: little office girls, emerging from the tight courtyards of the north of the city, quick tick of heels, black leather handbags swinging, filling elevators, shooting upward like a swarm of swallows.

Men striding out, purpose in their eyes, enterprise in their loose limbs; machine rattle and clatter of conveyances; shouted order of command; the even beat of mechanical perplexity, working toward a common end.

And up above God is disturbed in his everlasting tranquillity, and compelled to take an interest in our tiny destinies.

man exiles as Mies van der Rohe, whose Seagram Building (1958) became an instant classic, modernist structures shaped the skyline. In postwar Europe modernism was embodied in such major civic buildings as the New National Gallery of Berlin (1968), another Mies van der Rohe design; Hans Scharoun's Berlin Philharmonic Hall (1963), composed of irregular forms and capped by a sweeping, tentlike roof; the Pompidou Center in Paris (1976), Richard Rogers and Renzo Piano's quirky art museum and tourist magnet, seemingly all exoskeletal pipes, ducts, and escalators; and I. M. Pei's Pyramid of the Louvre Museum (1989), a glass-and-steel entryway to a royal palace under intermittent construction from the twelfth through the eighteenth centuries.

No sooner had modernism established its dominance than it came under attack. Especially in the soaring skyscrapers of Manhattan, the revolutionary ambitions of the Bauhaus were transmuted into the self-aggrandizing ambitions of the American corporation. In the 1950s and 1960s one sleek glass-and-steel tower after another sprang up along the avenues of New York, corporate headquarters likened by their detractors to gigantic filing cabinets—sterile, geometric, and boring.

As early as the 1960s a revolt against modernism set in. Paradoxically, the postmodern revolt in architecture came out in favor of tradition, although a tradition expressed ironically, quoting tongue in cheek from neo-classicism and other styles. The ornamentation shunned by the modernists returned, playfully rendered in garlands, friezes, and, more unexpectedly, the curlicues of Thomas Chippendale, the eighteenth-century cabinet-maker. Voiced in the work of the American architects Robert Venturi, Michael Graves, and Philip Johnson, postmodernism accommodated itself to modernism. Soon it appeared that rather than posing a brash challenge to the older movement, postmodernism was carrying it on in a modified form.

A prime expression of modernism—and certainly its most famous monument—was the World Trade Center, designed by the Japanese architect Minoru Yamasaki and built between 1966 and 1977. Its twin towers of steel, glass, and concrete reprised the favored building materials of modernists from Louis Sullivan on. Its unadorned spareness, save for the fluted skin that served to emphasize its verticality, restated the modernists' aesthetic principles. The World Trade Center's 110 stories dominated the lower Manhattan skyline, to the extent that in its early years some critics dismissed it as an architectural dinosaur, out of date, out of step with the times, too big for its environment. Then in just under two hours of the morning of September 11, 2001, the towers came to a horrific end. Having come to represent New York's muscular pride in itself, the Trade Center's sudden absence from the cityscape was felt as an almost unbearable loss.

No tasks seemed more urgent than memorializing the thousands who died in the destruction of the World Trade Center and erecting a suitable replacement. The design of such a replacement was thrown open to an international competition whose entrants included some of the world's most accomplished architects. The winning design, announced in February 2003, belonged to the firm of the Polish-born American architect Daniel Libeskind.

Born in Germany at the close of World War II, Anselm Kiefer made his international reputa-
tion as a critical commentator on themes in German history that gave rise to the Third
Reich. Deutschlands Geisteshelden (Germany's Spiritual Heroes), *a huge painting of*
oil and charcoal on burlap, depicts a room that is at once memorial hall and crematorium.
Eternal fires burn along the walls in memory of German heroes, but the wooden building
itself appears ready to go up in smoke, taking with it Germany's mythic past and Germans'
capacity for self-delusion. A critic of the virulent nationalism that the Nazis both embodied
and exploited, Kiefer himself came under critcism in some artistic circles for his preoccupa-
tion with such themes.   (Keiefer, Anselm, Deutschlands Geisteshelden, *1973. Oil and charcoal on*
burlap mounted on canvas, 120½ x 267¾ inches. The Broad Art Foundation, Santa Monica. Photo
credit: Douglas M. Parker Studio.)

Libeskind made his reputation as a deconstructivist. Although postmodern
in the literal sense that they come after the modernists, the deconstructivists
do not share postmodern architecture's historicist bent. Their work is more of
a riff on modernism than a repudiation of it. Libeskind's best known design,
the Jewish Museum in Berlin, is a statement, in the heart of the capital of a
new Germany, on the central calamity of Europe in the twentieth century. To
the eye of a visitor it appears to have been taken apart, stretched, compressed,
folded, twisted, and then reassembled in arresting and surprising ways. It is
nonlinear and almost anti-geometric, a mournful structure devoted to an
inescapably mournful and anguished remembrance. By unhappy coinci-
dence the museum opened to the public in September 2001.

　　The Freedom Tower, the heart of Libeskind's idea for the World Trade Center site, is a work of affirmation, renewal, and defiance. Twisting skyward
1776 feet, a number quoting the year America declared its independence, the
tower echoes in its shape the nearby Statue of Libery and in its suspension
system the cables of the Brooklyn Bridge. "Sculptural," a word often used to
describe the work of Libeskind's fellow deconstructivist Frank Gehry, applies
equally well to the design of Freedom Tower. Libeskind kept the pressures of
wind and the needs of security uppermost in mind. How well his design

would withstand the combined pressures of money, power, influence, commerce, and municipal politics remained to be seen.

After Modern Art

In 1933 the Reichstag, seat of the German parliament, suffered large-scale damage in a great fire. In 1945 it was almost destroyed in the bombing and shelling of Berlin. In 1995 the restored Reichstag of a reunified Germany was wrapped in more than a million square feet of silver polypropylene fabric. The Reichstag fire was probably set by Martinus van der Lubbe, a young Dutch communist, but the Nazis, who had come to power weeks earlier, pinned it on the Germany communist party. The war damage was the work of the Allies. The Reichstag was wrapped by the sculptor Christo and his crew, to great popular and critical acclaim.

The Reichstag's fate reflected Europe's turbulent and tortuous history from Hitler to the present, not only in politics but also in the arts. For no sooner had the Nazis taken power than they intensified their hounding of artists they identified with modernism, in their eyes a degenerate, "Jewish," un-German movement. Many modernists fled to America where, along with other refugees from Nazi Germany and the war, they enlivened American culture. By welcoming Christo's wrapping of the Reichstag the German government embraced everything playful, democratic, and humane in the work of a leading contemporary artist. Its gesture was the antithesis of the Nazi treatment of the arts.

A German painter who commented on the Nazi past as unflinchingly as the novelists Günter Grass and Heinrich Böll was Anselm Kiefer, born the year the regime died. Especially in the 1970s and early 1980s such large Kiefer paintings as *Shulamite* and *The Meistersinger* expressed the savagery of the Nazis and the bleakness of their times.

Among the artists who fled Nazism and war for America were three who became mentors of a loosely affiliated group of young American painters later termed Abstract Expressionists. The Germans Max Ernst and Hans Hoffman and the Dutch Piet Mondrian arrived with their reputations already made. Mondrian, whose work was characterized by intersecting vertical and horizontal lines laid out in designs of knife-edge precision and clarity, was said to have been especially invigorated by the gridlike pattern of New York City's streets. They affirmed, perhaps, his vision of the world.

New York was the home of Abstract Expressionism, which also came to be called the New York School. In the eyes of some American critics, at least, it proclaimed the city's displacement of Paris as the art capital of the world. The New York School was certainly a declaration of exuberance and energy. Rejecting the idea of representation almost entirely, the Abstract Expressionists, of whom Jackson Pollack was the most aggressive (and famous), splashed their huge canvases with heroic quantities of paint, working rapidly in the hope of capturing on the fly the spontaneity of their creative emotions.

Not all were as "wild" as Pollack. Mark Rothko, for instance, was known for his cool, mysterious, blurry-edged squares and rectangles, iconlike in their inducement to contemplation; Helen Frankenthaler for her elegant deployment of pastels, which she exchanged for brighter, more vivid colors as her career wore on; and Ad Reinhardt for a series of paintings entirely in black.

The New York School lasted longer than a New York minute, but the contemporary art world is insatiable in its appetite for the new. By the early 1960s (by 1956 Pollock was already dead), Abstract Expressionism was no longer at the center of attention. Ours is an era in which more artists are at work than lived in all three centuries of the Renaissance. Perhaps it would be truer to say that contemporary art no longer had a center. Instead it resembled a many-ringed circus. As your gaze wanders from one ring to another your eyes alight on many interesting and original things, all different and hard to categorize, all worthy of the spotlight.

Pop artists burst on the scene in the early 1960s with the brashness and lack of subtlety of a carload of circus clowns. Both a celebration and a send-up of popular culture, Pop Art, like Abstract Expressionism, was a largely American movement inspired by European artists. A distant influence was the French Dadaist Marcel Duchamp, who in 1917 famously transformed a urinal into an art object by calling it one. A close progenitor was the Englishman David Hockney, whose early work most clearly displayed his affinities with Pop, a label he rejected and a style he turned away from in the 1970s and 1980s.

The most influential Pop artist was undoubtedly Andy Warhol, whose paintings of Campbell's soup cans epitomized the movement. Rebelling against what they regarded as the Abstract Expressionists' remoteness and pretension, the Pop artists rendered with nearly photographic exactitude paintings of the everyday products of a consumer society (Warhol); enormous statues of such products (Claes Oldenburg's *Lipstick (Ascending) on Caterpillar Tracks*; collages and silk-screen prints combining familiar images, like sporting events, with painted brushstrokes (the renegade Abstract Expressionist Robert Rauschenberg); an almost obsessive series of American flags (Jasper Johns, another Abstract Expressionist renegade); and oil paintings as cartoonish as any cartoon (Roy Lichtenstein). It required a great mastery of technique—to say nothing of breath-taking self-confidence—to make extraordinary paintings of soup cans and other ordinary objects. Warhol's prediction that "in the future everybody will be famous for 15 minutes" itself became one of the most famous pronouncements of our time. Critics of "reality" television and other artifacts of popular culture have taken it as prophesy.

In 1971 Warhol produced and directed an underground film called *Women in Revolt*, a little-noticed, ill-tempered, and badly received jibe at the nascent women's liberation movement. With some notable exceptions, Abstract Expressionism and, in its early years, Pop Art, were dominated by male artists. In the late 1970s, and with gathering force in the 1980s and 1990s, women artists who addressed feminist themes emerged. In *Untitled Film Stills*, a series of black-and-white photographs in which she served as her own model, the American Cindy Sherman explored myths of femininity in postwar popular culture. Casting herself as a blond bombshell, Sherman portrayed the sexual clichés of Hollywood fantasy. In later sculptures, composed of dismembered medical mannequins with grossly enlarged breasts and predatory-looking genitalia, fantasy turned dark.

Sarah Lucas, a younger British artist, in the 1990s employed Sherman's device, the self-portrait photograph, in a more aggressive way. Her defiant, androgynous stare provokes an observer to ask, is she joking or not? Lucas's sculptures address stereotypical ideas about male and female bodies. For instance, in *Au Naturel* (1994), which purports to be a still life, a cucumber, two oranges, a bucket and two melons are wittily deployed across an old mattress. The German Rosemarie Trockel was no less witty than Lucas. *The Painting Machine* (1990) commented on the idea that female artists had historically been perceived as mere painters-by-the-numbers. As though she felt obliged to dismantle this stereotype herself, Trockel steadily produced a diverse body of work across a wide range of artistic mediums. The French-born sculptor Louise Bourgeois was among the European artists who emigrated to the United States on the eve of World War II and found a place among the Abstract Expressionists. From the 1960s she moved in a feminist direction, sculpting sexually ambiguous or androgynous human figures or parts of figures, especially hands and forearms, themes said to evoke her childhood.

Christo, wrapper of the Reichstag and other public monuments, like the Pont Neuf in Paris, was himself a Pop artist. He also could be grouped with the performance artists, who shared the paradoxical ambition of creating ephemeral objects of beauty. The Reichstag housed the German parliament year in and year out; it became a work of art for seventeen days. The Pont Neuf had spanned the Seine for centuries; in the fall of 1985, following fifteen days in Christo's wrapping, it became a bridge once more.

History, Fiction, Film, and Social Criticism After 1945

World War II opened wounds in European politics, society, and culture so deep they are still healing. Historians have created an enormous literature on all aspects of the war. Books on the German experience alone fill libraries. In *The German Catastrophe*, published in 1946, the elderly German historian Friedrich Meinecke suggested the Nazi dictatorship had come out of the blue, catching the Germans unaware, as if overtaken by a storm or some other force of nature they were helpless to resist. In 1960 the American journalist William L. Shirer brought out *The Rise and Fall of the Third Reich*, which located the roots of Nazism deep in the German past. In Shirer's account, for instance, the anti-Semitism of Martin Luther, the sixteenth-century religious reformer, foreshadowed the anti-Semitism of Hitler and his henchmen. If Meinecke saw the Nazi era as an aberration from the course of German history, Shirer saw in it many continuities with the past.

The historians' debate has continued within this frame. One influential group discerned in nineteenth-century German history a "special path" (*sonderweg*), away from the liberal democratic tendencies of France and Britain and toward the authoritarian, racist nationalism that manifested itself in Nazism. Another group insisted Germany's history departed in no significant way from that of the liberal democracies; the seeds from which Nazism bloomed had to be located elsewhere.

Some historians saw the destruction of Europe's Jews as the intentional outcome of longstanding Nazi policy; others considered the Holocaust less a consequence of the will of the Nazi leadership than of the structure of the Nazi regime. A small group of so-called historical revisionists put forward the wholly untenable argument that the Holocaust had not happened at all. In the 1980s in Germany the debate between "intentionalists" and "structuralists" was overtaken by the *historikerstreit*, or historians' battle, over whether the Holocaust was horrifically unique in world history or had parallels in other genocides. To this deeply emotional issue some historians attached a new reminder that in the last year of World War II the Soviet army had wreaked on Germans, civilians, and soldiers alike a vengeance out of proportion to the suffering the Germans had inflicted on the Russians earlier in the conflict.

In the mid-1990s the American Daniel Goldhagen rekindled the debate on whether Nazism was an aberrant force in German history or a deep-seated continuity. By virtue of an anti-Semitism that took hold in the nineteenth century, Goldhagen asserted, the Germans were "Hitler's willing executioners," eager participants in the Final Solution. Goldhagen's views met with wide popular acclaim in Germany, at least in part because he went on to argue that the democratic reforms of the postwar era had extirpated Nazism. In effect, what Daddy and Granddaddy had done during the war was their business, not an ineradicable legacy passed on to succeeding generations. Goldhagen's thesis was less well-received by other academic historians, who found holes in his evidence and in the logic of his argument.

The war also fired the imagination, the realm of fiction. From the 1950s into the new century, a preoccupation with the Nazi period dominated the German literary scene, from Günter Grass's magic realist novel *The Tin Drum* (1959), purportedly the autobiography of a self-induced dwarf who recounts his fantastical adventures at the center of the all-too-real history of Germany in the Nazi years and after; through Heinrich Böll's *Billiards at Half-Past Nine* (1959), whose protagonist relives in a single day's flashbacks the trauma of war and the Nazis; to Bernhard Schlink's *The Reader* (1995), in which an adolescent boy learns his much older lover was once an SS concentration camp guard; and beyond.

French film-makers took the lead in plumbing the moral ambiguities of life in France under the German Occupation of 1940–1944. Marcel Ophuls's 1971 documentary *The Sorrow and the Pity* explored the selective forgetting, remembering, and reinventing that overtook the French when confronted with their own recent past. The film helped demolish the myth of the Resistance—the idea that a majority of the French actively opposed the German occupier. Louis Malle delivered another blow to the myth with *Lacombe, Lucien* (1974), in which the eponymous protagonist, turned down by the Resistance, joins the collaborationist Vichy police instead; it's all the same to him. Another Malle film, *Au Revoir, les Enfants* (1987), portrays the enormous consequences that can follow in wartime from a small, unthinking moment. Julien (meant to be seen as a young Louis Malle) unintentionally betrays to the Nazis the Jewish identity of his best friend, hidden by his parents at Julien's rural boarding school.

Algerian-born Albert Camus belonged to the tiny band whose credentials as members of the French Resistance were impeccable. Following the war he found himself identified with the existentialists who gathered around Jean-Paul Sartre. Existentialism came in many varieties. In Sartre's version the universe was without meaning, God did not exist, and life was absurd. Nevertheless, man was free to make choices and, once he had made them, was obliged to struggle on their behalf. Camus denied he was an existentialist, even though his stance was similar to that of Sartre, who embraced the term. Camus preferred the older label of "humanist." In his short but prolific life (he was killed in a car crash in 1960), his novels and essays made him one of the most influential literary figures in postwar France. Among the great twentieth-century themes to which he repeatedly returned were war, revolution, the nature of freedom, and colonialism. No one expressed their dilemmas and conundrums more lucidly and acutely. And no one left the reader freer to make up her own mind.

Take, for instance, his novel *The Plague* (1948), which recounts what happens when a mysterious and deadly disease ravages the Algerian port city of Oran. Dr. Rieux, the protagonist, responds heroically to the rat-borne plague. Most Oranians do not, and many of their responses—treacherous, selfish, fearful, ignorant, and all too human—are disheartening in the extreme. Is Camus's novel an allegory of the German Occupation of France? Is it really about colonialism (the subject of another Camus novel, *The Fall* [1957])? Or should it be taken at face value, as a fictional account of the plague in a North African city? It has been read all three ways. It could be read all three ways at once.

The son of working-class European settlers in Algeria, Camus did not set foot on the French mainland until he was twenty-five. His friendship with the writers Jean-Paul Sartre and Simone de Beauvoir already badly strained by their defense of Stalinism, Camus broke with them and their like-minded friends over the Algerian War. Firmly on the side of the rebels, for them Algerian independence from France was a matter of justice. For Camus, Algeria was as much his homeland as France. For him the preferred solution was a third way—neither an old French Algeria nor a new Algerian Republic, but a community built by settlers and Muslims together. Such a solution was probably never in the cards, but it estranged Camus from the French Left. In Sweden to accept the Nobel Prize for Literature in 1957, the height of the Algerian War, Camus told a heckling student, "I have to denounce blind terrorism in the streets of Algiers, which might one day strike my mother or my family. I believe in justice but I'll defend my mother before justice." Camus's old companions in literature and the Resistance wrote him off. In fact, none had a mother in Algiers, and they refused to countenance the views of someone who did. Camus's fondness for the concrete, expressed in all his writing, clashed with the Parisian intelligentsia's preference for the abstract.

Camus's almost exact contemporary, the much longer-lived Marguerite Duras (1914–1996) was, like Camus, a francophone writer who was born and reared in a French overseas territory—in her case Indochina. Her past was far more ambiguous and politically sinuous than Camus's—and her portrayal of that past in her writings more ambiguous still; in this respect she more closely resembled the majority of her countrymen than Camus did. Having made her way to France on the eve of World War II from her birthplace near Saigon, she held a minor post in the collaborationist Vichy government before joining the Resistance shortly after the Allied landing in Normandy. Having converted to the winning side in the nick of time, Duras emerged in the postwar era as one of the writers identified with the *nouveau roman*, or new novel, a group that included Nathalie Sarraute and Alain Robbe-Grillet. The new novel abandoned such conventions of the old novel as plot, character development, and chronology. Duras's own style was cinematic, characterized by abrupt cuts and flashbacks; not surprisingly, she wrote a number of scripts for films, notably Alain Resnais's *Hiroshima Mon Amour* (1959).

Among the most prolific of postwar French writers, Duras published forty novels, of which her most widely read, *The Lover* (1984), appeared late in life. Like many of her books, *The Lover* was highly autobiographical. Set in French Indochina in the 1930s, when cracks were already appearing in the foundations of empire, it relates an affair between a fifteen-year-old European girl and a much older Chinese man. Nearly everything in the story is topsy-turvy. For instance, the girl is the seducer of an Asian who is scarcely less an outsider in the dominant Vietnamese culture than she. For all the novel's reputation as a critique of colonialism, Duras's blend of the erotic and exotic narrowly skirted the European stereotyping of Asians that Edward Said deplored in his classic *Orientalism* (1978).

When the tide of European imperial rule receded from the lands it had overflowed, the language of the imperialists stayed behind. Native francophone and anglophone writers created new literatures. For some, like the Martiniquean psychiatrist Frantz Fanon, French was a weapon in the struggle against colonial rule. Such books as *Black Skin, White Masks* (1967) and *The Wretched of the Earth* (1961) made Fanon the preeminent thinker on colonial liberation. Others, like Salman Rushdie, born in Bombay of a Muslim family that soon repaired to Pakistan, were far less committed to a particular line of politial activism than was Fanon. Rushdie wrote of the end of British rule in India in a way that combined magic realism with a tone of ironic detachment. *Midnight's Children* (1968) established Rushdie's literary reputation long before the Iranian religious authorities put a price on his head for his allegedly blasphemous novel, *The Satanic Verses* (1988). Chinua Achebe (*Things Fall Apart*,

Albert Camus, French resistance fighter, existentialist philosopher, Nobel prize–winning novelist, and essayist. Born in a settler family in French Algeria, Camus was torn between the struggle for justice that French supporters saw in the cause of the Algerian nationalist revolutionaries and the right of his own working-class mother to a place in the only country she knew. He proposed reconciling the settler and native communities, a "third way" that appealed neither to die-hard revolutionaries nor to died-hard settlers. Camus was killed in an automobile accident in 1960. Algeria became independent in 1962. (Getty Images.)

1958) and Wole Soyinka (*The Interpreters*, 1965) were two Nigerian writers who did not hesitate to portray the evils not only of colonialism but also of the indigenous postcolonial governments that succeeded them. Rushdie, Achebe, and Soyinka were also good examples of the limitations of postcolonial theory, which became fashionable in the academy from the 1980s on. None of the three writers—and many others like them—fit into the rather arbitrary analytical and classificatory schemes of the postcolonial theorists. The writings of Fanon, which sanctioned the use of violence in a just cause and sided unequivocally with the wretched of the earth, were better suited to the theorists' liberationist and anti-European tendencies.

Among European intellectuals foremost in championing the work of francophone and anglophone writers indigenous to the disintegrating European empires were Jean-Paul Sartre and his close friend Simone de Beauvoir. Sartre introduced to a white European audience the Martiniquean poet Aimé Césaire's concept of "Négritude," or blackness. Césaire and the Senegalese poet Leopold Senghor, the first president of Senegal, imbued with a sense of pride and militancy a cultural identity formerly associated with feelings of shame and inferiority.

Beauvoir also found a cause of liberation much nearer home. Her book *The Second Sex* (1949) became one of the most famous and influential books published in the second half of the twentieth century. It shared with similarly influential works, like Rousseau's *Social Contract* (1763) or Marx's *Capital* (1867) the quality of being hard to understand. Beauvoir was a Marxist-leaning, existentialist philosopher. In her writings she made no concessions to her readers. They took from *The Second Sex* what they wanted from it, as Rousseau's and Marx's readers had done earlier (that the meaning of a text belongs to readers as much as it does to authors was later elevated into a dictum of postmodern literary theory). If *The Second Sex*, *The Social Contract*, and *Capital* were written as philosophical treatises, they could all be understood as calls to action. Their arguments could be reduced to a single, ringing phrase. In Rousseau's case it was, "Man is born free, and everywhere he is in chains." In Beauvoir's it was, "One is not born a woman, one becomes one."

Beauvoir's claim relied on what later became known as social-construction theory. Being a woman was not a function of being a member of the female sex but of being a member of a society. In Western society, men had historically held all the face cards, and women had played the hand they were dealt. They had no other choice. Their subordination derived from their place in a male-dominated society, not from their sex. Men reserved the public sphere for themselves; they relegated women to the private sphere, where they performed roles that mainly put them in service to men—as wives, mothers, servants, sexual partners for hire (prostitutes), and so on. Beauvoir's discourse on the secondary status of the second sex was a grim accounting indeed. It was written as a statement of how things were in 1949 and how things had been for centuries, not as a declaration of how Beauvoir wanted them to change. As much as she was an activist—if an activist of the pen—in such causes as colonial liberation, she never truly became an activist in the cause of women's liberation. There can be little doubt she intended no irony in calling her autobiographical observations *Memoirs of a Dutiful Daughter* (1974). By the time of her death in 1986 Beauvoir had become an icon. Her claim that "woman" was made, not born, was nearly as commonplace—if still contested—in society as in the women's studies departments that proliferated in American and European universities in that decade and later.

There was in fact a hiatus of a generation between the publication of *The Second Sex* in 1949 and the birth of the feminist movement in the early 1970s.

Much of the immediate response to Beauvoir's book took the form of character assassination. What was to be expected of a dissolute, unmarried woman who lived in a hotel with Jean-Paul Sartre? Feminist action lagged behind feminist thought for more than twenty years. In the student upheavals of 1968, young women leftists were still making coffee and sandwiches for the guys.

The women's movement arose not only in response to the ideas of Beauvoir and younger thinkers like Julia Kristeva and Susan Sontag, but also in reaction to changing economic conditions. There were many feminisms, not one, just as earlier there were many socialisms. Just as these socialisms had often been profoundly at odds with each other, especially from the late nineteenth century on, so, too, were the varieties of feminism. To take but one example, some feminists were bitter antagonists of pornography; other feminists thought women ought to enjoy a pornography of their own.

It was bread-and-butter issues, however, that tended to distinguish the feminist movement from the broader and more inclusive women's movement. Perhaps the starkest and most powerful of these issues, in terms of its power to shape the destinies of women, was the need to earn more than one income to support one family. Across Europe and the United States women entered the work force in steadily increasing numbers from the early 1970s on. Two-income households had long been commonplace in the working class. That mothers and fathers both had to work hard to support a family had been known to peasants for generations (true, both parents usually stayed at home and worked family holdings). To middle-class households, however, the need to put two earners into the workplace was something new. Putting large numbers of middle-class women to work for salaries or wages carried great consequences for families, society, and the women themselves. Child care became a pressing need to which European governments, with their strong tradition of state benevolence, responded better than governments elsewhere. The restaurant and fast-food industries soared. The care of elderly parents grew vastly more complicated and expensive. Paradoxically, single-parent households steadily increased. As had often been the case in times of rapid and emotionally fraught social and economic change, prophets of doom emerged, decrying what had happened and calling for a return to a presumptive golden age.

World War II had scarcely ended when Italian neo-realist film made its first bold statement. Roberto Rossellini's *Rome, Open City* (1945), a story based on an actual event, had the grainy quality of newsreel footage (a technique Gillo Pontecorvo later brilliantly employed in his classic *The Battle of Algiers* [1966]). Like all neo-realist films, *Open City* is about people for whom life is a daily struggle. Rossellini's ordinary people are caught up in extraordinary events—the Italian Resistance's battle with the Germans, who took over the war against the Allies when Mussolini's government collapsed in 1943. Together the resisters put aside their antagonisms to fight an evil that threatens them all.

Vittorio de Sica's *The Bicycle Thief* (1949), is the embodiment of neo-realist themes, techniques, and devices: in its everydayness, its exploration of the culture of poverty, its reliance on nonprofessional actors, its use of locations instead of sets, and its simplicity. The critic André Bazin once remarked, "The dream of [Cesare] Zavatinni [the film's script writer] is just to make a ninety-minute film of the life of a man to whom nothing ever happens." It is not that nothing ever happens in *The Bicycle Thief*, but not much does. An unemployed man, played by Lamberto Maggiorani, needs a bicycle for a job. He pawns what little he has to get one. The bicycle is stolen. The man knows who stole it; accompanied by his young son, he tries to get it back. He is rebuffed on all sides. Insofar as the film makes a point, it is that a juster society might more fairly distribute its wealth.

Rossellini and De Sica were prime heroes of the young French film-makers of the *Nouvelle Vague*, or New Wave, which broke upon the world in the late 1950s. Jean-Luc Godard, Claude Chabrol, Jacques Rivette, Eric Rohmer, and François Truffaut, the group's innermost circle, all wrote film criticism for the magazine *Cahiers du Cinéma*. They were bursting with ideas and opinions about film-making and eager to try their hands at it. They took a cerebral approach that verged on pretension. Friendly critics credited them with being deeply influenced by the existentialism then in vogue in Paris. Perhaps, it was said, their world-weary, marginalized anti-heroes expressed this tendency. Perhaps the casino-owner Rick, Humphrey Bogart's character in *Casablanca*, served as a more obvious archetype than Jean-Paul Sartre.

Despite their contempt for glossy studio productions, the New Wave directors admired certain Hollywood directors. In their guise as critics for *Cahiers du Cinéma* they elaborated their *auteur* (author) theory of film-making. Making a movie might be an industrial enterprise calling on the skills of hundreds of craftsmen and technicians, but a movie that rose to the level of art nevertheless bore a distinctive stamp: the guiding vision and intelligence of its author, the director. The director's style marked his entire body of work, as could be seen in the films of Alfred Hitchcock, Howard Hawks, and others whom they revered.

The *Cahiers du Cinéma* group might have spent their careers as film geeks instead of film-makers had not the newly established French Fifth Republic created subsidies for film-making. The government proved willing to underwrite even the films of artists who were no friends of the regime.

True, the subsidies proved relatively modest, so the New Wave directors found themselves making films on a shoestring. Necessity was the mother of many of their innovations. Their films had a spontaneous, rough, and unpolished look, a quality that was much praised, at least partly because they could not afford to make them pretty. They shot on location, sometimes in their own or their friends' apartments, because they could not afford to rent sound stages. The jump cuts that characterized such Jean-Luc Godard films as *Breathless*, were partly the result of low budgets for film stock. New Wave directors could not afford the countless takes of their studio counterparts.

The technological breakthrough the New Wave directors most fruitfully exploited was the hand-held camera. Such a camera opened up film-making in innumerable ways. Cheaper than the older behemoths, requiring less ambient light and less cumbersome supporting equipment, hand-held cameras, combined with shooting on location, encouraged innovation. Improvisation in New Wave films extended to acting, where dialog took on the meandering, hesitating, and repetitious quality of natural speech.

New Wave films were critical and box-office successes, both at home and abroad. This was especially true of the work of François Truffaut, from *The Four Hundred Blows* (1959) through *Shoot the Piano Player* (1960) to *Jules and Jim* (1961) and beyond. By the mid-1960s the New Wave had come near to expending itself. Its members went off in new directions. Godard, for instance, was drawn into radical politics and Truffaut moved toward traditional film-making, as in *Day for Night* (1973), his homage to the artifices of studio films. Perhaps it was less a case of the New Wave exhausting itself than of the big studios adopting its techniques and devices. New Wave ideas and influences lived on especially in the world of independent or "indy" films, whose faithful make an annual pilgrimage to the Sundance Film Festival in Idaho.

Since the 1960s no school or movement has achieved the prominence once accorded the New Wave. Instead, directors whom the *Cahiers du Cinéma* would undoubtedly have accorded the status of *auteurs* established long and distinguished careers. The Swede Ingmar Bergman, the Pole Andrzej Wajda, and the Spaniard Pedro Almodóvar are but three examples.

If these artists and their predecessors held the creative edge in film-making, the box-office advantage belongs to the big Hollywood studios. Their dominance is frequently cited as a example of the power of the forces of globalization. Take, for instance, *The Return of the King*, released in late 2003. For the first time in history a film opened all over the world on the same day. The distributors were striving to discourage film pirates, not to flex their globalizing muscles, but the point was made anyway.

Hollywood has dominated the European market for years. In 2002 in the then-fifteen-member European Union, U.S.-made films accounted for 71 percent of the tickets sold. French films accounted for 11 percent, British 7 percent, Italian 3 percent, German 2 percent, "other European" 5 percent, and the rest of the world 1 percent. In 2002 only three European films landed in the European box-office top twenty; the other seventeen were American. The European share of the American market is feeble. In 2001 only slightly more than 5 percent of tickets sold were to European films. Devotees flocked to art houses to see the latest Almodóvar, but they flocked in small numbers compared to the total number of moviegoers. The qualitative judgment that European films were better than their American counterparts did not register in the weekly grosses.

Popular Music from 45 RPM to I-Pod

In the decades following World War II, how people listened to music changed as radically as what they listened to. The half century that opened with the introduction of vinyl records spinning forty-five revolutions per minutes closed with I-Pods downloading tunes from the Internet.

The first great music revolutionary of the postwar era was Elvis Presley, the king of rock and roll. Early Presley hits like "Heartbreak Hotel" and "Hound Dog" melded several black and white musical forms, especially the blues, rhythm & blues, and country. Presley and other innovators broke with the thematic, tonal, and rhythmic conventions that had ruled white popular music since the birth of radio in the 1920s.

Such a hybrid musical genre as rock and roll (or rock 'n roll) has never been easy to characterize. At its purest it consists of three repetitive chords, a powerful back beat, and a punchy melody, all driven forward by drums, voices, and electric guitars. In the half-century after Presley burst on the scene, however, rock music assumed a riotous diversity. The Beatles, perhaps the most original, prolific, and influential rock band of all time, in 1964 led the so-called British Invasion of the United States, followed closely by the edgier, scarier—if you were a parent—Rolling Stones. By 1970 the Beatles had gone their separate ways, but the Rolling Stones, masters of the concert tour, rolled on, playing to sellout crowds into the new millenium.

With the loss of the powerful gravitational force the Beatles had exerted, the newer stars in the rock-music galaxy flew in every direction, creating a firmament no style, or constellation of styles, dominated for long. Some groups of the 1970s, like Bruce Springsteen and the E Street Band, or the harsher punk movement, typified by the Sex Pistols, self-consciously sought to restore rock to its simple but hard-driving origins. The heavy-metal style exemplified by Black Sabbath in the 1970s and 1980s combined with punk to provide the foundations of grunge, the Seattle-based style of which Nirvana became, in the 1990s, the most influential exponent.

Rock music was dominated by whites. Rap or hip-hop was African-American and Caribbean-American in origin. Edgy, wary, by turns playful and in-your-face, hip-hop was an urban genre. In the work of early stars like Kool Herc, Grandmaster Flash, and Africa Bambaata, it was a discourse on life in the Bronx. Musically simple at first, featuring DJ-inspired sampling, scratching, and a heavy beat, it grew increasingly complex. Hip-hop's clever rhymes came under attack for their homophobic, misogynistic, and gangsta themes; whether these lyrics were meant in earnest or ironically, as challenges to authority or cartoonish send-ups, was an open question.

In the 1980s rock and rap inhabited parallel universes; crossovers were rare until the sudden emergence, at century's end, of the white hip-hop artist Marshall Mathers, better known as Eminem. In Eminem, a white performer mainstreaming black music, could be seen the Elvis Presley of the new millenium. A break-out African-American group was Outkast, as popular among whites as blacks.

Hip-hop bands emerged in Europe in the 1990s, trailing a cloud of cultural-studies scholars. The early bands especially admired the Americans Public Enemy, Ice-T, and NWA. In France and Germany, the new hip-hop artists belonged to and spoke for the substantial Muslim and Yugoslav immigrant communities; in Italy and Greece, scarcely any immigrant musicians were involved. In either case, European musicians quickly moved from imitating their American sources to making hip-hop their own. If their lyrics borrowed

The Written Record

"SGT. PEPPER'S LONELY HEARTS CLUB BAND"

If there is an epochal moment in the history of rock, the dominant popular music form from the mid-1950s to the late 1970s, it is the making, release and reception of the Beatles' album "Sgt. Pepper's Lonely Hearts Club Band." Recorded at the soon-to-be legendary Abbey Road studio in early 1967, the title song was the work of Paul McCartney. The eleven other tracks on the album, including "With a Little Help from My Friends," "Lucy in the Sky with Diamonds," "Getting Better," "When I'm Sixty-Four," "Lovely Rita," and "Good Morning Good Morning," all became enormously popular. Acclaimed by critics, the album, along with "Revolver," another Beatles long-playing record, or LP, was embraced by the youth culture of the 1960s. At the height of their fame when "Sgt. Pepper" was released, the Beatles continued their remarkably prolific career until 1970, when the band broke up.

It was twenty years ago today,
Sgt. Pepper told the band to play
They've been going in and out of style
But they're guaranteed to raise a smile.
So may I introduce to you
The act you've known for all these years,
Sgt. Pepper's Lonely Hearts Club Band.
We're Sgt. Pepper's Lonely Hearts Club Band,
We hope you will enjoy the show,
Sgt. Pepper's Lonely Hearts Club Band,
Sit back and let the evening go.
Sgt. Pepper's lonely, Sgt. Pepper's lonely,
Sgt. Pepper's Lonely Hearts Club Band,
It's wonderful to be here,
It's certainly a thrill.
You're such a lovely audience,
We'd like to take you home with us,
We'd love to take you home.
I don't really want to stop the show,
But I thought that you might like to know,
That the singer's going to sing a song,
And he wants you all to sing along.
So let me introduce to you
The one and only Billy Shears
And Sgt. Pepper's Lonely Hearts Club Band.

heavily from idiomatic American English, the themes of gangsta rap were as conspicuously absent from their songs as the cultural context that inspired such themes was missing from their own lives.

Like Presley (and other pop stars) before him, Eminem was construed as a corrupter of youth. By the turn of the century recording-industry executives had come to see the young themselves as amoral pirates, downloading from the Internet songs for which they had once willingly paid a pretty penny. Pop music artists were more popular than ever but sales of their recordings stagnated. How to safeguard intellectual property rights in an age of ubiquitous electronic copying devices was a vexing question. Few good answers could be had.

In the meantime, classical or elite music gave off conflicting signs of robustness and frailty. In the work of such composers as Philip Glass and Charles Wuorinnen, experimentation flourished and new music drew enthusiastic devotees. By and large, however, the preponderance of the audience for elite music remained devoted to the traditional repertory of operatic, symphonic, and chamber works. At the new millenium, the graying of this audience, the mounting costs of producing works composed for large ensembles, and slumping sales of classical recordings, which accounted for only 3 percent of the annual sales of the music recording industry, caused some observers to worry about the long-term future of music whose roots ran deep into the European past. Other observers countered that elite music had never been so accessible to so many people, either as audiences for great professional musicians or as amateur performers themselves. In the United States, the composer John Adams pointed out, opera attendance had never been higher or the commissioning of new works greater.

Postmodern Literary Theory

When you compare Frank Gehry's Guggenheim Bilbao Museum with the Empire State Building, or Andy Warhol's *Consommé Soup* with Picasso's *Les Desmoiselles d'Avignon*, you immediately see the differences between postmodern and modern architecture and postmodern and modern art. The visual arts speak to the eye. Explanation surely enhances understanding and enjoyment, but it is not essential; the uninstructed eye readily discerns how the forms and materials of postmodern art and architecture depart from those of their modern predecessors. It is hard to mistake one style for the other.

Beyond the realm of art and architecture, however, disagreement about the meaning of postmodernism sets in and confusion abounds. This is especially the case in the realm of the written word and its province of academic literary criticism. Postmodernism is a famously unstable concept, not least because its foremost adherents insist on the instability of all knowledge—including, when they come under attack, their own views. Temporally, postmodernism comes after modernism. But is it an assault on modernism or modernism in a new guise? It has been understood both ways.

Literary postmodernism dates from the 1970s, when theorists—and it is a movement long on theory—began issuing statements later taken as manifestos. Starting out in France, it spread to Britain and elsewhere in Europe. By the early 1980s postmodernism was receiving increasing attention in the United States. Within a decade the postmodernist stance had won many adherents in literature and such other disciplines as sociology, anthropology, women's studies, art history, and, to a lesser extent, history. What people took—or mistook—postmodernism for had become the subject of heated debate in circles far removed from research and teaching in the social sciences and humanities.

One of the most influential theorists in the founding years of postmodernism was the French philosopher François Lyotard. To Lyotard and his many disciples the great touchstone of modernism, and so the focus of their criticism, was the Enlightenment. From the Enlightenment stemmed the modernist advocacy of reason as method and guide in all human endeavor; the conviction that truth is knowable; the certitude that the procedures of science provide the model for discovering the truth; and the assumption that, once discovered, truth or knowledge may be universally applied.

Critics had been blasting away at the foundations of the Enlightenment long before the postmodernists came along. The modernists regarded themselves as rebels against the orderly Enlightenment worldview and its chief sponsor and beneficiary, the bourgeoisie. In the eyes of the literary postmodernists, the modernists had not gone far enough. They had actually been renovators of Enlightenment thought—modernizers, it might be said—when what was needed was a wrecking crew.

Lyotard and his disciples sought to demolish the Enlightenment edifice. Their point of attack was the great buttresses that, in their view, held the whole structure up. These buttresses were the "grand narratives" or "master narratives", stories a culture tells itself about its beliefs and practices. A master narrative in Western liberal societies, especially the United States, is the conviction that democracy is the most rational form of government and the pursuit of happiness is a worthy goal. The master narrative of Marxism was the certainty that capitalism would destroy itself and a utopian socialist society would emerge from the ruins. And so on.

Concealed behind the order such master narratives portray and strive for, Lyotard insisted, is disorder. Postmodernism at its most general is a critique of all master narratives in favor of the contradictions and instabilities such stories are devised or "constructed" to mask. The postmodernist stance insists on the provisional, contingent, situational character of knowledge. Not only does it make no claims to reason, truth, or universality; it disparages such claims. Language itself is not a window on reality but a mirror of the fractured state of knowledge and consciousness. In the case of the written word, a text derives meaning not from its author but from its readers, all of whom are free to invest it with such interpretations as they see fit. In some hands, postmodernism has been an invitation to a radical subjectivity verging on nihilism, or the conviction that nothing has a real existence.

Most postmodernists have refused this invitation, but their playfulness with respect to all knowledge claims, as well as the opacity of their own critical lexicon, have sometimes landed them in trouble. A famous instance is the Sokal Affair. In 1996 Alan Sokal, a physicist at New York University, submitted to *Social Text*, a cultural-studies journal, a paper called "Transgressing the Boundaries: Toward a Transformative Hermeneutics of Quantum Gravity."

On the same day the journal published his paper, Sokal announced it was a hoax. The article *Social Text* printed was not a contribution to super-string theory, or any other important field in physics. It was a string of nonsense, a cruel joke played on the assumptions and pretensions of postmodernism. Taken in, the editors charged Sokal with a breach of ethics; by submitting an article he knew to be false, he had betrayed their trust. The story of the hoax received wide attention in the press, leaving the friends of postmodernism feeling wounded and misunderstood and their critics sharing an unedifying sense of glee at their embarrassment.

Despite this and other unhappy excursions into realms of theory even more abstruse and difficult than their own, the postmodernists could be credited with making a report on the state of the world today. It is no accident, as Sigmund Freud liked to say, that postmodernism emerged with the onset of the computer revolution. In the World Wide Web were expressed all the contradictions, paradoxes, and instabilities of culture, politics, economics, and society that postmodernism sought to capture. The Web is the most gigantic text the world has ever seen, infinitely manipulable, infinitely open to interpretation. Still, one of the Web's most popular features, the search engine Google, represented the continuing power of the movement of which many postmodern thinkers have been so critical. In their dedication to finding order in a seemingly chaotic universe, in their thirst for knowledge and their aim of satisfying the thirst of everyone else, Google's creators were the intellectual heirs of the writers Denis Diderot recruited to produce the *Encyclopédie*, or *Encyclopedia*, both the embodiment of the Enlightenment and its greatest achievement. In search of enlightenment, eighteenth-century readers thumbed the *Encyclopedia*. Twenty-first century readers Google the Web.

SUMMARY

In papers of 1905 and 1916, Albert Einstein announced the theories of special and general relativity, respectively. Together they overturned the Newtonian explanation of the physical universe that had prevailed for more than two centuries. For Newton's absolute space and absolute time, constant everywhere and forever, Einstein's theories proposed a relative spacetime, in which the great English physicist's two concepts were shown to be inextricably knotted into one. At the onset of the twenty-first century, an Anglo-American research team announced the sequencing of the human genome. This was an astounding leap forward, yet it was utterly dependent on Francis Crick and James Watson's announcement a half-century earlier that DNA alone was the only substance capable of storing all the information required to create a living being.

If the arts did not revolutionize our understanding either of the universe or of life on our home planet, they delighted, awed, ennobled, entertained, instructed, and sometimes shocked. They challenged received opinion and enhanced our understanding of ourselves. They kept us in touch with earlier times and introduced us to the new. Sometimes they did both at once, as when eighteenth-century operas were transplanted to twenty-first-century settings.

In the aftermath of World War II, literature and film probed the terrible wounds that Nazism inflicted on Europe and the world. At the same time, they declined to remain fixated on the past. In Europe, especially, novelists experimented with new forms and film-makers with new ways of telling stories. Architects reinvigorated the Bauhaus style they had inherited from the 1920s and struck out in new directions—or did they instead reach more deeply into the past?—when they rediscovered ornamentation and exploded the modernists' commitment to geometric forms. Meanwhile, the Abstract Expressionists abandoned representation altogether, only to see the Pop artists embrace it in their depictions of a mass-consumption society. If rock 'n roll musicians meant to entertain they also managed to shock, as did the hip-hop artists who came along later, until both were absorbed into the deep and onflowing mainstream of popular culture. Insisting on the unstable meaning of all texts, postmodern literary critics found their theories applied to their own work. They fared less well in the mainstream than did hip-hop and rock 'n roll.

SIX

Europe Since 9/11

Globalization

Globalization is an abstract and fuzzy term for a huge and complex reality. History is replete with such terms. The past that each generation struggles to make sense of is a realm of instability, imprecision, disagreement, and confusion. We make do with labels like "middle class" and "globalization" because they make themselves indispensable. They are rough but they are ready; they give us a purchase on the world.

The term "globalization" is much newer than the reality it seeks to describe. Some economic historians locate its beginnings as long ago as the sixteenth century. Economists are content to look to the early 1970s, when economic integration, the main engine or driving force behind globalization, gained traction. The collapse of fixed exchange rates and the dismantling of controls on capital allowed ever larger sums of money to flow unimpeded across borders. By the end of the twentieth century the volume of world trade was sixteen times greater than it had been in 1950, although world output, or GDP, was only five-and-a-half times larger. In a series of agreements culminating in the creation of the World Trade Organization (WTO) in 1993, governments set aside tariffs, import quotas, and other trade barriers. At first confined to removing barriers against the flow of goods, such as bulldozers, in the 1990s agreements were extended to services, such as building airports. The WTO also made it more difficult for its 132 member nations to break the rules, which under earlier trade agreements was easily done.

Sharply reduced shipping costs also propelled globalization. Computer hard drives, digital cameras, and other products of an electronic era are light and compact, far cheaper to ship than coal, iron, and other heavy, bulky materials of the industrial age. Packing goods in containers easily transferred between trucks and ships drastically reduced the time and labor required to send cargo by sea. Linking trucks to airplanes as the fast-freight business did broke down longstanding barriers between different modes of transportation.

The hero or villain of globalization, depending on your point of view, is the multinational corporation. Such a company owns and acquires other companies, employs workers, and does business in many countries beyond its own. Coca Cola is a good example of a multinational; Toyota, General Electric, and Nestlé are others. Critics regard multinationals as exploitative, selfish,

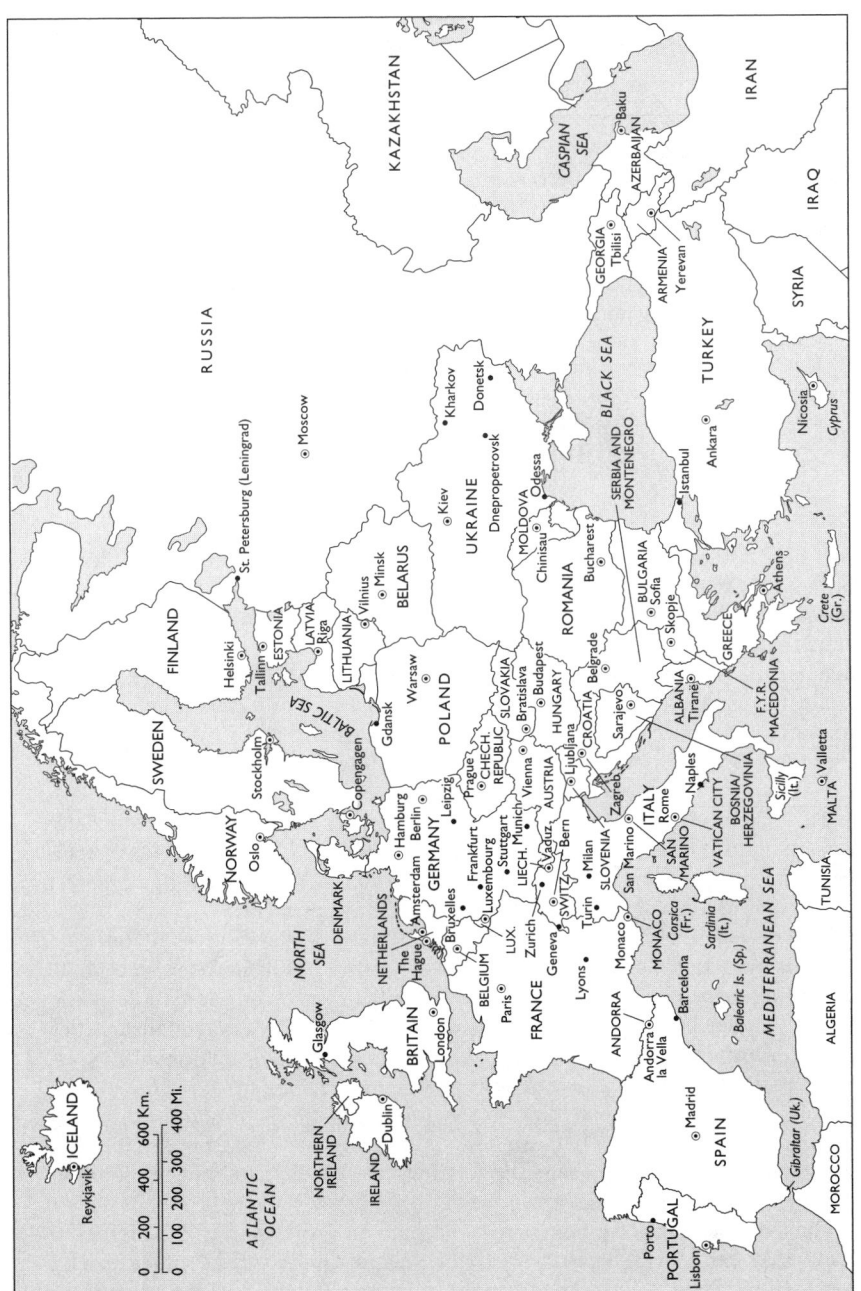

Europe in the Early Twenty-First Century.

Doing History

BENJAMIN BARBER ON JIHADISM AND GLOBALISM

Writing what the Oxford University scholar and journalist Timothy Garton Ash calls "the history of the present" can be a risky business. "Who follows truth too closely at the heels," it has been said, "may have his brains kicked out." Still, even the history of the fairly distant past is provisional, subject to almost incessant revision and reinterpretation. New interpretations of the causes of the French Revolution, for instance, continue to be put forward. The history of our own fast-moving times is hard to capture, yet vital to our understanding of the world in which we live. The pinpointing of dominant trends in the recent past tends to be the work of nonhistorians, but it still requires a historical understanding. Here is one such effort by the American political scientist Benjamin R. Barber, who identifies what he calls "the two axial principles of our age." His essay, published in the early 1990s, shows its age. The world no longer looks quite as he suggests. But every piece of historical writing is like that; it reflects the times in which it was written.

Just beyond the horizon of current events lie two possible political futures—both bleak, neither democratic. The first is a retribalization of large swaths of humankind by war and bloodshed: a threatened Lebanonization of national states in which culture is pitted against culture, people against people, tribe against tribe—a Jihad in the name of a hundred narrowly conceived faiths against every kind of interdependence, every kind of artificial social cooperation and civic mutuality. The second is being borne in on us by the onrush of economic and ecological forces that demand integration and uniformity and that mesmerize the world with fast music, fast computers, and fast food—with MTV, Macintosh, and McDonald's, pressing nations into one commercially homogenous global network: one McWorld tied together by technology, ecology, communications, and commerce. The planet is falling precipitantly apart *AND* coming reluctantly together at the very same moment.

These two tendencies are sometimes visible in the same countries at the same instant: thus Yugoslavia, clamoring just recently to join the New Europe, is exploding into fragments; India is trying to live up to its reputation as the world's largest integral democracy while powerful new fundamentalist parties like the Hindu nationalist Bharatiya Janata Party, along with nationalist assassins, are imperiling its hard-won unity. States are breaking up or joining up: the Soviet Union has disappeared almost overnight, its parts forming new unions with one another or with like-minded nationalities in neighboring states. The old interwar national state based on territory and political sovereignty looks to be a mere transitional development.

The tendencies of what I am here calling the forces of Jihad and the forces of McWorld operate with equal strength in opposite directions, the one driven by parochial hatreds, the other by universalizing markets, the one re-creating ancient subnational and ethnic borders from within, the other making national borders porous from without. They have one thing in common: neither offers much hope to citizens looking for practical ways to govern themselves democratically. If the global future is to pit Jihad's centrifugal whirlwind against McWorld's centripetal black hole, the outcome is unlikely to be democratic—or so I will argue.

McWorld, or the Globalization of Politics

Four imperatives make up the dynamic of McWorld: a market imperative, a resource imperative, an information-technology imperative, and an ecological imperative. By shrinking the world and diminishing the salience of national borders, these imperatives have in combination achieved a considerable victory over factiousness and particularism, and not least of all over their most virulent traditional form—nationalism. It is the realists who are now Europeans, the utopians who dream nostalgically of a resurgent England or Germany, perhaps even a resurgent Wales or Saxony. Yesterday's wishful cry for one world has yielded to the reality of McWorld. . . .

Jihad, or the Lebanonization of the World

OPEC, the World Bank, the United Nations, the International Red Cross, the multinational corporation . . . there are scores of institutions that reflect globalization. But they often appear as ineffective reactors to the world's real actors: national states and, to an ever greater degree, subnational factions in permanent rebellion against uniformity and integration—even the kind represented by universal law and justice. The headlines feature these players regularly: they are cultures, not countries; parts, not wholes; sects, not religions; rebellious factions and dissenting minorities at war not just with globalism but with the traditional nation-state. Kurds, Basques, Puerto Ricans, Ossetians, East Timoreans, Quebecois, the Catholics of Northern Ireland, Abkhasians, Kurile Islander Japanese, the Zulus of Inkatha, Catalonians, Tamils, and, of course, Palestinians—people without countries, inhabiting nations not their own, seeking smaller worlds within borders that will seal them off from modernity.

A powerful irony is at work here. Nationalism was once a force of integration and unification, a movement aimed at bringing together disparate clans, tribes, and cultural fragments under new, assimilationist flags. But as Ortega y Gasset noted more than sixty years ago, having won its victories, nationalism changed its strategy. In the 1920s, and again today, it is more often a reactionary and divisive force, pulverizing the very nations it once helped cement together. The force that creates nations is "inclusive," Ortega wrote in *The Revolt of the Masses*. "In periods of consolidation, nationalism has a positive value, and is a lofty standard. But in Europe everything is more than consolidated, and nationalism is nothing but a mania . . ."

This mania has left the post-Cold War world smoldering with hot wars; the international scene is little more unified than it was at the end of the Great War, in Orgega's own time. There were more than thirty wars in progress last year, most of them ethnic, racial, tribal, or religious in character, and the list of unsafe regions doesn't seem to be getting any shorter. Some new world order! . . .

The passing of communism has torn away the thin veneer of internationalism (workers of the world unite!) to reveal ethnic prejudices that are not only ugly and deep-seated but increasingly murderous. Europe's old scourge, anti-Semitism, is back with a vengeance, but it is only one of many antagonisms. It appears all too easy to throw the historical gears into reverse and pass from a Communist dictatorship back into a tribal state.

despoiling bullies; advocates see them as representing the triumph of global capitalism, bringing high technology to poor countries and cheap goods to rich ones. Although most of the assets and employees of even the most far-flung multinationals remain in the home country, they have been the main force behind the freely flowing rivers of capital, goods and services that make up the global economy.

Instantaneous communications have created the "global village" the Canadian writer Marshall McLuhan envisioned four decades ago. The telegraph, the telephone, wireless radio, and television have been around a long time. The computer-based Internet, however, dates only from the early 1980s and the World Wide Web from the early 1990s. In 1993 alone traffic on the brand-new Web increased by more than 300,000 percent. Yet as recently as 1995 Bill Gates, president of the Microsoft Corporation, had yet to recognize what an important platform for communicating, disseminating knowledge, and marketing goods and services the Internet had become.

Enthusiasts claimed the Internet would prevent wars, reduce pollution, and promote equality. Similarly grand claims greeted the laying of the first transoceanic telegraph cable in 1858. Such claims probably underestimate the complexity of historical change. If the Internet has not met the more extravagant expectations of visionaries, its unparalleled capacity for creating and sustaining worldwide networks makes it a major promoter of globalization. To take one example, a computer programmer in Bangladore, India, can work for a software company anywhere in Europe, without leaving home. Seemingly overnight, networking tied together stock markets, currency and commodities exchanges, and banks and businesses throughout the globe.

At the close of 2003 *The Return of the King*, the last film in the *Lord of the Rings* trilogy, opened on the same day in theaters around the world. Although the decision for simultaneous release was prompted more by fears of piracy than by a rush to reach a worldwide market, the global box-office appeal of the Tolkien fantasy affirmed Hollywood's dominance of the international film industry. The long history of American movie-making had created a huge library of popular films and television shows. Communications satellites, launched to enable the United States to gather intelligence around the globe, came to be used to transmit television signals; the creation of digital television enabled a several-fold increase in the number of programs that could be transmitted simultaneously.

The American culture portrayed in movies and television shows had great appeal abroad, often to the dismay of champions of local cultures. English, the language of globalization, gave the American entertainment industry an edge over rivals. No German or Japanese film could hope to reach an international audience as large as a film made in America. By the close of the twentieth century Europe bought about $2 billion of American television programs annually, and sold to America a tiny fraction of that amount. Still, television viewers around the world preferred to watch their own country's shows; American imports were always a second choice.

Huge increases in world trade, the transportation and communications revolution, the rise of the multinational corporation, the emergence of a

GLOBAL TRADE AND GLOBAL POLITICS: THE CASE OF THE KALASHNIKOV ASSAULT RIFLE

A major issue of globalization has been the attempt to protect intellectual and material property from "piracy": the illegal production and sale of cheap copies of CDs and DVDs, for instance; computer software of all kinds; or knockoffs of name-brand luxury goods. American and European companies have portrayed themselves, accurately enough, as defenders of property rights against Russian and Asian pirates. The case of the famous AK-47, recounted in C. J. Chivers's article, turns the tables. Here international trade and international politics intermingle in complex ways.

Zhevsk, Russia, July 24—The bazaar in this industrial city shows why Western companies regard Russia as a land of piracy.

Bootlegged copies of new American movies—"King Arthur," "Troy" and "Spider-Man 2"—sell for $3. Photoshop CS, a $600 program in Western stores, fetches $2.75.

Markets like this, found throughout Russia, have been a longstanding subject of diplomatic complaint. Washington contends Russian intellectual-property pirates cost the United States more than $1 billion a year.

Now Russia is striking back. A Russian industry and product designer are asserting that the United States has been abetting intellectual-property pirates to suit its own needs, by directing copies of Russian merchandise around the world.

The complaint is not about software or music. It makes no mention of movies or video games. It is about the Kalashnikov assault rifle, the most prolific firearm ever made.

"We see a great number of products which are named after Kalashnikov, my name," said Mikhail T. Kalashnikov, the weapon's original designer. "They are buying Kalashnikovs from other countries," he added.

Since the collapses of the Taliban in Afghanistan and Saddam Hussein's army in Iraq, the United States has been purchasing or arranging the transfer of thousands of knockoffs of Kalashnikovs commonly referred to as AK-47's, to outfit new military and security forces in Kabul and Baghdad.

These rifles have not been made in Russia, where the arms industry holds patents for the weapon in several nations. Instead they have originated in weapons plants controlled by Eastern European states, each of which was a partner of Moscow's in Soviet days.

So begins an argument at once curious, impassioned and bizarre, involving the legacy of cold war influence jockeying, secretive arms deals, recent efforts to defeat modern Islamic insurgencies, and international business and patent law.

The automatic Kalashnikov, made in a factory here, is in many ways Moscow's Ford. It is a quintessential national product: extraordinarily successful, widespread, a name closely connected to the identity of a state.

It was designed by Mr. Kalashnikov, a former Russian tank sergeant, in classified Soviet weapons trials shortly after World War II, and was promptly embraced by Soviet soldiers for its simplicity and reliability under almost any condition. It is regarded as a weapon that rarely, if ever, fails.

Russian arms officials say that no other nation has a valid license to make the AK-47 and its many derivatives and clones, and that to defeat insurgents and terrorists, Washington has been encouraging violations of intellectual property rights. Russia is suffering losses in income, jobs and damage to the Kalashnikov name, the officials say, and would like the United States to shop for the weapons directly from here.

"We would like to inform everybody in the world that many countries, including the United States, have unfortunately violated recognized norms," said Igor Sevastyanov, who leads a division of Rosoboronexport, Russia's state-controlled arms export company. American officials confirm that non-Russian Kalashnikov rifles have been provided with American assistance to Afghanistan and Iraq. Sometimes the weapons have been transferred via purchases on international arms markets, they say, other times via the solicitation of donations from friendly states as a gesture of cooperation with the Bush administration's war and reconstruction efforts.

The officials also say that they are aware of the Russian complaints, which raise questions of provenance that remain unresolved.

"We have taken the position that there are important issues with respect to the production, intellectual property rights and conditions of export of these weapons, and it is important that we strengthen controls in all of these areas," a State Department official said. Officials from Rosoboronexport and Izhmash, the Russian company holding patents on the rifle, say American-coordinated transfers include Kalashnikov clones made in Romanian, Bulgarian and Hungarian plants that have continued to be sold despite Russian complaints.

Another transfer, arranged by the American-led Coalition Provisional Authority in Iraq last year, involved the purchase of Kalashnikovs from Jordan. The weapons were believed to be excess stock from the Jordanian army, and to have been manufactured years ago by the former East Germany, another State Department official said.

The transfers have been diplomatically delicate; the Jordanian deal drew complaints from across the political spectrum.

American business representatives have said that American-made rifles should be bought to preserve American jobs. Others questioned the wisdom of shipping more automatic rifles to countries already awash in such guns.

Congressman have asked why American forces did not save money by reissuing to friendly forces the thousands of Kalashnikov rifles confiscated in both wars.

(Last spring, journalists from The New York Times watched United States marines collect tens of thousands of mint-condition Kalashnikovs in a cache in a hospital in Tikrit. The weapons were still in their original packing crates.)

In spite of complaints, the transfers continued, American officials say, in part because the automatic Kalashnikov is inexpensive and requires less training to master than modern American rifles. Several officials noted that many young Iraqi and Afghan men already know how to use it.

Izhmash and Rosoboronexport agree with this position; their officials are even proud that the Pentagon prefers the Kalashnikov for its new allies.

But they say Washington's deals have come at the expense of Izhmash and Izhevsk, where mass production of the rifles began in 1949, and where orders and the work force have shrunk since the Soviet Union broke up in 1991.

More than 12,000 people worked on the gun lines then; roughly 7,000 work there today, and at fewer shifts, said Andrei Vishnyakov, an Izhmash official.

The officials noted that the low price of Kalashnikov knockoffs can make it impossible to sell the genuine item, a phenomenon resembling the underselling of software and DVD's, albeit on a different scale.

For example, the Jordanian rifles sold for about $60 each—less than one-fourth of the price of a new Kalashnikov from the Izhmash plant, according to Rosoboronexport data.

"They are selling these rifles at dump prices," said Alexander G. Likhachev, a former Izhmash director who is now an official with the state arms agency.

He added that Russia wants that business. "We are prepared to manufacture the genuine weapons, in big quantities, because we know there is a demand," he said.

The legal standing of Rosoboronexport's complaint is uncertain. American officials, analysts and trade representatives said issues surrounding each transfer would require intensive legal research to resolve.

The task would be daunting. In the 1950's, in a mix of collaborative revolutionary spirit and jockeying against the West, the Soviet Union began exporting the rifles and the technology to manufacture them to states in its sphere of influence. Ultimately, Moscow entered licensing agreements with 18 states, according to Rosoboronexport.

"We transferred and gave them all the technical documentation, all the know-how about the design," Mr. Kalashnikov, now 84, said in an interview at his dacha in the Russian woods. "Representatives of these countries came here. They studied our production line."

Moreover, once the rifle's utility became well known, another 11 countries began making derivatives and clones without Moscow's approval, the state agency said.

Russia says that all former licenses have expired. But to make this case, the old licenses would have to be studied, as would Izhmash's more recently acquired patents as well as intellectual property laws in each Kalashnikov-manufacturing state.

A third American official said several former Soviet-bloc countries that formerly made Kalashnikovs with Moscow's approval contend they retain rights to the weapon today. "There is a dispute among all the parties involved," the official said.

Still, whatever the legal merits, analysts agree: the complaint's symbolic power is great.

"I'm not a big fan of guns, but that said, if the creators of this intellectual property have rights to enforce, I really do hope they can get them enforced in every country," Eric Schwartz, a vice president of the International Intellectual Property Alliance, said in a telephone interview. "And I hope that the United States government would comply and set a good example."

The alliance represents American companies with products protected by copyright laws.

The complaint also faces the unrelenting realities of the market. After decades in production in Plants in Asia, Africa, the Middle East and Europe, the automatic Kalashnikov has spread far beyond Izhevsk's reach.

Analysts estimate that 70 million to 105 million of the weapons have been made.

It has been used not only by more than 55 state armies, but also by the Viet Cong, militias in Beirut, Palestinian insurgents in Gaza City, guerrillas in Iraq and child soldiers in Asian and African states. A Kalashnikov is on the seal of Hezbollah and the flag of Mozambique. It features prominently in the symbolism of jihad.

Even the United States long ago entered in the Kalashnikov business, in the 1980's when it surreptitiously bought Chinese and Egyptian Kalashnikovs for Islamic guerrillas battling the Red Army in Afghanistan.

American purchases of Kalashnikovs have continued intermittently since then. A few years ago, according to officials at the State Department and the Pentagon, Washington purchased Kalashnikovs for a Nigerian peacekeeping force in Sierra Leone.

With so many of the weapons in circulation, one analyst said Russia's complaint could prove to be an almost impossible fight.

Rosoboronexport's position is like "the Chinese saying they have a royalty right on every firearm, because that's where it all started with the invention of gunpowder 700 years ago," said Dr. Aaron Karp, a professor at Old Dominion University in Virginia who specializes in weapon proliferation issues.

Mr. Kalashnikov, who said the Russian versions of his rifle are superior, and who expressed deep fondness to Russian workers who have long made them, recognized the difficulties in the state agency's complaint.

He remembered that years ago President Boris N. Yeltsin vowed to defend the weapon from market infringement, to no avail. "President Yeltsin said he would do everything," Mr. Kalashnikov said. "But it's not so easy."

transnational entertainment industry and international capital markets —all were among the interacting forces driving globalization forward. As a reality and as a concept meant to describe a reality, globalization provoked intense controversy. Feelings against it ran high enough to send throngs of demonstrators into the streets of cities where such putatively globalizing organizations as the WTO, the International Monetary Fund (IMF), or the World Bank chose to meet.

Enthusiasts saw globalization as a force for peace and stability—breaking down walls, bridging divides throughout the world, easing poverty. Their optimistic vision mirrored the rationalist, scientific, universalist views of the Enlightenment. The fiercest opponents, especially those who took to the streets, saw globalization as a force for exploitation, oppression, and injustice. Governments, in their view, were merely the pliant hand-maidens of capitalism.

Skeptics believed the enthusiasts had not only overstated the benefits and beneficence of globalization but had also exaggerated its newness, geographical reach, and transformative power. Economic historians insist that global economic integration is an old process, although they disagree on just how old it is. Some trace it to the sixteenth century when, they say, powers were prosperous and at peace. Yet the edifice of interdependence came crashing down when war broke out in 1914, not to be rebuilt for decades—not, in fact, until the 1970s. A sustained depression in the United States, skeptics remind us, could undercut globalization as effectively as the Great Depression of the 1930s arrested the advance of world economic integration.

9/11

Early in the morning of September 11, 2001, terrorists seized four jet airliners flying from Boston, Newark, and Washington, DC. Out of the clear blue sky two flew into the north and south towers of the World Trade Center; the third slammed into the Pentagon; the fourth crashed in rural Pennsylvania, apparently after passengers tried to wrest control of the aircraft from the hijackers. Less than two hours after the twin towers were struck, they collapsed. The attack killed more than three thousand people—more than have died violently in America on any day but September 17, 1862, when Union and Confederate troops fought at Antietam and more than twice as many died. Many Europeans died in the attacks on the World Trade Center; some European countries lost more citizens than they had in any previous terrorist attack.

The hijackers brilliantly exploited the openness of American society, the laxity of prevailing security measures, and inattentiveness and breakdowns on the part of American intelligence agencies. Armed with box-cutters, simple but lethal tools, the hijackers seized control of the airplanes and rammed them into targets apparently chosen both for their symbolic value and for the likelihood of killing large numbers of people.

The surprise attack plunged the United States into war, just as the Japanese surprise attack on Pearl Harbor had done sixty years earlier. The war on terrorism promises to be far longer than the modern wars Americans and Europeans have fought separately and together—less conventional, in terms of weapons and strategies; more shadowy, in terms of enemies; less well-defined, in terms of geography; more uncertain in terms of objectives and even in terms of knowing when—or if—victory has been won.

The New York Times characterized September 11 as "one of those moments in which history splits, and we define the world as 'before' and 'after.'" True, as the shock of 9/11 wore off, continuities reemerged between the time the World Trade Center dominated the lower Manhattan skyline and the time it was no more. The split in history was incomplete. Still, the discontinuities were enormous. As *The Economist* put it, 9/11 was "The Day the World Changed."

Europe immediately rallied to America's support. "We are all Americans," declared an editorial in *Le Monde*, a leading Paris daily frequently critical of

The twin towers of the World Trade Center in Manhattan within half an hour of being struck by two hijacked airliners on the morning of September 11, 2001. The attack plunged the United States into a war on terrorism in general and wars in Afghanistan and Iraq in particular. Europeans rallied to the Americans in the days following 9/11, but tendencies in American policy estranged some European states and peoples from their transatlantic ally. (Time Life Pictures/Getty Images.)

the United States. For the first time in its history NATO invoked Article 5 of its charter, which declared that an attack against one member was to be regarded as an attack against all. Germans by the hundreds of thousands took to the streets to express their sympathy and solidarity with the Americans. As emotions cooled, however, so did European enthusiasm for American leadership of the war on terrorism.

For Europeans the great rift in history remained the fall of the Berlin Wall in 1989, the collapse of the communist regimes of central and eastern Europe, and the reunification of Germany. Nothing better captured the hope that 1989 inspired than the Berlin Philharmonic Orchestra's year-end performance of

Beethoven's Ninth Symphony. "All Men are Brothers" proclaims the symphony's exuberant choral movement. For Europeans the fall of the Berlin Wall continued to mark a watershed between a century of wars and hardships and a new era of peace and prosperity, exemplified and promoted by the European Union. For Americans, the collapse of the World Trade Center announced the end of the American sanctuary. No longer did they live free of the warlike violence that had so badly disfigured the rest of the world.

As harbingers of the future, 1989 and 9/11 offered a contrast between light and shadow. If Europeans continued to take their bearings from a symbol of hope, Americans took theirs from a disaster. Declaring a war on terror, the U.S. government recommended courses of action that European governments were not always inclined to follow. Before long, deep fissures opened in the old transatlantic alliance.

On September 13 Secretary of State Colin Powell blamed the 9/11 attacks on al Qaeda, a terrorist network hitherto little known to the public. Al Qaeda espoused an Islamist, or fundamentalist, form of Islam, in which "violence, including killing civilians, is justified as a means to restore *sharia* (Islamic law) and maintain Islamic cultural identity. Adherents to this brand of Islamist activism say they are engaged in a *jihad* (holy struggle) against Islam's enemies, including even fellow Muslims who have abandoned what the extremists view as 'true' Islam." Like the International Committee of the Red Cross, al Qaeda was a worldwide nongovernmental organization, or NGO. Instead of offering succor to victims of war and disaster, as the Red Cross did, al Qaeda was dedicated to dealing death and creating victims.

Some observers regarded 9/11 and earlier attacks as episodes in a radical Islamist assault against the infidel West, especially the United States. Others saw al Qaeda's campaign of terror as directed at remaking the Middle East by destroying Israel, overthrowing the Saudi monarchy, undermining the government of Egypt and other secular Arab states, and eliminating Western influence in the region.

Investigators quickly traced the Egyptian Mohammad Atta and a handful of his 9/11 accomplices to Hamburg, Germany, where they had established an al Qaeda cell in the 1990s. European police and intelligence agencies turned up other accomplices, fellow-travelers, and sympathizers in Holland, Belgium, France, Italy, Britain, and Spain. If agents and followers of al Qaeda were spread across Europe, the leaders, notably the Saudi millionaire Osama bin Laden, were to be found in Afghanistan, where they took haven in the mid-1990s.

One of a number of failed states around the world, Afghanistan had been wracked by civil war since the Soviet withdrawal in 1989 (see Chapter 4, pp. 78–80). By 1996 the Islamist Taliban had established control over most of the country. Only a ragged tribal coalition called the Northern Alliance continued to contest its authority. To their like-minded al Qaeda brethren the Taliban gave not only sanctuary but also a free hand in establishing terrorist training camps on Afghan soil. Crossing into Afghanistan from Pakistan, whose Inter-Service Intelligence agency (ISI) maintained ties with an assort-

---

The Written Record

OSAMA BIN LADEN AND LIEUTENANTS, *FATWA* OF FEBRUARY 1998

On February 23, 1998, Osama bin Laden and his chief lieutenants issued a *fatwa*, or Islamic religious ruling, requiring the Muslim faithful to kill Americans, both civilian and military, whom they held responsible for conducting a war against Islam. Calling their organization the World Islamic Front, they later changed its name to al Qaeda, Arabic for "the base." In August 1998 al Qaeda obeyed its own injunction by setting off bombs in Kenya and Tanzania that killed a dozen American diplomats and killed and wounded hundreds of Kenyans and Tanzanians. In October 2000 al Qaeda bombed the U.S. destroyer *Cole*, killing seventeen sailors. The 9/11 attack on the World Trade Center killed nearly three thousand and set in motion what the Bush administration called "the war on terror." If Osama bin Laden regarded Americans as the main enemy, he and his lieutenants also employed the broader term "Crusaders," a reference to allies of the United States, who were chiefly represented by the nominally Christian states of Europe.

Praise be to Allah, who revealed the Book, controls the clouds, defeats factionalism, and says in His Book: "But when the forbidden months are past, then fight and slay the pagans wherever ye find them, seize them, beleaguer them, and lie in wait for them in every stratagem (of war)"; and peace be upon our Prophet, Muhammad Bin-'Abdallah, who said: I have been sent with the sword between my hands to ensure that no one but Allah is worshipped, Allah who put my livelihood under the shadow of my spear and who inflicts humiliation and scorn on those who disobey my orders.

The Arabian Peninsula has never—since Allah made it flat, created its desert, and encircled it with seas—been stormed by any forces like the crusader armies spreading in it like locusts, eating its riches and wiping out its plantations. All this is happening at a time in which nations are attacking Muslims like people fighting over a plate of food. In the light of the grave situation and the lack of support, we and you are obliged to discuss current events, and we should all agree on how to settle the matter.

No one argues today about three facts that are known to everyone; we will list them, in order to remind everyone:

First, for over seven years the United States has been occupying the lands of Islam in the holiest of places, the Arabian Peninsula, plundering its riches, dictating to its rulers, humiliating its people, terrorizing its neighbors, and turning its bases in the Peninsula into a spearhead through which to fight the neighboring Muslim peoples.

If some people have in the past argued about the fact of the occupation, all the people of the Peninsula have now acknowledged it. The best proof of this is the Americans' continuing aggression against the Iraqi people using the Peninsula as a staging post, even though all its rulers are against their territories being used to that end, but they are helpless.

Second, despite the great devastation inflicted on the Iraqi people by the crusader-Zionist alliance, and despite the huge number of those killed, which has exceeded 1 million . . . despite all this, the Americans are once against trying to repeat the horrific massacres, as though they are not content with the protracted blockage imposed after the ferocious war or the fragmentation and devastation.

So here they come to annihilate what is left of this people and to humiliate their Muslim neighbors.

Third, if the Americans' aims behind these wars are religious and economic, the aim is also to serve the Jews' petty state and divert attention from its occupation of Jerusalem and murder of Muslims there. The best proof of this is their eagerness to destroy Iraq, the strongest neighboring Arab state, and their endeavor to fragment all the states of the region such as Iraq, Saudi Arabia, Egypt, and Sudan into paper statelets and through their disunion and weakness to guarantee Israel's survival and the continuation of the brutal crusade occupation of the Peninsula.

All these crimes and sins committed by the Americans are a clear declaration of war on Allah, his messenger, and Muslims. And ulema have throughout Islamic history unanimously agreed that the jihad is an individual duty if the enemy destroys the Muslim countries. This was revealed by Imam Bin-Qadamah in "Al-Mughni," Imam al-Kisa'i in "Al-Bada'i," al-Qurtubi in his interpretation, and the shaykh of al-Islam in his books, where he said: "As for the fighting to repulse [an enemy], it is aimed at defending sanctity and religion, and it is a duty as agreed [by the ulema]. Nothing is more sacred than belief except repulsing an enemy who is attacking religion and life."

On that basis, and in compliance with Allah's order, we issue the following fatwa to all Muslims:

The ruling to kill the Americans and their allies—civilians and military—is an individual duty for every Muslim who can do it in any country in which it is possible to do it, in order to liberate the al-Aqsa Mosque and the holy mosque [Mecca] from their grip, and in order for their armies to move out of all the lands of Islam, defeated and unable to threaten any Muslim. This is in accordance with the words of Almighty Allah, "and fight the pagans all together as they fight you all together," and "fight them until there is no more tumult or oppression, and there prevail justice and faith in Allah."

This is in addition to the words of Almighty Allah: "And why should ye not fight in the cause of Allah and of those who, being weak, are ill-treated (and oppressed)?—women and children, whose cry is: 'Our Lord, rescue us from this town, whose people are oppressors; and raise for us from thee one who will help!'"

We—with Allah's help—call on every Muslim who believes in Allah and wishes to be rewarded to comply with Allah's order to kill the Americans and plunder their money wherever and whenever they find it. We also call on Muslim ulema, leaders, youths, and soldiers to launch the raid on Satan's U.S. troops and the devil's supporters allying with them, and to displace those who are behind them so that they may learn a lesson.

Almighty Allah said: "O ye who believe, give your response to Allah and His Apostle, when He calleth you to that which will give you life. And know that Allah cometh between a man and his heart, and that it is He to whom ye shall all be gathered."

Almighty Allah also says: "O ye who believe, what is the matter with you, that when ye are asked to go forth in the cause of Allah, ye cling so heavily to the earth! Do ye prefer the life of this world to the hereafter? But little is the comfort of this life, as compared with the hereafter. Unless ye go forth, He will

> punish you with a grievous penalty, and put others in your place; but Him ye
> would not harm in the least. For Allah hath power over all things."
>   Almighty Allah also says: "So lose no heart, nor fall into despair. For ye must
> gain mastery if ye are true in faith."

ment of Afghan warlords, Islamists, and terrorists, recruits from around the
world made their way to al Qaeda's camps.

The War in Afghanistan

In the aftermath of 9/11 President George W. Bush rallied international support for a war on terrorism. True, some of the support amounted to lip service. British Prime Minister Tony Blair offered his country's assistance in
military operations against al Qaeda. Other European allies were more circumspect, condemning the attack and redoubling the hunt for terrorists in
their countries, but without committing themselves to engaging their own
military forces. President Vladimir Putin seized the opportunity to portray
Russia's faltering struggle against the separatist insurrection in Chechnya as
part of the war on Islamist terrorism. Russia also acquiesced in the establishment of American military bases in the former Soviet states of Uzbekistan
and Tajikistan, which bordered on Afghanistan. How the world had changed
since the height of the cold war!

President Bush demanded the Taliban turn over Osama bin Laden "dead
or alive." The Taliban equivocated, prevaricated, and in the end declined.
Meanwhile, the United States pressured Pervez Musharraf, president of Pakistan, into aligning his country with the anti-terrorist campaign, despite
strong Pakistani sympathies for al Qaeda. On October 10 the United States
launched air strikes against Taliban and al Qaeda targets in Afghanistan. Several NATO countries as well as Finland and Russia provided combat support
and logistical assistance.

American special-operations forces—some mounted on horseback—called
in devastating air strikes in support of the Northern Alliance—an informal
coalition of Afghan warlords—which bore the brunt of the fighting against
the poorly trained and badly equipped Taliban.

By November the Taliban were fleeing their urban strongholds in disarray
and by December they had lost control of the country. They melted away
among their fellow Afghans, but the Arab fighters of al Qaeda had fewer
places to hide. Most dashed for the high country near the porous Afghan
frontier. Many escaped into the friendly and lawless borderlands of Pakistan.
The biggest question of all was the fate of Osama bin Laden. From time to
time tape recordings of a voice purporting to be bin Laden's turned up at the
offices of Aljeezera, the Arab television channel. CIA analysts pronounced the
tapes authentic, but the whereabouts of the man himself remained unknown.

Driven from power, the Taliban regrouped in hideouts along the Afghan/Pakistani frontier. They posed a serious threat to the new government. Formed under UN auspices and led by President Hamid Karzai, its authority barely reached beyond the capital city of Kabul. The UN-mandated International Security Assistance Force (ISAF), with only five thousand troops at its command, was incapable of keeping order beyond the city limits.

In the countryside, warlords fought each other, exploiting ethnic tensions for various ends of their own, siding with the Americans and their allies when it suited them, making trouble when it did not, and determined to be masters in their own neighborhoods, whatever happened in Kabul. A few thumbed their noses at a government incapable of acting effectively against them. A United States force of roughly eighteen thousand had its hands full battling surviving elements of al Qaeda and the Taliban, who stepped up raids in southern and eastern Afghanistan.

In August 2003 NATO took over the ISAF's peacekeeping responsibilities. NATO had recent peacekeeping experience in Bosnia and Kosovo, but the mission to Afghanistan was the first it had ever assumed beyond the Euro-Atlantic area of its birth. The NATO commitment to Afghanistan recalled Western solidarity in the early days of the war on terrorism. Nearly a year later, however, the modest force of five thousand had increased to a scarcely more robust sixty-five hundred, of which nearly a third were German, a quarter Canadian, and a tenth French; NATO's twenty-three other members and eleven other countries together accounted for the remaining twenty-five hundred troops. Except for a small German contingent garrisoned in Kunduz, the ISAF had still not budged from Kabul.

At a meeting in Istanbul, Turkey, in June 2004, NATO leaders pledged to send another four thousand soldiers to Afghanistan, some distributed in packets as Provincial Reconstruction Teams (PRTs), others charged with providing security for already postponed parliamentary and presidential elections. Whether all would make good on their pledges seemed doubtful at best. Several NATO member states had little enthusiasm for peacekeeping operations far from home; they had little interest in sending men and money to a country that seemed on the verge of sliding back into the disorder that had plagued its previous quarter-century. Moreover, even when they had substantial forces on the ground, as in the German case, NATO governments saddled them with restrictions that limited their effectiveness. Instead of narrowing the gap between European states and their American ally over how best to fight the war on terror, NATO's role in Afghanistan threatened to widen it. Resurgent warlords and a resurgent Taliban were enemies, but together they endangered the existence of the fledgling national government.

The Afghan presidential election of November 2004, however, confounded the worst fears of foreign observers. Hamid Karzai secured a majority against a big field of candidates in voting largely free of both violence and fraud. Still, no sooner had election results been certified than the UN issued a report stating that the production of opium, Afghanistan's leading cash crop, had soared in the years since the ouster of the Taliban. The report deepened fears that one of the poorest countries in the world, only recently a haven for terrorists, risked becoming a so-called narco-state. In 2004, for instance, 95 percent of the heroin sold in Europe derived from opium poppies cultivated in Afghanistan.

The Crisis over Iraq

Speaking early in 2002, President George W. Bush identified Iraq, Iran, and North Korea as members of an "Axis of Evil." All three possessed or were seeking to develop, he charged, weapons of mass destruction (WMD), a category that included biological weapons like anthrax and botulinum, chemical weapons like sarin and mustard gas, and nuclear and radiological weapons. Furthermore, Bush went on, all three regimes were willing to make such weapons available to terrorist organizations like al Qaeda. Iraq under Saddam Hussein was soon singled out as the offender against which something had to be done. In the 1991 Gulf War the United States drove Iraq from Kuwait without driving Saddam from office. The Iraqi dictator crushed challenges to his rule, tightened his grip on power, and, the United States charged, continued to pursue an ambitious program to develop weapons of mass destruction. The United States appeared ready to oust Saddam Hussein on its own.

At the new century the United States had the most powerful military the world had ever seen. Annual U.S. military expenditures equaled the defense spending of the next nine largest military powers combined. No state rivaled the United States in its ability to project force overseas.

European governments were acutely aware of the disparity between what they could achieve militarily, even if they pooled their resources, and what the Americans could achieve by themselves. They were to the United States as the Lilliputians were to Gulliver. In a multilateral approach to terrorism they saw a means of restraining their gigantic friend. They preferred working within NATO and the EU to the Bush administration's preference for going it alone. They did not share the Americans' newfound taste for preemptive war. The Americans, an EU official complained, were in "unilateralist overdrive." With an eye to assuaging the Europeans' fears, Secretary of State Colin Powell persuaded President Bush to seek the UN Security Council's backing for action against Iraq.

Addressing the UN in September 2002, Bush emphasized that Saddam had been defying UN directives on WMD ever since the Gulf War. His pattern of denials, evasions, and stonewalling were proof he had something to hide. The Security Council obliged Bush on the WMD issue. On November 8, by a vote of 15-0, it passed Resolution 1441, declaring Iraq "in material breach of its obligations" to disarm and threatening "serious consequences" should its defiance continue.

Iraq readmitted UN weapons inspectors it had expelled in 1998. Iraqi spokesmen continued to deny American allegations of WMD and the regime's purported links with al Qaeda. In the meantime, the United States steadily built up its military forces in the Middle East. As the deadline for Iraqi compliance neared, the rift in the Atlantic alliance widened.

France took the lead in opposing the United States, closely seconded by Germany, where sentiment ran strongly against America's hard-line stance and Chancellor Gerhard Schroeder faced a tough election campaign. French President Jacques Chirac and his foreign minister, Dominique de Villepin, forcefully asserted that Iraq did not pose to the world the threat the United States described. Joined by China and Russia, France and Germany called for more intrusive weapons inspections but saw no need to insist on a deadline for Iraqi compliance; they believed the policy of containment—keeping Iraq hemmed in—was continuing to work.

Public opinion polls revealed that a substantial majority of Europeans, even in Britain, Spain, and Italy, whose governments sided with the United States, opposed invading Iraq. Huge crowds gathered across Europe to demonstrate against the looming prospect of a U.S.-inspired war. Acrimonious exchanges among NATO foreign and defense ministers over the wisdom of U.S. policy were amplified by name-calling in the media.

The prospect of war over Iraq also revealed divisions within the EU. The leaders of ten central and eastern European countries set to join the EU in 2004 lined up behind the United States. President Chirac intemperately advised the ten EU candidates to be quiet. Speaking out, he hinted, might harm their candidacies for membership. His annoyance betrayed fears that expansion would erode France's historical dominance. Both Paris and Berlin, the chief paymaster of the EU, let it be known that the less-developed regions of the union might not receive the subsidies they had been hoping for were they to continue siding with the United States on Iraq.

Meanwhile, at the UN, the struggle over Iraqi WMD played itself out. In early February 2003, Secretary of State Colin Powell appeared before the Security Council, PowerPoint presentation in hand, to charge that Iraq was still hiding WMD. Skeptics countered that Powell's intelligence data were ambiguous and sketchy, and Powell himself eventually expressed regret for having relied on them. Later in February, the chief UN weapons inspector reported that his teams had so far found no WMD, but many weapons-related materials remained unaccounted for.

Determined to head off the impression they were bent on going to war no matter what, Britain, the United States, and Spain submitted a "second" resolution declaring Iraq in violation of 1441 and setting March 17 as a deadline to disarm. In January France had already declared it would veto *any* UN resolution that would trigger the use of force and foreign minister Villepin continued to pursue this line. Concluding they did not enjoy sufficient Security Council support, the United States and its allies withdrew their resolution.

Diplomacy at the United Nations collapsed. The United States reverted from seeking to disarm Iraq to ousting Saddam Hussein by force.

The Iraq War

On March 20, 2003, the United States and Britain (Australia and Poland also contributed small numbers of combat troops) attacked Iraq from Kuwait, nearby ships, and aircraft near and far. Coalition troops were almost constantly on the move. Speed enabled them to exploit their edge in discipline and training over the Iraqis. Superior weapons, especially precision guided munitions, further magnified the coalition's advantages. Employed to devastating effect against command, control, and communications systems, or what the armed forces call "C3", they severed contact between the Iraqi authorities and their combat forces in the field.

Bypassing as many cities and towns as they could, the Americans raced up the main roads toward Baghdad while a smaller British force attacked Basra, a key city in southeastern Iraq. In the face of this relentless assault the Iraqi forces—poorly equipped, poorly led, largely unprotected from air attack—lost heart. Abandoning weapons, equipment, uniforms, and the boots on their feet (nothing gives away soldiers like their boots), they headed for home. Some units stood their ground. In Nasiriya and elsewhere on the road up to Baghdad, coalition forces fought fierce battles against Iraqi paramilitary units.

On April 9 Baghdad fell to the Americans. Widespread looting on the part of Iraqi civilians stripped the city bare. Saddam Hussein was nowhere to be found. Few European critics of American actions denied that he was a murderous tyrant, responsible for killing hundreds of thousands of Iraqis—including gassing to death upward of eight thousand Iraqi Kurds in the town of Halabja—and jailing, torturing, and maiming thousands more. Most persisted in their doubts and reservations, however, about the wisdom of going to war against the regime and the manner in which the Americans had done so.

Capturing Baghdad did not end the war. Defeated in the conventional campaign, elements loyal to Saddam Hussein turned to an insurgency against the largely American occupation. The insurgency bore elements of terrorism, in the form of urban bombings, and guerrilla warfare, in the form of hit-and-run attacks on coalition troops and Iraqi police. Surprised by the ferocity and persistence of the insurgency, the Americans were not well prepared to deal with it, although critics insisted they should have been.

Despite a diligent search, the Americans did not turn up the weapons of mass destruction that had been the main justification for going to war. In January 2004 David Kay, head of the U.S. Iraq Survey Group, told a U.S. Senate committee that his large team of searchers had found no WMD in Iraq. Hans Blix, the chief UN weapons inspector, initially assumed Iraq was concealing WMD; the Iraqis' foot-dragging and evasions seemed to confirm Saddam was hiding something. Beyond a handful of missiles, however, Blix's inspectors failed to find anything. At length he concluded, as David Kay did, that Iraq abandoned its weapons development program sometime in the 1990s. In a memoir on his experience Blix reserved his sharpest criticism for American policy makers, wrong in virtually every claim they made about Iraqi WMD throughout the run-up to war.

The failure to find any WMD brought the Bush administration under harsh attack. Both European and American critics charged the American leadership with cooking up phony allegations against the regime of Saddam Hussein.

WMD, they contended, were a pretext for attacking Iraq. The real reasons lay elsewhere—in Iraq's oil deposits, in the desire to establish a strong American strategic presence in the Middle East, and so on. In their own eyes, at least, the absence of Iraqi WMD vindicated President Chirac, Chancellor Schroeder, and other European opponents of war. They had urged allowing weapons inspectors more time to do their work; they had claimed the old policy of containment would keep Saddam in check. The American claim that Iraq posed a fearsome threat to the stability of the Middle East had proved false. If the failure to turn up WMD appeared to vindicate Chirac and Schroeder, it badly damaged the standing of Tony Blair with British voters, of whom a majority opposed Britain's going to war alongside the United States.

Assuming that Iraqi WMD are never found, why did the Bush administration and the Blair government prove to be wrong about them? The case each made for war was based on the reports of its respective intelligence agencies, and these reports, as the American weapons inspector David Kay put it, were "almost all wrong." Official inquiries into the intelligence failures of both countries found that the strong conclusions of intelligence officials rested on flimsy evidence. Having few spies of their own in the region, they trusted the second- and third-hand claims of unreliable sources. Consequently, "the two intelligence dossiers presented to the American and British people by their leaders, just before the war, exaggerated the likelihood that Saddam's regime was a serious threat to the West."

Aside from WMD, the main justification for war against Iraq was the presumption of links between Saddam Hussein's regime and terrorist organizations. The Bush administration portrayed the coming war with Iraq as a campaign in the larger war on terror (in general, the Blair government did not pursue this line). In the run-up to war, administration officials repeatedly tied al Qaeda and Saddam Hussein's regime together. Critics pointed out that secular Muslim rulers like Saddam were the sworn enemies of the Islamist Osama bin Laden; they charged that a war with Iraq would actually distract from the war on terrorism. At length, inquiries by the Bush-appointed National Commission on Terrorist Attacks upon the United States (also known as the 9/11 Commission,) and by the Senate Select Committee on Intelligence found no formal ties between Iraq and al Qaeda.

Absent incontrovertible proof that Iraq threatened the region and the West, the U.S. government shifted its justification for going to war from weapons to politics. The war, spokesmen pointed out, rid the Iraqi people of a brutal dictatorship. The forcible removal of Saddam, they contended, was a necessary prelude to the creation of the first Arab democracy in the Middle East. In mid-December 2003 came the galvanizing news that American troops had captured Saddam Hussein alive in a dismal hideout near his hometown of Tikrit. His capture offered one of those rare moments when everything seemed to change and everything appeared to remain the same. The guerrilla war continued, yet the myth of the elusive and invincible warrior had shattered and the fearsome prospect of his return to power evaporated.

First responders, as fire, police, and emergency medical personnel are now generally called, attend to some of the victims of the Madrid railway bombings of March 11, 2004. Deaths in the morning rush-hour attacks eventually mounted to 191; scores more were wounded. Facing an election in three days, the conservative Spanish government immediately blamed a Basque separatist group. It quickly emerged that the bombings were the work of al Qaeda. Angered by their government's duplicity, a majority of Spanish voters handed the socialists a parliamenatary majority. The new socialist government promptly withdrew Spanish troops from Iraq. If the withdrawal represented the will of the Spanish people, some observers suggested al Qaeda also got what it wanted.   (Associated Press.)

Responding to international pressure, continued violence in Iraq, and the urgings of influential Iraqi politicians and religious leaders, the United States announced it would hand over sovereignty on June 30, 2004 (and actually did so on June 28). It welcomed the participation in Iraqi affairs of a UN it had previously spurned. Coalition troops were to remain in the country at least until the end of 2005.

Al Qaeda Strikes in Europe

On March 11, 2004, a series of bombs ripped through four packed commuter trains in Madrid, killing nearly two hundred people. The center-right government of Jose Maria Aznar immediately pinned the blame for the bombings, which came three days before parliamentary elections, on the Basque separatist group ETA. Evidence quickly emerged that al Qaeda, not the ETA, was responsible. Voters took out their anger at the government's duplicity, many analysts thought, by returning a socialist majority to parliament. Polls showed that voters threw out the Aznar government because they believed Spain's participation in the Iraq War had provoked the al Qaeda bombings in Madrid. The new socialist prime minister, José Zapatero, promptly carried out his campaign promise to remove some twelve hundred Spanish troops from Iraq.

Analysts saw in the Madrid bombings an attempt by al Qaeda to deepen the wedge between the United States and Europe over the war on terrorism. Stop supporting the American war on Islam, the bombings appeared to tell European governments, or you risk being next. The corollary was that if Europeans followed Spain's good example and withdrew their troops from Iraq, they might be spared such attacks.

In the wake of Madrid, the resolve of some European members of the U.S.-led coalition did indeed soften. Poland, previously second only to Britain in its support for America, momentarily wavered in its determination to keep troops in Iraq. Such reassessments may have been provoked more by the disquiet over events in Iraq than by threats from al Qaeda. Bombings, shootings, and the taking and beheading of hostages pressed the governments of countries where the war was unpopular to remove their soldiers from harm's way. Norway withdrew its military engineers in July 2004; the Netherlands signaled its intention to pull out in early 2005; Italian parliamentary deputies expressed strong reservations about extending Italy's troop commitment; in Hungary the opposition called for the withdrawal of Hungarian troops. Thailand, the Dominican Republic, Honduras, Nicaragua, the Philippines, and Singapore all brought their small detachments home. Still, in several East European and former Soviet countries, including Azerbaijan, Georgia, Albania, and Macedonia, the commitment to staying in Iraq remained strong. "We benefited in our recent history from foreign peacekeepers," a Macedonian official said, "so we understand the value of action. Our stand on Iraq is firm, and our participation is not questionable."

The United States sustained a considerable self-inflicted wound to its moral authority when well-substantiated allegations that American military personnel had abused Iraqi prisoners surfaced in the press.

The original European anti-war trio of France, Germany, and Russia continued to be sharp critics of the United States. Singly and in concert they insisted that the Americans cede management of postwar Iraq to the UN None of the three pledged any new funds to help rebuild Iraq, but they offered assurances they would help find ways to reduce its huge burden of foreign debt. The United States argued that loans contracted by the despotic Saddam should be forgiven. France, Germany, and Russia, owed billions by the Iraqi dictator, were determined to get some of their money back. Germany, however, still nervous about straying too far from its historically close relationship with Washington, hinted from time to time that it was not quite as adamant in these demands as its EU colleague was. NATO agreed to play a role in training the security forces of a newly sovereign Iraq, although France declined to send any of its own troops to that country. French-trained Iraqi forces, President Chirac declared, would need to be trained in France.

Overnight, 9/11 made terrorism the main preoccupation of the U.S. government. If Europeans poured out their feelings of solidarity in the days following the attack, their governments shared neither the American government's assessment of the gravity of the terrorist threat nor its views on what should be done about it. Perhaps it is not too far-fetched to suggest that Europeans responded to 9/11 and the ensuing war on terrorism as Americans reacted to the war in Europe between 1939 and 1941. It took the attack on Pearl Harbor, as far from Europe as far could be, to bring the United States into the European war. Europeans have so far suffered no comparable blow to their sense of relative security. Among them skepticism about U.S. policy remained widespread.

Europeans who shared none of the premises driving American policy in the U.S.-declared war on terror nevertheless worried about the encroachment of Islamism on politics and society in western Europe. Over the last two decades, Muslim immigration to Europe has accelerated, bringing the Muslim population to 23 million, or 5 percent of the general population. The birth rate among Muslims is three times the rate among non-Muslims. Consequently, Muslim communities across Europe are considerably younger than the non-Muslim population, and it is precisely among the young, according to some observers, that the attractions of the extremist ideology of Islamism are greatest. The agents of 9/11 and the Madrid bombings alike were all young men in their twenties and thirties.

In late 2004 vague worries about the impact of Muslim immigration on the Europe of the future were suddenly transformed into acute anxieties about the threat of Islamism in the present. On November 2 Theo van Gogh, a well-known Dutch film-maker, was shot off his bicycle on an Amsterdam street by an Islamist who nearly severed van Gogh's head before plunging into his chest a knife bearing a five-page letter attacking the enemies of Islam. Van Gogh had directed a short television film, a mocking documentary written by a Somali-born Muslim woman (and member of the Dutch parliament) critical of Islam for its treatment of women. His Muslim assailant, himself a Dutch citizen of Moroccan origin, had several accomplices who, like him, belonged to an Islamist network and were swiftly arrested by the Dutch police.

Shock and anger over van Gogh's murder fueled an already burning debate over the place of Islamism in particular and the Muslim community in general in the Netherlands, generally regarded as one of Europe's most tolerant and liberal societies. Expressions of outrage against a brutal killing over an expression of free speech were punctuated by threats against Muslims, the fire-bombing of a Muslim school, and calls by more than one Dutch politician for setting far greater limits on Muslim immigration. In this atmosphere of heightened mutual fear—of newcomers on the part of the Dutch and the Dutch on the part of newcomers, issues that might have been separable in calmer times were tangled together. Acts of terrorism put into question longstanding immigration policies; in turn, the presence of Islamists within the Muslim community shook confidence in how well foreigners could be assimilated into Dutch culture and society. In the Netherlands and elsewhere, issues of terrorism, immigration, and assimilation were unlikely to be untangled soon.

The Enlargement of the European Union

Britain's partnership with the United States on Iraq and the war on terrorism obscured its ties with Europe and the EU. The special relationship with the United States fostered by prime ministers from Winston Churchill on was but one expression of a longer-standing British aloofness from the European continent. Prime minister Blair insisted his country could nurture both its transatlantic and cross-Channel alliances. The gravitational pull of the EU, however, increasingly drew Britain into alignment with its partners on a range of issues that put it at odds with the United States.

A case in point was the Kyoto Protocol on global warming. Signed in 1997, "Kyoto" pledged industrialized countries to make drastic cuts in their emissions of greenhouse gases. Although the Americans from the beginning sought to make changes in the Kyoto targets, the Bush administration expressed such strong reservations when it came to office in 2001 that it was blamed for torpedoing the agreement. A disproportionate share of the burden for reducing emissions, U.S. officials claimed, fell to the United States. Some members of the EU were not much closer to meeting the Kyoto targets than the United States, but the American action allowed Brussels to take the high ground of principle. EU spokesmen excoriated the Americans for their irresponsibility in the face of a mounting environmental crisis.

The EU also parted company with the United States over the International Criminal Court (ICC). In the 1990s war crimes tribunals were established under UN auspices to try perpetrators of genocide in Rwanda and the former Yugoslavia. Despite the arrest of such high-profile politicians as Slobodan Milosevic, ex-president of Serbia, who went on trial in The Hague in 2002, most of those indicted remained at large. The war-crimes tribunals were ad hoc arrangements, slated to go out of business when they completed their work, and the United States supported them.

In March 2003 the International Criminal Court, set up by a 1998 treaty, was inaugurated at The Hague. Its mandate was to try charges of genocide, war crimes, and mass atrocities arising from war that no national court was willing or able to prosecute. Unlike the tribunals on Rwanda and the former Yugoslavia, the ICC was meant to be permanent. True to its internationalist bent, the EU unanimously supported the new court, which was also backed by dozens of other countries, including all the European members of NATO except Turkey. The United States, however, refused to recognize the ICC, citing fears that politically motivated charges might be brought against American soldiers. So fierce was U.S. opposition that it pressed countries to agree they would not hand over to the ICC any wanted Americans found within their borders. The EU resisted these blandishments, but the United States kept up the pressure. At odds once again were the EU's confidence in multilateralism and the U.S. preference for unilateralism.

At the turn of the century, the United States and the EU were the world's largest traders. Trade between the two neared $400 billion a year, of which 95

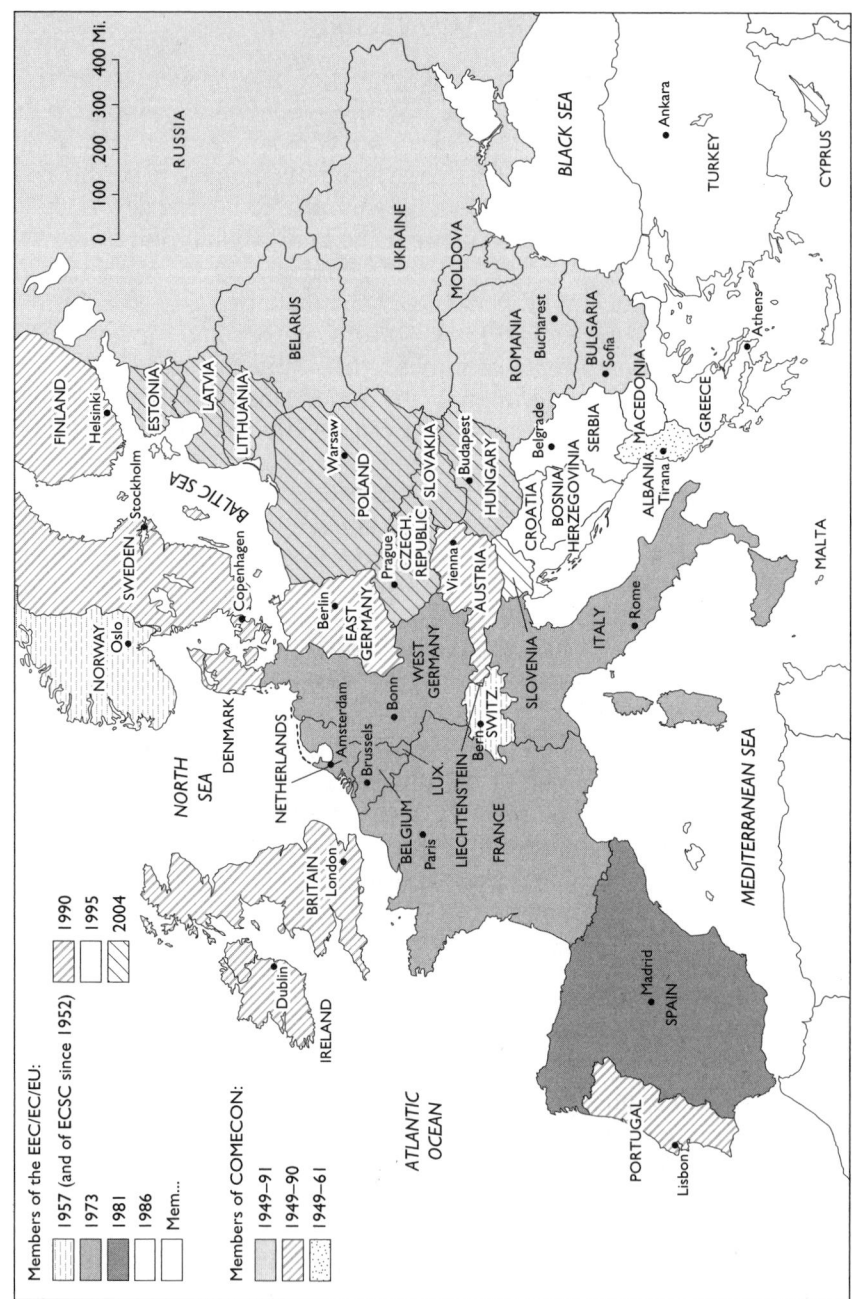

The Economic Integration of Europe, 1957–2004.

percent went to and fro without incident. The remaining 5 percent, however, was the subject of disputes so longstanding and acrimonious as to threaten from time to time the whole edifice of transatlantic trade. The details of the issues that put the United States and the EU at odds were often complicated, arcane, and stupefyingly boring to all but a handful of experts. In their implications, however, they affected the lives and livelihoods of innumerable producers and hundreds of millions of consumers.

This became immediately apparent when in March 2003 the United States slapped tariffs mounting to 30 percent on that quintessential industrial product, steel. The Bush administration claimed this was a temporary measure, aimed at giving an inefficient American steel industry time to put its house in order. Outraged at tariffs it regarded as illegal and harmful to European steelmakers, the EU appealed to the World Trade Organization (WTO), arbiter of world trade rules. The WTO upheld the EU's appeal. Armed with this ruling, the EU threatened to retaliate with tariffs on American products ranging from Harley Davidson motorcycles to Florida orange juice. The EU was playing a game of diplomatic chicken, for it listed products with an eye to the geography of American electoral politics. The Bush administration had either to back down on steel tariffs or risk the ire of voters whose jobs might be threatened by the EU's retaliatory tariffs. In December 2003 President Bush agreed to dismantle the tariffs on steel, although without conceding the EU had made him blink.

The year 2004 was what one journalist called, after the reigning theory on the origins of the universe, a "big-bang" enlargement of the European Union. Ten countries joined, at a stroke increasing membership from fifteen to twenty-five and making for the largest expansion since the creation of precursor institutions a half century earlier (see Chapter 3). The expansion was the first to take in countries formerly dominated by the Soviet Union. Estonia, Latvia, Lithuania, Poland, Hungary, the Czech Republic, and Slovakia had all been on the eastern side of the Iron Curtain. Joining these seven were Slovenia, once part of the former Yugoslavia, and the Mediterranean islands of Cyprus and Malta. Russia expressed no interest in becoming a member. Expansion increased the area of the EU by a quarter and its population by a fifth, or 80 million people.

Concurrent with expansion, but moving along a separate track, was the drafting of an EU constitution. This was a document of devilish length and complexity, subject to wrangling among the members and requiring ratification by all, including the new ones. There were many bones of contention over the proposed constitution and just as many angles of attack. The debaters, however, were generally arrayed under one of two banners. Under the first banner were champions of the integrationist or federalist tendency, who since the Treaty of Rome in 1957 had pushed for a political union, a supranational body with the power to tax and a unified foreign and military policy. Under the second banner marched the Euroskeptics, content with what the EU has tended to become in recent years—a free-trade area or glorified customs union whose members retained most, if not all, of their own political institutions.

Constitution-making ran aground late in 2003 on a reef of contention over how representation should be distributed between large and small states. The U.S. Constitutional Convention of 1787 resolved this dilemma by creating a bicameral legislature. The House of Representatives bowed to the force of numbers and the Senate to the notion that small states should carry as much legislative weight as large states. For the EU, however, no such solution seemed to be in the cards. Although the draft constitution was shelved for the time being, French President Chirac reminded observers that the project of Europe had "a history of crises overcome."

It was unclear whether the integrationists or the Euroskeptics would ultimately prevail. In the middle of the nineteenth century it had been just as unclear whether the German *Zollverein*, or customs union, was an end in itself or a step along the path to German unification. True, the *Zollverein* proved in the long run to be a step toward a united Germany, but this was by no means a foregone conclusion.

The big-bang enlargement went a long way toward completing what the fall of the Berlin Wall had begun. If the fall of the wall marked the beginning of the end of the Soviet Union, the enlargement of the EU finally erased the cold war's longstanding frontiers and restored to popular usage the old geographical expression "central Europe." The cold war had put this phrase in cold storage. The long face-off between the United States and the Soviet Union divided Europe into East and West. There was no in-between. It was if the Midwest had been incorporated into the eastern United States, made into a "non-area," with all references to its variety and distinctiveness suppressed. In resurrecting "Central Europe," EU enlargement acknowledged not only the end of an era but also the realities of physical geography, regional culture, and the preferences of people who live there.

Enlarging eastward potentially shifted the EU's center of gravity eastward as well. The Union's main institutions (the European Commission, the European Parliament, and the European Central Bank) arose and remain in the Franco-German borderlands of Belgium and Luxembourg. Their location between the two dominant powers of the old EU nicely represented their real influence on its affairs. Demands could arise to put these governing institutions nearer the center of the new EU, just as, following reunification, the capital of Germany reverted from Bonn to Berlin. Both France and Germany have already manifested their fear that enlarging the EU will dilute their own power and influence within. Currently the two countries together account for half the economic output of the euro zone and wield at least as much political influence. Being two of fifteen has not been much different from being two of the original six; being two of twenty-five may not be the same. A Czech official, however, insisted that "Germany and France have always been the engines of the Union, and we don't have a problem with that. It's the reality."

Joining a rich club is not going to make the new members rich overnight. Once they wrested free of the Soviet thumb, some made impressive economic strides. The Baltic states of Latvia, Estonia, and Lithuania, for instance, enjoyed increases in national incomes of 5 to 6 percent a year. The "Visegrad" group (so-called after a joint declaration signed in that Hungarian town) of Poland, Hungary, the Czech Republic, and Slovakia, joined by Slovenia, lagged behind at a still respectable 3 to 4 percent annually. Yet without exception, the new members of the EU have a lot of catching up to do. According to one set of calculations, if the fifteen countries of the 2003 version of the EU were to experience economic growth of 2 percent a year, and the ten newcomers were to grow at 4 percent annually, it would require these ten an average of fifty years to reach the average income per person of the fifteen. True, economic forecasting over such long spans of time is as uncertain as long-term weather forecasting. Still, these calculations highlight the disparity between the relative wealth of old EU members and the relative poverty of the newcomers.

The big-bang enlargement will change the EU, for change is always at the heart of human affairs, but it is too soon to tell what will happen. Some guesses about broad tendencies can be made, however. One guess is that the EU, already one of the world's most complex bureaucratic enterprises, will become even more complex. It will require a large fund of goodwill and imagination to ward off gridlock. Another guess is that the far greater diversity of an enlarged EU in terms of history, politics, language, wealth, and geography will register in a much greater diversity of interest among the members. Such diversity could be a source of innovation; it could also encourage the development of internal blocs pushing their own interests at the expense of others, thereby endangering Union-wide policies. Still another guess is that an enlarged EU will be more U.S.-friendly than the EU of fifteen was in the recent past. As their support for the U.S. position on Iraq suggested, most of the newcomers were more sympathetic to the United States than were the old EU critics, disinclined to see themselves as rivals, and grateful to the transatlantic power for its support in the transition from communism to democracy.

Europe's Demographic Prospects

Three guesses about the future are enough—perhaps too many—for a history book to make. Demographic predictions—statements about population growth—are better than guesses because they extrapolate from data already in hand. The data gathered both by the UN and by national censuses show that the European population is shrinking and aging, and this is not a good omen. European fertility rates—the average number of children a woman can expect to have in her lifetime—have fallen sharply since 1970, and especially since 1985. By 2000 the rate had fallen to less than 1.4, far below the replacement level of 2.1 (the number required to keep the population steady), and it is projected to continue falling for another decade. At the same time birth rates have declined, life expectancy has risen, and this combination makes for an aging population. The effect has many implications for public policy, not the least of which is a growing burden on the public purse to provide for pensions and health care.

Baby boomers will soon be retiring in droves on both sides of the Atlantic, but in the United States other demographic tendencies mitigate the fiscal and economic consequences of an aging population. Soon, in fact, the U.S. population will be getting younger. The fertility rate is rising, and immigration to America, the historical source of the replenishment and rejuvenation of the American population, far outpaces immigration to Europe. Moreover, immigrants are reproducing at a greater rate than native-born Americans. The elderly in Europe face the prospect of a dwindling number of workers supporting them and an even fewer number of children entering the work force. In the absence of a dramatic growth in productivity, fewer workers will bring a decline in GDP.

Demographic trends have political and psychological implications as well as fiscal and economic consequences. The U.S. trends of higher immigration and fertility rates will produce a population not only larger than Europe's but also a younger one, more ethnically diverse and, in all likelihood, more dynamic. The young tend to be exuberant risk-takers; the old to be cautious, and risk-averse. These different casts of mind evince themselves not only behind the wheels of automobiles, but in all the diverse activities essential to sustaining the vitality and vibrancy of an advanced consumer society. As the United States replenishes itself with Latin American and Asian immigrants, American culture will be reshaped, and its political attention, still strongly drawn toward Europe, may be pulled in new directions.

SUMMARY

The deeper demographic projections are cast into the future, the more uncertain they become. In the landscape of the past, the ground seems more solid under your feet, better explored, in some respects downright familiar. This is almost invariably an illusion. Much about the past remains unknown, and some of it remains unknowable. What is thought to be worth knowing changes and what is thought to be known is subject to almost ceaseless revision. The terrain of history turns out to be unstable.

"Change," the American playwright Tony Kushner recently remarked, "is not the substitution of one static state for another. The meanings of September 11 continue to be fought over, and the prevailing interpretations will direct future action." Kushner's remark about 9/11 holds true for Europe since 1945—and for far remoter stretches of Europe's past, for that matter. What is truly astonishing about European history since World War II is the sweep and scope of change. At the end of the war European rule, although weakened substantially and wielded fitfully, stretched over great swaths of Africa, Asia, and the Middle East. Scarcely a decade later, with a couple of notable exceptions, the Europeans had withdrawn to their own continent; a decade after that, in the 1960s, even the notable exceptions had yielded to indigenous rule. For nearly three more decades still, however, the Soviet

Union held under its thumb most of central Europe, the great territorial prize of the war. Finally in 1989, following periods of intermittent restiveness, the Berlin Wall fell, leading in short order to the Soviet Union's collapse and the spread of democracy throughout the European lands the Soviet Army had occupied. A more precarious democracy took root in Russia. Only in the Balkans (and for a much shorter time, in Romania) did violence accompany the end of authoritarian rule. Throughout most of the 1990s the implosion of Yugoslavia disturbed the peace but only intermittently caught the worried attention of governments to the west and north.

If the collapse of communism and the spread of democracy drastically altered the face of Europe between 1945 and our day, by far the greatest contrast in the lot of Europeans then and now lies in the economic realm. It is simplifying only slightly to say that Europe in 1945, Britain included, was a ruin in which hope barely stirred. By the century's end Europe in the form of the EU was a mighty engine of industry and commerce, the world's largest market-place, challenging the United States all across the board. Europe had accomplished the remarkable feat of retreating within its narrow geographic confines and emerging transformed. Worries over terrorism supplanted fears of nuclear war, but Europe in the first decade of the twenty-first century was more the master of its own destiny than it had been since the first decade of the twentieth century.

Suggested Readings

CHAPTER 1: Europe in a Bipolar World

Surveys and National Histories

Craig, Gordon A. *The Germans*. New York: Meridian, 1991. A somewhat dated but still insightful account by the dean of American historians of Germany.

Davies, Norman. *Europe, A History*. New York: Oxford University Press, 1996. Widely acclaimed and remarkably long history of Europe from early times to the early 1990s.

Gilbert, Felix, and David Clay Large. *The End of the European Era, 1890 to the Present*. New York: Norton, 2002. An able survey of the "long" twentieth century.

Hitchcock, William I. *The Struggle for Europe; The Turbulent History of a Divided Continent, 1945 to the Present*. New York: Doubleday and Co., Inc., 2003. Surveys the political and economic history of Europe since World War II.

Holborn, Hajo. *The Political Collapse of Europe*. New York: Alfred A. Knopf, 1962. A brilliant brief survey of how and why Europe lost its mastery of international politics.

Howard, Michael. *The Invention of Peace; Reflections on War and International Order*. New Haven, CT: Yale University Press, 2000. A leading military historian's essay on war and peace in the affairs of nations.

Mazower, Mark. *Dark Continent; Europe's Twentieth Century*. New York: Alfred A. Knopf, 1999. A history of Europe as a struggle among liberal democracy, fascism, and communism.

Roberts, J. M. *The Penguin History of Europe*. New York: Penguin Books, 1996. An able survey of European history from earliest times to the present.

———. *The Twentieth Century: The History of the World, 1901 to 2000*. New York: Viking, 1999. The best of the many world histories that appeared toward the end of the second millenium.

Taylor, A. J. P. *The Course of German History*. New York: Routledge, 2001. Reprint of a classic account by a leading British historian.

Wright, Gordon. *France in Modern Times; From the Enlightenment to the Present*. New York: W.W. Norton, 1995. A somewhat dated but still invaluable interpretive synthesis on modern French history.

The Impact of World War II

Burrin, Philippe. *France Under the Germans; Collaboration and Compromise*. Trans. Janet Lloyd. New York: The New Press, 1996. Recounts the remarkable variety and ambiguity of French responses to the German Occupation of 1940–1944.

Buruma, Ian. *The Wages of Guilt; Memories of War in Germany and Japan*. New York: Farrar, Straus & Giroux, 1994. Compares the history of guilt in the two principal aggressor nations of World War II.

Craig, Gordon A. *The Politics of the Prussian Army, 1640–1945*. Oxford: Oxford University Press, 1955. The definitive work on the army that created Prussia, unified and defended Germany, and was defeated in World War II.

Douglas, Lawrence. *The Memory of Judgment; Making Law and History in the Trials of the Holocaust*. New Haven, CT: Yale University Press, 2001. Legal responses to the crimes of the Holocaust.

Dower, John W. *Embracing Defeat: Japan in the Wake of World War II*. New York: Norton/The New Press, 1999. Continuity and change in Japanese culture and society in the period of the postwar American occupation.

Evans, Richard J. *The Coming of the Third Reich*. New York: Penguin Press, 2003. The first of a projected three-volume history of Nazi Germany by a leading British historian.

Fest, Joachim. *Plotting Hitler's Death; The Story of the German Resistance*. Trans. Bruce Little. New York: Metropolitan Books, 1996. The fullest available account of the resistance to Hitler, culminating in the assassination attempt of July 20, 1944.

Gilbert, Felix. *A European Past; Memoirs, 1905–1945*. New York: Norton, 1988. Memoirs of a major European historian and refugee from Nazi Germany.

Goldhagen, Daniel Jonah. *Hitler's Willing Executioners; Ordinary Germans and the Holocaust*. New York: Alfred A. Knopf, 1996. A controversial revisionist account of the Holocaust. Argues that a deep historical anti-Semitism underlay German support for Nazi crimes against the Jews.

Hastings, Max. *Armageddon: The Battle for Germany, 1944–1945*. New York: Random House, 2004. The last eight months of World War II in Europe surveyed by a leading military historian and journalist.

Heiber, Helmut, and David Glanz, eds. *Hitler and His Generals: Military Conferences, 1942–1945*. Trans. Gerhard L. Weinberg, Roland Winter, Krista Smith, and Mary Beth Friedrich. New York: Enigma, 2003. A transcription of the detailed minutes of Hitler's wartime conferences with Nazi Germany's principal military commanders.

Jackson, Julian. *The Fall of France: The Nazi Invasion of 1940*. New York: Oxford University Press, 2003. The most recent account of what the great French historian Marc Bloch called "the strange defeat."

Langer, Lawrence L. *Admitting the Holocaust; Collected Essays*. New York: Oxford University Press, 1995. Essays on victims' and observers accounts of the Holocaust in memoirs, fiction, films, and plays.

Lukacs, John. *The Hitler of History*. New York: Alfred A. Knopf, 1997. Surveys the enormous literature on Hitler.

Merridale, Catherine. *Night of Stone; Death and Memory in Twentieth-Century Russia*. New York: Viking, 2000. The impact on the psyche of ordinary Russians of the great traumas of Russian history.

Overy, Richard. *The Dictators: Hitler's Germany, Stalin's Russia*. New York: W. W. Norton, 2004. A comparison of the two principal totalitarian states and societies of the twentieth century and the men who shaped and led them.

———. *Why the Allies Won*. New York: Norton, 1996. If the Germans had the superior army, the Allies had the superior establishment for providing the sinews of war.

———. *Russia's War; A History of the Soviet War Effort: 1941–1945*. New York: Penguin Books, 1997. The best short, one-volume account of the impact of World War II on the nation that bore the brunt of the German military onslaught.

Paxton, Robert O. *Vichy France: Old Guard and New Order, 1940–1944*. New York: Alfred A. Knopf, 1972. This standard work sees Vichy policy as initiated by the French authorities, not imposed by the German occupiers.

————. *The Anatomy of Fascism*. New York: Alfred A. Knopf, 2004. A brief, lively, and deeply perceptive analysis of fascism: what it is and how, where, and why fascists came to power. A major statement by a major historian.

Rhodes, Richard. *The Making of the Atomic Bomb*. New York: Simon and Schuster, 1986. An exhaustive account of the Manhattan Project, the wartime American effort to create and employ an atomic bomb.

Sebald, W. G. *On the Natural History of Destruction*. Trans. by Anthea Bell. New York: Random House, 2003. A German novelist's meditation on the silence Germans long maintained on the Allied bombing of their cities in World War II.

The Cold War

Allison, Graham, and Philip Zelikow. *Essence of Decision: Explaining the Cuban Missile Crisis*, 2d Ed. New York: Longman, 1999. Remains the best study of the Cuban missile crisis of 1962.

Freedman, Lawrence. *Kennedy's Wars; Berlin, Cuba, Laos, and Vietnam*. New York: Oxford University Press, 2000. An overview of President John F. Kennedy's cold war military and foreign policy, based on recently opened archives.

Gaddis, John Lewis. *The United States and the Origins of the Cold War, 1941–1947*. New York: Columbia University Press, 1972. A major statement on how and why the United States and the Soviet Union, allies in World War II, became enemies in the postwar era.

————. *The United States and the End of the Cold War: Implications, Reconsiderations, Provocations*. New York: Oxford University Press, 1992. Examination of how and why the cold war ended by a leading cold war historian.

————. *We Now Know: Rethinking Cold War History*. New York: Oxford University Press, 1997. Reflections on the cold war in light of the opening in the 1990s of the archives of the former Soviet Union.

Hanhimake, Jussi M., and Odd Arne Westad, eds. *The Cold War; A History in Documents and Eyewitness Accounts*. New York: Oxford University Press, 2004. A comprehensive documentary anthology covering a broad spectrum of cold war issues.

Harrison, Hope. *Driving the Soviets Up the Wall; Soviet-East German Relations, 1953–1961*. Princeton, NJ: Princeton University Press, 2003. A revisionist study of the keystone to the Soviet bloc. Argues that the East Germans pushed the Soviets into building the Berlin Wall instead of being pushed.

Logevall, Fredrik. *Choosing War; The Lost Chance for Peace and the Escalation of War in Vietnam*. Berkeley: University of California Press, 1999. The leading account of how and why President Lyndon B. Johnson escalated the American war in Vietnam.

Naftali, Timothy, and Aleksandr Fursenko. *"One Hell of a Gamble:" Khruschev, Castro, and Kennedy, 1958–1964*. New York: Norton, 1997. A comprehensive and authoritative study of the origins, course, and consequences of the Cuban missile crisis of 1962.

Rhodes, Richard. *Dark Sun: The Making of the Hydrogen Bomb*. New York: Simon and Schuster, 1995. A sequel to the author's prize-winning book on the atomic bomb, showing how the Soviet Union's acquisition of a thermonuclear weapon shaped subsequent American weapons programs.

Taubman, William. *Khruschev; The Man and His Era*. New York: W.W. Norton & Company, 2003. Pulitzer prize–winning biography of the leader who loosed the grip of Stalin on Soviet foreign and domestic policy.

Van Creveld, Martin. *The Sword and the Olive; A Critical History of the Israeli Defense Force*. New York: PublicAffairs, 1998. The best one-volume study of a key Israeli institution.

CHAPTER 2:   The Loss of European Empire

Betts, Raymond F. *France and Decolonization*. New York: St. Martin's, 1991. A concise overview by a leading student of colonial history.

———. *Decolonization; The Making of the Contemporary World*. Routledge, 1998. A brief, well-informed, and comprehensive survey.

Birmingham, David. *The Decolonization of Africa*. Athens: Ohio University Press, 1996. A short and accessible treatment of the end of European rule in a huge and diverse continent.

Brown, Judith M. *Gandhi and Civil Disobedience: The Mahatma in Indian Politics, 1928–1934*. Cambridge: Cambridge University Press, 1977. Gandhi as the pragmatist of nonviolent resistance to British rule of India.

———. *Modern India; The Origins of an Asian Democracy*. New York: Oxford University Press, 1994. The history of India from the establishment of British rule in the eighteenth century to its emergence as the most stable democracy in the non-Western world.

Chamberlain, M. E. *Decolonization: The Fall of the European Empires*, 2d ed. Oxford: Blackwell, 1999. A succinct account of the end of an era.

Dalloz, Jacques. *The War in Indochina*. Lanham, MD: Rowman & Littlefield, 1990. The French colonial background, the Japanese interlude, and the outbreak of war against French rule through the defeat at Dien Bien Phu in 1954.

Darwin, John. *Britain and Decolonization: The Retreat from Empire in the Postwar World*. New York: St. Martin's, 1988. An introduction to the rise and fall of the largest seaborne empire of modern times.

Devillers, Philippe, Jean Lacouture, and Adam Roberts, trans. *End of a War: Indochina, 1954*. New York: Praeger, 1969. An account by an academic expert (Devillers) and a veteran journalist (Lacouture) with long experience in Indochina.

Fall, Bernard B. *Hell in a Very Small Place; The Siege of Dien Bien Phu*. Philadelphia: Lippincott, 1967. The best account in English of the decisive battle of the French war in Indochina.

Ferguson, Niall. *Empire: The Rise and Demise of the British World Order and the Lessons for Global Power*. New York: Basic Books, 2003. Argues the British Empire benefited not only Britain but also the overseas lands Britain ruled.

Gifford, Prosser, and William Roger Louis, eds. *Decolonization and African Independence: The Transfer of Power, 1960–1980*. New Haven, CT: Yale University Press, 1988. Essays on how colonial rulers struggled to hold onto advantages in postcolonial Africa without accepting obligations.

Gorst, Anthony. *The Suez Crisis*. London: Longmans, 1997. The background, unfolding, and consequences of the last Franco-British attempt to exert great-power influence in the Middle East.

Hochschild, Adam. *King Leopold's Ghost; A Story of Greed, Terror, and Heroism in Colonial Africa*. Boston: Houghton Mifflin, 1999. A riveting account of the Belgian king's ruthless exploitation of one of the largest and richest European colonial acquisitions in Africa.

Horne, Alistair. *A Savage War of Peace: Algeria, 1954–1962*. New York: Viking, 1978. A comprehensive account of the French and Algerian sides of the Algerian War.

Jalal, Ayesha. *The Sole Spokesman: Jinnah, the Moslem League, and the Demand for Pakistan*. Cambridge: Cambridge University Press, 1994. Explores the partitioning of British India, the creation of Pakistan, and the central role of the Muslim leader Mohammed Ali Jinnah.

Karnow, Stanley. *Vietnam; A History*. New York: Penguin, 1983. A standard account of the American war in Vietnam and its French antecedents.

Lancaster, Donald. *The Emancipation of French Indochina*. New York: Octagon Books, 1975. A history of French Indochina from its origins to the Geneva Conference of 1954.

Louis, William Roger. *The British Empire in the Middle East, 1945–1951: Arab Nationalism, the United States, and Postwar Imperialism*. New York: Penguin, 1987. The British Labour government's ultimately futile attempt to hold onto power in the Middle East as a gauge of great-power status.

Low, D. A. *Eclipse of Empire*. Cambridge: Cambridge University Press, 1993. The end of the British Empire in India and Africa.

Oren, Michael B. *Six Days of War; June 1967 and the Making of the Modern Middle East*. New York: Oxford University Press, 2002. Currently the best account of the Israeli-Egyptian war and its long-lasting impact on the Middle East.

Panikkar, K. M. *Asia and Western Dominance*. London: Allen & Unwin, 1953. Established the idea of the "Vasco da Gama" era, or the rise of European hegemony in Asia and other non-European territories.

Schalk, David L. *War and the Ivory Tower: Algeria and Vietnam*. New York: Oxford University Press, 1991. A comparison of the response of French and American intellectuals to the wars in North Africa and Southeast Asia, respectively.

Sheehan, Neil. *A Bright Shining Lie: John Paul Vann and America in Vietnam*. New York: Vintage, 1989. A brilliant case study of how and why things went wrong for the United States in Vietnam.

Springhall, John. *Decolonization Since 1945: The Collapse of European Overseas Empire*. New York: Palgrave Macmillan, 2001. Deals with each major European overseas colony in succession.

Talbott, John. *The War Without a Name; France in Algeria, 1954–1962*. New York: Alfred A. Knopf, 1980. Emphasizes the political dimension of the French war in Algeria.

CHAPTER 3:　Western Europe

National Histories and Political Leaders

Annan, Noel. *Changing Enemies: The Defeat and Regeneration of Germany*. New York: W.W. Norton, 1996. The postwar occupation and de-Nazification era.

Ardagh, John. *France in the New Century: Portrait of a Changing Society*. New York: Viking, 1999. France today, with careful attention to France yesterday.

Brubaker, Rogers. *Citizenship and Nationhood in France and Germany*. Cambridge, MA: Harvard University Press, 1992. A comparative study of two major dimensions of advanced liberal democracies.

Dahrendorf, Ralf. *Society and Democracy in Germany*, 2 Vols. Reprint ed. London: Ashgate Publishing, 1967. A still valuable study of how the thoroughness of the Nazi defeat opened the way to the establishment of a German democracy.

Duggan, Christopher. *A Concise History of Italy*. Cambridge: Cambridge University Press, 1994. Concentrates on Italy's difficulties over the last two centuries in establishing a workable nation-state.

Ginsborg, Paul. *A History of Contemporary Italy, 1943–1988*. London: Palgrave Macmillan, 2003. The standard account.

Jenkins, Roy. *Churchill; A Biography*. New York: Farrar, Straus & Giroux, 2001. An exhaustive, authoritative, and likely-to-be definitive biography by a distinguished writer and politician.

Keegan, John. *Winston Churchill*. New York: Penguin, 2002. A brief and masterful "life" by Britain's leading military historian.

Lacouture, Jean. *De Gaulle*. New York: Norton, 1990. The authoritative biography.

Nicholls, Anthony J. *The Bonn Republic: West German Democracy, 1945–1990*. New York: Longman, 1997. A brief survey of the history of West Germany.

Robbins, Keith. *The Eclipse of a Great Power: Modern Britain, 1870–1992*. London: Longman, 1994. Britain's evolution from leading imperial power to regional power allied to the United States.

Schwarz, Hans-Peter. *Konrad Adenauer*, 2 Vols. New York: Berghahn Books, 1995–97. The definitive biography.

NATO

Kaplan, Lawrence S. *The Long Entanglement: The United States and NATO After Fifty Years*. Westport, CT: Praeger, 1999. A survey of NATO on its fiftieth anniversary.

———. *NATO and the United States: The Enduring Alliance*. New York: Twayne Publishers, 1999. A standard work on NATO.

International Crises and Wars

Chandler, David, exec. ed., Ian Beckett, ed. *The Oxford Illustrated History of the British Army*. New York: Oxford University Press, 1994. A survey by twenty experts on war and society.

Crile, George. *Charlie Wilson's War*. New York: Grove Press, 2003. An account of the CIA's covert support for the guerrilla war of 1979–1989 against the Soviet invasion of Afghanistan. Wilson was a maverick Texas congressman who played an important role in U.S. funding of the Afghan mujahedeen.

Freedman, Lawrence. *Kennedy's Wars; Berlin, Cuba, Laos, and Vietnam*. New York: Oxford University Press, 2000. An overview of Kennedy's cold war military and foreign policy, based on recently opened archives.

Hastings, Max, and Simon Jenkins. *The Battle for the Falklands*. New York: Norton, 1983. The best book on Britain's successful 1983 war with Argentina for control of the Falkland Islands, more than seven thousand miles distant from Britain.

Logevall, Fredrik. *The Origins of the Vietnam War*. New York: Longman, 2001. A short account, accompanied by important documents, of the origins of the Vietnam War, from the French withdrawal in 1954 to the major American escalation of 1965.

Maier, Charles, ed. *The Cold War in Europe*. New York: M. Wiener, 1996. Essays on the domestic and international dimensions of the cold war.

Naftali, Timothy, and Aleksandr Fursenko. *"One Hell of a Gamble": Khruschev, Castro, and Kennedy, 1958–1964*. New York: Norton, 1997. A comprehensive and authoritative study of the origins, course, and consequences of the Cuban missile crisis of 1962.

Rubin, Barnett R. *The Fragmentation of Afghanistan*. 2d ed. New Haven, CT: Yale University Press, 2002. Afghanistan from the Soviet invasion of 1979 through the war against the Taliban.

Russian General Staff. *The Soviet-Afghan War; How a Superpower Fought and Lost*. Ed. & trans. Lester W. Grau and Michael A. Gress. Lawrence: University Press of Kansas, 2002.
The Russian General Staff's candid appraisal of the Soviet debacle in Afghanistan.

1968

Caute, David. *The Year of the Barricades: A Journey Through 1968*. Reprint ed. New York: Perennial, 1988. An impassioned narrative by a keen-eyed leftist observer.
Marwick, Arthur. *The Sixties: Cultural Revolution in Britain, France, Italy, and the United States*. New York: Oxford University Press, 1998. The "long" sixties (1958–1974) interpreted as a sweeping cultural revolution. Case studies of Great Britain, France, Italy, and the United States.

European Integration

Gillingham, John. *Coal, Steel, and the Rebirth of Europe*. Cambridge: Cambridge University Press, 1991. The beginnings of European integration.
Milward, Alan S. *The European Rescue of the Nation State*. 2d ed. New York: Routledge, 2000. European integration seen as driven by national self-interest.
Urwin, Derek W. *The Community of Europe: A History of European Integration*, 2d ed. The beginnings and course of the movement toward a European Union. New York: Longman, 1995.
Willis, F. Roy. *France, Germany, and the New Europe, 1945–1967*. New York: Oxford University Press, 1968. A somewhat dated but still valuable study of the early years of the integration movement.

CHAPTER 4:   The Collapse of Communism in Central and Eastern Europe and the Soviet Union

Batt, Judy. *Economic Reform and Political Change in Eastern Europe: A Comparison of the Czechoslovak and Hungarian Experiences*. New York: St. Martin's Press, 1988. Political reform as a necessary prelude to economic reform.
Bearden, Milt, and James Risen. *The Main Enemy; The Inside Story of the CIA's Final Showdown with the KGB*. New York: Random House, 2003. The last years of the long struggle between the intelligence agencies of the two superpowers. By a former chief of the CIA's Moscow station and a *New York Times* reporter.
Clark, Wesley K. *Waging Modern War; Bosnia, Kosovo, and the Future of Conflict*. New York: PublicAffairs, 2001. A firsthand account of the war by the then supreme allied commander in Europe.
Cohen, Roger. *Hearts Grown Brutal; Sagas of Sarajevo*. New York: Random House, 1998. A riveting account of the siege of Sarajevo, 1992–1995, by a Pulitzer prize–winning reporter for the *New York Times*.
Daalder, Ivo H., and Michael E. O'Hanlon. *Winning Ugly; NATO's War to Save Kosovo*. Washington, DC: Brookings Institution Press, 2000. An early and still the best general history of the war over Kosovo.
Garton Ash, Timothy. *The Uses of Adversity: Essays on the Fate of Central Europe*. New York: Random House, 1989. Central Europe on the brink of the revolution of 1989.
———. *The Magic Lantern: The Revolution of '89 Witnessed in Warsaw, Budapest, Berlin, and Prague*. New York: Random House, 1990. A journalist's eyewitness account of events in the major revolutionary cities of central Europe in 1989.

————. *The File; A Personal History.* New York: Random House, 1997. History and analysis of the dossier the East German Stasi (secret police) kept on the author when he was a graduate student in East Berlin in the late 1970s.

————. *History of the Present; Essays, Sketches, and Dispatches from Europe in the 1990s.* New York: Random House, 1999. The evolution of post–cold war Europe by a leading scholar-journalist.

————. *The Polish Revolution: Solidarity,* 3d ed. New Haven, CT: Yale University Press, 2002. The best history of the Polish Revolution available in English.

Glenny, Misha. *The Fall of Yugoslavia; The Third Balkan War.* 3d ed. New York: Penguin, 1996. An expert journalist's account of the roots of war in the Balkans, 1990–1992.

Goldman, Marshall I. *The Piratization of Russia: Russian Reform Goes Awry.* New York: Routledge, 2003. How the self-styled oligarchs created immense personal fortunes by helping themselves to the major economic and financial resources of the former Soviet state.

Graham, Thomas E., Jr. *Russia's Decline and Uncertain Recovery.* Washington, DC: Carnegie Endowment for International Peace, 2002. A pessimistic assessment of Russia's prospects after more than a decade of post-Soviet political and economic turmoil.

Gray, William Glenn. *Germany's Cold War: The Global Campaign to Isolate East Germany, 1949–1969.* Chapel Hill: University of North Carolina Press, 2003. A history of West Germany's relentless and reasonably successful effort to isolate East Germany and to keep in doubt the legitimacy of the East German regime.

Halberstam, David. *War in a Time of Peace; Bush, Clinton, and the Generals.* New York: Scribner, 2001. A leading American journalist's account of American military and diplomatic responses to war in a post–cold war world.

Havel, Vaclav. *Disturbing the Peace; A Conversation with Karel Hvizdala.* Trans. Paul Wilson. New York: Alfred A. Knopf, 1990. Reflections of the leading anticommunist dissident under communist Czechoslovakia and the first president of the Czech Republic.

Hoffman, David E. *The Oligarchs: Wealth and Power in the New Russia.* New York: PublicAffairs, 2002. The former Moscow bureau chief of *The Washington Post* focuses on six leading oligarchs as a means of illuminating the dubious role in post-Soviet Russia of the rest.

Holbrooke, Richard. *To End a War.* Rev. ed. New York: Modern Library, 1999. The chief American negotiator's account of the negotiation of the 1995 Dayton Accords, which ended the Bosnian War.

Ignatieff, Michael. *The Warrior's Honor: Ethnic War and the Modern Conscience.* New York: Metropolitan Books, 1997. Reflections on the moral dilemmas of modern war, based on Ignatieff's travels in the Balkans in the 1990s.

————. *Virtual War; Kosovo and Beyond.* New York: Metropolitan Books, 2000. The ethics of employing precision-guided munitions in modern war.

Jelavich, Barbara. *History of the Balkans.* 2 Vols. Cambridge: Cambridge University Press, 1983. Volume 2 offers the standard account of the region in the twentieth century.

Judah, Tim. *The Serbs; History, Myth & and the Destruction of Yugoslavia.* New Haven, CT: Yale University Press, 1997. Emphasizes the Serbians central role as both victims and perpetrators of politically and culturally inspired violence in the Balkans.

————. *Kosovo; War and Revenge.* New Haven, CT: Yale University Press, 2000. An historical perspective on the war over Kosovo, by an observer who lived in Belgrade from 1990 to 1995.

Lendvai, Paul, *The Hungarians: A Thousand Years of Victory in Defeat*. Ann Major, trans. Princeton, NJ: Princeton University Press, 2004. How Hungary has survived as a nation-state for more than a thousand years, despite linguistic uniqueness and cultural isolation.

Lieven, Anatol. *The Baltic Revolution; Estonia, Latvia, Lithuania, and the Path to Independence*. Rev. ed. New Haven, CT: Yale University Press, 1994. A well-informed study of the anti-Soviet revolution most neglected beyond the region itself.

Loyd, Anthony. *My War Gone By, I Miss It So*. New York: Penguin Books, 1999. A freelance journalist's idiosyncratic treatment of the Bosnian War.

Maass, Peter. *Love Thy Neighbor; A Story of War*. New York: Alfred A. Knopf, 1996. A deeply personal account of the Bosnian War based on the writer's firsthand experience as a reporter for *The Washington Post.*

Marx, Anthony W. *Faith in Nation: Exclusionary Origins of Nationalism*. New York: Oxford University Press, 2003. A revisionist account stressing the authoritarian, state-building side of nationalism against the more familiar association of the origins of nationalism with liberalism.

Matlock, Jack F., Jr. *Reagan and Gorbachev: How the Cold War Ended*. New York: Random House, 2004. An authoritative account by a former ambassador to the Soviet Union and participant in discussions between Reagan and Gorbachev.

Mazower, Mark. *The Balkans; A Short History*. New York: The Modern Library, 2002. An accessible review of a deeply complex history, characterizing conflict in the Balkans as in the nature of a long civil war.

McFaul, Michael, Nikolai Petrov, and Andrei Ryabov. *Between Dictatorship and Democracy; Russian Post-Communist Political Reform*. New York: Carnegie Endowment for International Peace, 2004. A collection of well-informed essays on trends in Russian politics since the end of the Soviet Union.

Naimark, Norman M. *Fires of Hatred; Ethnic Cleansing in Twentieth-Century Europe*. Cambridge, MA: Harvard University Press, 2001. Ethnic cleansing as a consequence of deeply twentieth-century attitudes, not ancient hatreds.

Neuffer, Elizabeth. *The Key to My Neighbor's House: Seeking Justice in Bosnia and Rwanda*. New York: Picador, 2002. Based on interviews with participants and observers in genocides in far-distant countries, one European, one African.

Oren, Michael B. *Six Days of War; June 1967 and the Making of the Modern Middle East*. New York: Oxford University Press, 2002. Currently the best account of the Israeli-Egyptian war and its long-lasting impact on the Middle East.

Rohde, David. *End Game; The Betrayal and Fall of Srebrenica: Europe's Worst Massacre Since World War II*. Boulder, CO: Westview Press, 1997. How outmatched UN peacekeepers failed to stop the massacre of more than seven thousand Bosnian Muslim men and boys by Bosnian Serb forces.

Rosenberg, Tina. *The Haunted Land; Facing Europe's Ghosts After Communism*. New York: Random House, 1995. The aftermath of communist rule in East Germany, the Czech Republic, and Poland.

Satter, David. *Darkness at Dawn: The Rise of the Russian Criminal State*. New Haven, CT: Yale University Press, 2003. Recounts the exploitation of the Russian people at the hands of a kleptocracy, or the rule of thieves.

Sell, Louis. *Slobodan Milosevic and the Destruction of Yugoslavia*. Durham, NC: Duke University Press, 2002. A political biography of the former communist turned nationalist who led Yugoslavia to war and ruin. By a former U.S. foreign service officer with long experience in the Balkans.

Shawcross, William. *Deliver Us from Evil; Warlords, Peacekeepers, and a World of Endless*

Conflict. New York: Simon and Schuster, 2000. A critique of humanitarian military interventions by a veteran British journalist.

Skilling, H. Gordon. *Czechoslovakia's Interrupted Revolution*. Princeton, NJ: Princeton University Press, 1976. The leading account in English of the "Prague Spring" of 1968 and its aftermath.

Talbott, Strobe. *The Russia Hand; A Memoir of Presidential Diplomacy*. New York: Random House, 2002. An account of the U.S. relationship with post-Soviet Russia under President Boris Yeltsin. By President Bill Clinton's deputy secretary of state (and close friend).

CHAPTER 5:   Arts and Sciences

Sciences

Cassidy, David C. *Uncertainty: The Life and Science of Werner Heisenberg*. San Francisco: W.H. Freeman, 1993. A biography of the German physicist who was a major figure in the development of quantum mechanics. Controversial for his ambiguous role in Nazi Germany's attempt to make an atomic bomb.

Feynman, Richard P., and others. *"Surely You're Joking, Mr. Feynman!" Adventures of a Curious Character*. New York: W.W. Norton, 1985. The amusing and deeply instructive memoirs of the great quantum theorist.

Greene, Brian. *The Fabric of the Cosmos; Space, Time, and the Texture of Reality*. New York: Alfred A. Knopf, 2004. Nonintuitive concepts of contemporary physics, such as string theory, explained to the nonspecialist reader.

Hawking, Stephen W. *A Brief History of Time*. New York: Bantam, 1988. Classic work for nonscientists on the origin, history, and future of the universe, by a leading theoretical physicist.

Judson, Horace Freeland. *The Eighth Day of Creation; Makers of the Revolution in Biology*. Cold Spring Harbor, NY: Cold Spring Harbor Laboratory Press, 1996. An authoritative account of the origins of molecular biology, in which the human side of the story receives as much attention as the scientific.

Pais, Abraham. *Subtle Is the Lord: The Science and the Life of Albert Einstein*. Philadelphia: American Philological Association, 1982. A biography by a physicist and colleague of Einstein.

Perutz, Max F. *I Wish I'd Made You Angry Earlier: Essays on Science, Scientists, and Humanity*. Expanded ed. Cold Spring Harbor, NY: Cold Spring Harbor Laboratory Press, 2002. Elegant and witty essays on twentieth-century science and scientists by the winner of the 1962 Nobel Prize in Biochemistry.

Ridley, Matt. *Genome*. New York: HarperCollins, 2000. Twenty-three chapters on the twenty-three pairs of chromosomes that comprise the human genome. A lucid and compelling account of the genetic history of the human species.

Watson, James D. *The Double Helix : A Personal Account of the Discovery of the Structure of DNA*. New York: Scribner, 1968. A riveting account by one of the chief discoverers of the structure of DNA.

Arts

Anderson, Perry. *The Origins of Postmodernity*. New York: Verso, 1998. A wide-ranging history.

Berman, Marshall. *All That is Solid Melts into Air; The Experience of Modernity*. New York: Penguin Books, 1988. On the varieties of the modernist sensibility.

Eagleton, Terry. *The Illusions of Postmodernism*. Oxford: Blackwell, 1996. A leftist critique by a leading literary critic.

Frampton, Kenneth. *Modern Architecture: A Critical History*. London: Thames & Hudson, 1992. A survey. Especially strong on twentieth-century architecture.

Guralnick, Peter. *Last Train to Memphis; The Rise of Elvis Presley*. Boston: Little, Brown, 1994. Who was Elvis before he became the king of rock 'n roll?

———. *Careless Love; The Unmaking of Elvis Presley*. Boston: Little, Brown, 1999. Explores Presley's greatness as a musician and the reasons for his decline. A nuanced and sensitive account.

Hopkins, David. *After Modern Art, 1945–2000*. New York: Oxford University Press, 2000. A compact and perceptive survey of a complex period in art history.

Leja, Michael. *Reframing Abstract Expressionism*. New Haven, CT: Yale University Press, 1993. A major revisionist statement.

Madoff, Steven. *Pop Art; A Critical History*. Berkeley: University of California Press, 1997. A collection of articles on the Pop movement in Europe and America.

Mason, Bobbie Ann. *Elvis Presley*. New York: Viking, 2003. A short and well-informed biography of the southern singer by a southern novelist.

Pells, Richard. *Not Like Us: How Europeans Have Loved, Hated, and Transformed American Culture Since World War II*. New York: Basic Books, 1997. The often-fraught cultural relationship between the United States and Europe.

Ross, Kristin. *Fast Cars, Clean Bodies: Decolonization and the Reordering of French Culture*. Cambridge, MA: MIT Press, 1995. The French resistance to American culture.

Ryback, Timothy W. *Rock Around the Bloc: A History of Rock Music in Eastern Europe and the Soviet Union*. New York: Oxford University Press, 1990. Rock culture in eastern Europe and the Soviet Union since 1954.

Seigel, Jerrold E. *The Private Worlds of Marcel Duchamp: Desire, Liberation, and the Self in Modern Culture*. Berkeley: University of California Press, 1995. A unifying study of the modernist artist who continues to influence several tendencies in contemporary art.

Sorlin, Pierre. *European Cinemas, European Societies*. New York: Routledge, 1991. A social history of European films.

Wagnleitner, Reinhold. *Coca-Colonization and the Cold War: The Cultural Mission of the United States in Austria After the Second World War*. Chapel Hill: University of North Carolina Press, 1994. A case study of American cultural imperialism in postwar Austria.

Wheeler, Daniel. *Art Since Mid-Century: 1945 to the Present*. New York: Vendome Press, 1991. A excellent introduction.

Wilder, Alec, and James T. Maher, eds. *American Popular Song; The Great Innovators, 1900–1950*. New York: Oxford University Press, 1972. A classic work.

Wood, Paul, Francis Frascina, Jonathan Harris, and Charles Harrison. *Modernism in Dispute: Art Since the Forties*. New Haven, CT: Yale University Press, 1993. Essays on modernism and postmodernism. Mainly on America but some attention to Europe.

CHAPTER 6:   Europe Since 9/11

Globalization

Barber, Benjamin R., and Andrea Schulz. *Jihad vs. McWorld: How Globalism and Tribalism Are Reshaping the World*. New York: Times Books, 1995. Transnational capitalism versus religious and tribal fundamentalism.

Bhagwati, Jagdish. *In Defense of Globalization*. New York: Oxford University Press, 2004. A defense by a distinguished international economist.

Emmott, Bill. *20:21 Vision: Twentieth-Century Lessons for the Twenty-First Century*. New York: Farrar, Straus & Giroux, 2003. What twentieth-century history has to suggest about major trends in the history of the twenty-first. By the editor-in-chief of *The Economist*, the influential British weekly.

Friedman, Thomas. *The Lexus and the Olive Tree: Understanding Globalization*. New York: Farrar, Straus, & Giroux, 2000. Globalization as the central tendency of the post–cold war world. An enthusiastic endorsement of that tendency by the foreign-affairs columnist of the *New York Times*.

James, Harold. *The End of Globalization; Lessons from the Great Depression*. Cambridge, MA: Harvard University Press, 2001. On the protectionist policies that threaten the prosperity of globalization just as they brought on the Great Depression of the 1930s.

Stiglitz, Joseph E. *Globalization and Its Discontents*. New York: W.W. Norton, 2003. An excellent account of what globalization means, how it works, and what, in the author's opinion, its deficiencies are. By the former chief economist of the World Bank and winner of the 2001 Nobel Prize in Economics.

9/11: Antecedents and Aftermath

9/ll Commission. *The 9/11 Commission Report: Final Report of the National Commission on Terrorist Attacks Upon the United States*. New York: W.W. Norton, 2004. Compelling and urgent reading. The most comprehensive study to date of the origins, course, and continuing consequences of 9/11.

Allison, Graham. *Nuclear Terrorism: The Ultimate Preventable Catastrophe*. New York: Times Books/Henry Holt and Co., 2004. In terms of potential loss of life, the most devastating of the so-called weapons of mass destruction. Allison argues that steps can be taken to keep nuclear devices out of the hands of terrorists.

Anderson, Jon Lee. *The Fall of Baghdad*. New York: Penguin Press, 2004. An American journalist's eyewitness account of events in Baghdad from the eve of the Iraq War through mid-June 2004.

Anonymous. *Imperial Hubris: Why the West Is Losing the War on Terror*. Washington, DC: Brassey's, 2004. A critique of current policy in the war on terror by a serving CIA officer with an intimate knowledge of al Qaeda and Afghanistan. The author, Michael Scheuer, disclosed his identity and resigned from the CIA several months after his book was published.

Baer, Robert. *See No Evil: The True Story of a Ground Soldier in the CIA's War on Terrorism*. New York: Three Rivers Press, 2002. A former CIA case officer's account of his service in the Middle East in the 1980s and 1990s.

———. *Sleeping with the Devil; How Washington Sold Our Soul for Saudi Crude*. New York: Three Rivers Press, 2003. A former CIA case officer and Middle East specialist insists on the danger to U.S. security posed by the current U.S.-Saudi relationship.

Bernstein, Richard. *Out of the Blue; The Story of September 11, 2001 from Jihad to Ground Zero*. New York: Times Books, 2002. An accessible and early account of 9/11.

Buruma, Ian, and Avishai Margalit. *Occidentalism; The West in the Eyes of Its Enemies*. New York: Penguin Press, 2004. A timely essay on the anti-Western stereotypes current in the Muslim world that have their origins in the West itself.

Coll, Steve. *Ghost Wars; The Secret History of the CIA, Afghanistan, and Bin Laden, from the Soviet Invasion to September 10, 2001*. New York: Penguin Press, 2004. A detailed and comprehensive account of the Afghan dimension of 9/11, from the Soviet invasion of 1979 to the eve of the attack on New York and Washington, DC.

Garton Ash, Timothy. *Free World: America, Europe, and the Surprising Future of the West.* New York: Random House, 2004. An optimistic perspective on the troubled relationship between the United States and its longstanding European allies.

Hedges, Chris. *War Is a Force That Gives Us Meaning.* New York: PublicAffairs, 2002. A veteran war correspondent's insights on the seductive powers of war.

Hoge, James F., Jr., and Gideon Rose. *How Did This Happen? Terrorism and the New War.* New York: PublicAffairs, 2001. An early and insightful collection of essays on 9/11 and its implications.

Howard, Michael. *The Invention of Peace; Reflections on War and International Order.* New Haven, CT: Yale University Press, 2000. A leading military historian's essay on war and peace in the affairs of nations.

Kagan, Robert. *Of Paradise and Power; America and Europe in the New World Order.* New York: Alfred A. Knopf, 2003. Explores the manifold tensions underlying the growing divergence between America and Europe over major issues of foreign policy in the last decade.

Keegan, John. *The Iraq War.* New York: Alfred A. Knopf, 2004. Focuses on the military operation that drove Saddam Hussein from power in 2003; scants the insurgency that followed.

Kepel, Gilles. *The War for Muslim Minds: Islam and the West.* Cambridge, MA: Belknap Press of the Harvard University Press, 2004. A leading Middle East specialist examines the struggle between the radical Islam that drove 9/11 and subsequent acts of global terrorism and the Western response to them. Neither the Islamists nor the Westerners, he suggests, are unified in thought and action. The most important battlegrounds in the struggle, Kepel argues, are the immigrant Muslim communities of Europe.

———. *Jihad; The Trail of Political Islam.* Trans. Anthony F. Roberts. Cambridge, MA: Belknap Press of Harvard University Press, 2002. Kepel's wide-ranging book bids fair to become the standard account on political Islam.

Lewis, Bernard. *What Went Wrong? Western Impact and Middle East Response.* New York: Oxford University Press, 2002. An account of how and why the Islamic world's encounter with modernity has been such a difficult and demoralizing struggle. By a leading Western student of Islam.

Miller, Judith, Stephen Engelberg, and William Broad. *Germs: Biological Weapons and America's Secret War.* New York: Simon and Schuster, 2001. Three *New York Times* reporters survey the recent history of biological weapons.

Moskos, Charles C., John Allen Williams, and David R. Segal. *The Postmodern Military; Armed Forces After the Cold War.* New York: Oxford University Press, 2000. Military sociologists examine the "postmodern"—i.e., volunteer, relatively small, and androgynous—armed forces of thirteen Western democracies.

Murray, Williamson, and Robert H. Scales, Jr. *The Iraq War; A Military History.* Cambridge, MA: The Belknap Press of Harvard University Press, 2003. Among the earliest and best of the already numerous histories of the Iraq War. By a military historian (Murray) and a recently retired career soldier (Scales).

Pollack, Kenneth M. *The Threatening Storm; The Case for Invading Iraq.* New York: Random House, Inc., 2002. Pollack, a member of President Bill Clinton's National Security Council and Middle East specialist, made the case that Saddam Hussein had weapons of mass destruction and was prepared to use them, a position he repudiated following the Iraq War, when no such weapons were found.

Randal, Jonathan. *Osama: The Making of a Terrorist.* New York: Alfred A. Knopf, 2004. More a history of the contemporary jihadi movement than a biography of Osama Bin Laden. By a longtime reporter for *The Washington Post.*

Rashid, Ahmed. *Taliban: Militant Islam, Oil and Fundamentalism in Central Asia.* New Haven, CT: Yale University Press, 2000. The authoritative account on the Taliban.

Sifry, Micah L., and Christopher Cerf, eds. *The Iraq War Reader: History, Documents, Opinions.* New York: Simon & Schuster, 2003. Documents the run-up to the Iraq War and its immediate aftermath.

Sterba, James, ed. *Terrorism and International Justice.* New York: Oxford University Press, 2003. Philosophical articles on terrorism and the appropriate ethical and moral response.

Talbott, Strobe, and Chanda Nayan, eds. *The Age of Terror; America and the World After September 11.* New York: Basic Books, 2001. A collection of articles on the impact of 9/11 on world affairs. Published soon after the attacks on New York and Washington, DC.

Walzer, Michael. *Arguing About War.* New Haven, CT: Yale University Press, 2004. A collection of previously published essays by a philosopher who has written widely on war. Topics include nuclear deterrence, humanitarian intervention, terrorism, and wars in the Persian Gulf, Kosovo, Afghanistan, and Iraq.

The European Union

Batt, Judy. *Economic Reform and Political Change in Eastern Europe: A Comparison of the Czechoslovak and Hungarian Experiences.* New York: St. Martin's Press, 1988. Political reform as a necessary prelude to economic reform.

Calleo, David. *Rethinking Europe's Future.* Princeton, NJ: Princeton University Press, 2001. An indispensable guide to Europe's prospects at the outset of the twenty-first century.

Guttman, Robert J., ed. *Europe in the New Century: Visions of an Emerging Superpower.* Boulder, CO: Lynne Rienner Publishers, 2001. A wide-ranging assessment of the EU on the eve of its expansion from fifteen to twenty-five members.

McCormick, John. *Understanding the European Union: A Concise Introduction,* 2d ed. New York: Palgrave Macmillan, 2002. An accessible introduction to the main themes of European integration.

Moravcsik, Andrew. *The Choice for Europe: Social Purpose and State Power from Messina to Maastricht.* Ithaca, NY: Cornell University Press, 1998. An excellent history of Europe's movement toward economic and political integration.

Ross, Georges. *Jacques Delors and European Integration.* New York: Oxford University Press, 1995. Concentrates on Jacques Delors's presidency of the European Commission as a means of exploring the European Union's strategy of economic and political integration.

Tiersky, Donald, ed. *Europe Today: National Politics, European Integration, and European Security.* 2d ed. Lanham, MD: Rowman & Littlefield, 2004. Case studies of Germany, France, the United Kingdom, and Poland discuss the domestic and foreign policies of each country, the introduction of the euro, and the implications of the Iraq War for NATO and the U.S.-European relationship.

Toukalis, Loukas. *The New European Economy Revisited.* New York: Oxford University Press, 1997. A somewhat dated but still useful examination of European economic integration.

Index